Planetary Politics

Logos

Perspectives on Modern Society and Culture
Michael J. Thompson, Series Editor

The books in the Logos series examine modern society, politics and culture, emphasizing the connections between these spheres rather than their academic separateness. Skeptical of what current intellectual trends call "interdisciplinary," titles in this series explore the ways that politics, economics, and culture inform one another, overlap, and weave the complex fabric of modern life in a global context. By putting forth bold ideas written to appeal to a broad range of interests, the series situates itself within the long tradition of intelligent social critique.

Islam and the West
Critical Perspectives on Modernity
Edited by Michael J. Thompson

Maverick Voices
Conversations with Political and Cultural Rebels
Edited by Kurt Jacobsen

Planetary Politics:
Human Rights, Terror, and Global Society
Edited by Stephen Eric Bronner

Planetary Politics

Human Rights, Terror, and Global Society

EDITED BY STEPHEN ERIC BRONNER

ROWMAN & LITTLEFIELD PUBLISHERS, INC.
Lanham • Boulder • New York • Toronto • Oxford

56065431

ROWMAN & LITTLEFIELD PUBLISHERS, INC.

Published in the United States of America
by Rowman & Littlefield Publishers, Inc.
A wholly owned subsidiary of The Rowman & Littlefield Publishing Group, Inc.
4501 Forbes Boulevard, Suite 200, Lanham, Maryland 20706
www.rowmanlittlefield.com

PO Box 317
Oxford
OX2 9RU, UK

British Library Cataloguing in Publication Information Available

Library of Congress Cataloging-in-Publication Data

Planetary politics : human rights, terror, and global society / edited by Stephen Eric
Bronner.
    p. cm. — (Logos)
  Includes bibliographical references and index.
  ISBN 0-7425-4198-3 (alk. paper) — ISBN 0-7425-4199-1 (alk. paper)
  1. Globalization. 2. Terrorism. 3. Human rights. 4. Internationalism. 5. United
States—Foreign relations—2001– I. Bronner, Stephen Eric, 1949– II. Series: Logos
(Rowman & Littlefield, Inc.)

JZ1318.P53 2005
327—dc22   2004017766

Printed in the United States of America

♾™ The paper used in this publication meets the minimum requirements of American
National Standard for Information Sciences—Permanence of Paper for Printed Library
Materials, ANSI/NISO Z39.48-1992.

Contents

Introduction

Stephen Eric Bronner

Global society has been analyzed in any number of ways: books dealing with its economic and cultural implications flood the market. But this volume highlights something relatively unique. It seeks to portray globalization with an eye on the transformation of politics into a planetary enterprise. Bringing together the work of major scholars with national and international reputations, much of which originally appeared in the interdisciplinary electronic journal *Logos*, this book aims to offer some new normative perspectives for dealing with the complexity of power in the planetary life of the new millennium.

Part I, "The Global Theater," sets the stage for this enterprise. Building on his classic work *Risk Society*, intent upon redefining the basic vocabulary of the new global order, Ulrich Beck sees both dangers ahead and the possibility for developing open multinational states. The certainty of progress and the refusal to consider various forms of political regulation, according to Manfred Steger, one of the most important participants in the debate on globalization, make the supposed Western consensus in support of globalization a phenomenon based less on "science" or objectivity than on certain ideological presuppositions grounded in particular material interests. Channeling globalization toward progressive ends cannot be taken as a given. According to David Held, among the most prominent theorists of globalization, it instead requires a cosmopolitan commitment predicated not merely on the economic interdependence of states but, more important, on an ethical decision to make sense of events in terms of an overlapping set of "collective fortunes" and a willingness to reason from the standpoint of others. That this is a choice rather than a necessity, indeed, is the point behind the essay of Douglas Kellner, who speaks of globalization as a "contested terrain."

Part II of this volume highlights the way in which planetary politics has given rise to "planetary perils." Terror on a new scale, carried on in a new way, has seized the popular imagination. It has reinforced provincial prejudices in dealing with world events and imbued our understanding and vocabulary with what Nadia Urbinati, a noted political theorist, has termed "the politics of exception and emergency." Deliberation and reflexivity, a willingness to engage the "other," are precisely what terror seeks to destroy. It generates fear and, in so doing, the call for security based on the use of force that can justify militarist excesses of the most powerful nations and the imperialist ambitions of the most influential elites. The essay by Carl Boggs, author of various works on American militarism, explores the ideological justifications employed to defend an increasingly ruthless militarism with planetary implications that world public opinion is increasingly resisting. A transnational phenomenon is seen as being generated in which the United States is being transformed from a traditional nation-state into the core of an empire. Imperialism of a new sort in which the old form of rivalry has essentially been supplanted by a historically unique economic and military integration of capitalist powers thus becomes the theme of the contribution by two internationally known political economists, Leo Panitch and Sam Gindin. The problems they see for the imperialist future, indeed, lie less with traditional notions of "overaccumulation" of capital than with the limits on coordinated planetary growth. Or, to put it another way, the most radical problems for imperialism lie "outside the capitalist core."

Whether or not one agrees with the assumptions behind this bold thesis, clearly, it has become necessary to rethink foreign policy with respect to its planetary implications. That is the purpose behind part III, "Planetary Foreign Policy." No longer is it possible to see international politics as based on the mechanical interactions between one state and another. This is especially the case when dealing with the relations between hegemonic and subaltern states. As I sought to show in "Anatomy of a Disaster," for example, the Iraqi War has undermined the global respect for the United States while increasing fear of its new ideology justifying "the preemptive strike." The implications of this war have both global and domestic consequences and, especially regarding elites of the hegemonic power, it is becoming increasingly difficult to distinguish economic from political aims and foreign from domestic ambitions. The Iraqi War illustrates the way in which the military quest for geopolitical advantage and a new set of imperialist goals are intertwined with the waging of a new domestic class war. Imperialism and militarism, however, require justification. The essay by Irene Gendzier, author of many publications dealing with diplomatic history and the Middle East, explores how the ideology produced by the "Islam industry"—unconcerned with actually educating the broader public about a very different and complex culture—both shapes the attitudes of policy makers and legitimates the foreign policy of the United States in an especially combustible region. Especially in a period marked by globalization and the emergence of a genuinely planetary politics with its international institutions, norms, diversity, and complexity, unilateral forms of constructing foreign policy are appearing ever more dangerous and anachronistic. Beginning to think about alternatives is therefore a matter of some importance. Drucilla Cornell and Philip Green are both noted political theorists, and they engage in this project by calling for a multilateral foreign policy that principally relies on international law and respect for international institutions. The philosopher Dick Howard explores other possibilities in what becomes an attempt to subject both unilateral and multilateral ideas of foreign policy to the contingent imperatives of furthering "democratic dynamics." Nevertheless, the question of how to understand the ethical imperatives and democratic aims of foreign policy remains.

"Cosmopolitan Hopes" is a fitting title for part IV, the concluding section of *Planetary Politics.* It should be noted that the prospects for building a cosmopolitan world are only now becoming realistic. The Enlightenment generated technological and scientific imperatives that are gaining increasing planetary acceptance. According to the editor of *Logos,* Michael Thompson, however, this acceptance has not been accompanied by the embrace of those normative or cultural imperatives—also generated during the Enlightenment—necessary for bringing a genuinely cosmopolitan society into existence. In a broader vision of politics, then, building a cosmopolitan world must become a matter of linking the scientific and the cultural dimensions of planetary life. But this invites the question of whether a global ethic is possible or even desirable. In reflecting on a conference marking the one hundredth anniversary of the 1893 Parliament of the World's Religions, the philosopher Karsten Struhl examines the difficulties associated with such an undertaking and whether, indeed, there is a transcendent position—akin to "God's eye"—that can privilege one ethical framework above others. This speculative discussion, I believe, actually intensifies the practical importance of dealing with human rights. And this needs to be done by linking its seemingly unyielding ideals with a contingent and interest-laden reality. That is the purpose behind the essay of Kurt Jacobsen and Alba Alexander. Long-time students of international relations and American politics, they provide a unique articulation of the tensions between the moral assertion of human rights and the interests associated with interventionist politics. Indeed, the contribution by Micheline Ishay—author of a seminal history of human rights—is also primarily concerned with the extent to which human rights can address the costs of globalization in what she calls an "age of empire."

Unifying this collection is a political purpose: the attempt to engage in progressive fashion the dominant trends, the terrible excesses, and the positive prospects of a decidedly new era marked by the transition from a corrosive interplay between nation-states to a burgeoning planetary politics. The point here is less to provide systematic definitions and finished conclusions than to raise some new perspectives and begin a new discussion. Given the interplay of unforeseen contingencies and conflicting ideals, that task, indeed, is difficult enough.

I

THE GLOBAL THEATER

1

The Silence of Words and Political Dynamics in the World Risk Society

ULRICH BECK

September 11, 2001, will stand for many things in the history of humanity. Among these, no less for the failure, for the silence of language before such an event: "war," "crime," "enemy," "victory," and "terror"—the terms melt in the mouth like rotten mushrooms. NATO summed up the alliance, but it was neither an attack from the outside, nor an attack of a sovereign state against another sovereign state. September 11 does not stand for a second Pearl Harbor. The attack was not directed toward the U.S. military machine, rather, toward innocent civilians. The act speaks the language of genocidal hate that knows "no negotiation," "no dialogue," "no compromises," and, lastly, "no peace."

The notion of "enemy" is misleading. It stems from an imaginary world in which armies conquer or get conquered and then sign "cease-fires" and "peace treaties." The terrorist attacks are, however, neither just a "crime" nor a simple case for "national justice." The notion and institute of "police" proves to be just as inadequate for acts whose results resemble military attacks, just as the police are in no position to dismiss a cadre of perpetrators who appear to fear nothing. Appropriately, the notion of "civil emergency services" seems to lose its meaning. We live, think, and act according to zombielike notions; according to notions that have died, but continue to rule our thinking and our actions. Yet if the military, trapped in its old notions, responds with conventional methods—such as surface bombings, for instance—then it is legitimate to fear that these are not only ineffective but also counterproductive: new Osama bin Ladens will be bred.

This is what makes suicide bombings, even months or years after they have occurred, incomprehensible. The notions on which our worldviews are predicated and the distinctions between war and peace, military and police, war and crime, internal and external security—particularly between internal and external in general—have been magnified. Who would have thought that internal security, even Germany's, for instance, would have to be defended in the remotest valleys of Afghanistan? "Defend!" Again, another false notion. Even the distinction between defense and attack does not hold up anymore. Can one still say that the United States is defending its internal security on foreign soil, in Afghanistan and so forth? What if all of these concepts are false and if language fails in the face of reality? What has really happened? No one knows. But would it be braver to be silent about it? The destruction of the Twin Towers in New York was followed by an explosion of chatty silence and meaningless action. To quote Hugo von Hofmannsthal: "I succeeded no longer in grasping reality with the simplifying gaze of familiarity. Everything broke down into pieces for me, and those pieces again into more pieces, and nothing else would let itself be encompassed under one concept. Single words would swim around me; they ran into eyes that stared at me and that I stared back into."[1]

This silence of words must finally be broken. We can no longer afford to keep quiet about this. If we could at least succeed in naming the silence of single ideas, to name the distance between idea and reality to presume and to prudently break the bridges of understanding to the novel reality that stems from our civilizing actions, most likely not much, but something, could be gained. In this article I would like to clarify the notion of world risk society and within this context criticize and redefine a series of notions:

1. the concepts of *war* and *terror*
2. the concepts of *economic globalization* and *neoliberalism*
3. the concepts of *state* and *sovereignty*

WHAT IS A WORLD RISK SOCIETY?

What do events and threats like Chernobyl, environmental catastrophes, discussions regarding human genetics, the Asian economic crisis, and current threats of terrorist attacks have in common? I will explain what I mean with an example. A few years ago the U.S. Congress contracted a scientific committee to develop a language to elucidate the danger of America's permanent sites for radioactive waste. The problem to be solved was the following: How do concepts and symbols have to be constructed in order to convey a single, unchanging message ten thousand years from now?[2]

The committee was made up of physicians, anthropologists, linguists, brain researchers, psychologists, molecular biologists, archeologists, artists, and so forth. It was supposed to answer the unavoidable question: Will the United States still be around in ten thousand years? For the government committee the answer was obvious: *USA forever!* To be sure, the central problem, as to how it is possible at a distance of ten thousand years to have a conversation with the future, gradually proved to be unsolvable. Scholars began searching for models among the oldest symbols of humanity. They began studying the construction of Stonehenge (1500 BC) and the pyramids, researching the history of the reception of Homer and the Bible, and wanting the life cycles of documents explained to them. But in any case, these were only enough for looking back a couple of thousand years, certainly not tens of thousands. The anthropologists recommended the symbol of the skull and crossbones. A historian remembered that to alchemists, the skull and crossbones meant resurrection. A psychologist performed an experiment with three-year-olds: when he pasted the skull and crossbones on a bottle, they yelled "poison" in fright, but if he pasted the same symbol on the wall, they animatedly yelled "pirates!"

Other scientists suggested literally plastering the ground around the permanent waste sites with ceramic, metal, and iron planks that contained all sorts of warnings. However, the judgment of the linguists was unambiguous: they would only be understood for a maximum of two thousand years! Precisely the scientific meticulousness with which the committee proceeded clarified what the concept of world risk society implies, uncovers, and renders understandable: human language fails before the task of informing future generations of the dangers that we inadvertently put into the world through the use of certain technologies. The modern world increases the worlds of difference between the language of calculable risks in which we think and act and the world of noncalculable uncertainty that we create with the same speed that we develop technology. With the past decisions on nuclear energy and our contemporary decisions on the use of genetic technology, human genetics, nanotechnology, computer sciences, and so forth, we set off unpredictable, uncontrollable, and incommunicable consequences that endanger life on earth.

What is new, then, about the risk society? Were not all societies, all people, all epochs always surrounded by dangers that prompted these societies to unite just in order to defend themselves? The concept of risk is a modern concept. It requires decisions and attempts to render the unpredictable consequences of civil decisions predictable and controllable. When one says, for example, that a smoker's risk for cancer is X amount high and the catastrophe risk of a nuclear power plant Y amount, then this means that risks are avoidable, negative consequences of decisions that appear predictable through the probability of accidents and diseases and thus are unlike natural catastrophes. The novelty of the world risk society lies in the fact that we, with our civilizing decisions, cause global consequences that trigger problems and dangers that radically contradict the institutionalized language and promises of the authorities in catastrophic cases highlighted worldwide (as in Chernobyl and now in the terrorist attacks in New York and Washington). The *political* explosiveness of the world risk society lies precisely in this fact. Its heart rests in the mass media, politics, and bureaucracy—not necessarily at the site of its happening. This political explosiveness does not allow itself to be described or measured in the language of risk, the number of victims dead and wounded, nor in scientific formulas. This causes it to "explode"—if the metaphor is permitted—with responsibility, demands of rationality, legitimizations through reality checks; for the other side of the present danger is the failure of institutions that derive their legitimacy through a declared mastery of danger. For this reason the "social birth" of a global danger is an equally improbable as well as dramatic, traumatic, world society–shaking event. In the shock highlighted by the mass media it becomes evident for a second in the world that the silence of words—or, according to one of Goya's etchings, "the slumber of reason"—generates monsters.

Three layers of danger can be identified in the world risk society. Each one either follows a different logic of conflict, circles around or represses other topics, or crushes or empowers certain priorities: first, ecological crises, second, global economic crises, and third—since September 11—the risk of transnational terrorist networks. Despite the differences, all three possibilities of danger present a common pattern of political opportunities and contradictions within the world risk society: in an age in which faith in God, class, nation, and the government is disappearing, the recognized and acknowledged global nature of danger becomes a fusion of relations in which the apparent and irrevocable constants of the political world suddenly melt and become malleable. At the same time, however, new conflict and political alternatives present themselves and once again question the unity of the world risk society: How could these dangers be overcome within the limits of historical nonsimultaneities of single nations and cultures?

This is how the horrific pictures of terrorism, these obscene images of a live mass murder and a live suicide, staged as a global television appearance, shook people worldwide and triggered a political reflexivity that contradicted all expectations. It was questioned and discussed over and over again: What could unite the world? The experimental answer is: an attack from Mars. This type of terrorism is like an attack from an "internal Mars." For a single historical blink of an eye, the disputed sites and nations stand united against the common enemy of global terrorism.

Precisely the universalization of terrorist threats against the nations of the world renders the battle against global terrorism a major political challenge in which opposing camps forge new alliances, regional conflicts are dammed, and the cards of world politics get reshuffled. Until recently, national arms reduction plans still dominated Washington's political actions and debates—now there is no more talk of this. Instead the view seems to have taken hold that not even a perfect arms reduction system could have prevented these attacks and that the way to ensure U.S. internal security is not through the United States acting on its own, but in a global alliance. Relations between former Cold War enemies, Moscow and Washington, play an outstanding role. U.S. unilateralism falls flat on its face in the world risk society and with respect to national interests. It is not possible for the United States to arrest Osama bin Laden in an isolated action by the CIA and the Pentagon without the rest of the world. The world risk society requires a multilateralism of the sort in which Russia comes out of the role of the petitioner and switches over to the role of nation to be wooed. Russian president Vladimir Putin's decision to completely and unmistakably place himself on the side of modernity, civilized and attacked, opened up new power and opportunities for refashioning himself as an important partner in the multipronged balance of power in the global alliance. However, this certainly does not create the illusion that the war against terrorism can underhandedly expand into a war against Islam, that is, a war that doesn't conquer terrorism, but feeds and increases it; or a war that might reduce important liberties or renew protectionism and nationalism and demonize cultural others.

In other words, the global nature of the perceived threat has two faces: it creates new forms for a political risk society *and* at the same time regional inconsistencies and inequalities with regard to those who are affected by those dangers. The fact that the collapse of global financial markets or the change of climate in single regions, for instance, has diverse effects, does not change the fact that in principle *everyone* could be affected, and that overcoming these problems in the present state necessitates global political efforts. Environmental problems such as global warming and the overpopulation of the world (of present and future generations) could promote the idea of a "community of common destiny."

However, this does not by any means occur without conflict. For example, the question arises as to what extent industrial nations have the right to demand that developing nations protect important global resources such as rain forests, while using a lion's share of energy resources for themselves. Yet, it is precisely these conflicts that form common ground by underlining the fact that global solutions need to be found and that these are to be brought about not through war but through negotiations.

However, this by no means implies that there is only *one* answer to the demands of the world risk society. The ways *into* the world risk society are for European and non-European nations and cultures just as different as the ways out of it can be. In this sense it becomes clear that in the future there will be *many* modernities. The debates surrounding an Asian modernity or a Chinese, Russian, South American, or African one are just beginning now. This type of discourse clears all doubt that the European monopoly on modernity is broken in the world risk society. Seen in such a manner, the radical critique of modernity in a non-European realm turns out to be one against "excessive individualism," against the loss of "cultural identity and worth," in short, against a "McDonaldization of the world," not a straightforward rejection of modernity, rather far more an attempt to test and try out *other modernities* that selectively hark back to the Western model of modernity.

The everyday realm of the world risk society does not come forth as a love affair between everyone and everything. It comes about and consists in the perceived necessity for global consequences to civilizing actions—regardless of whether or not these consequences create globality through information technology and networking, financial channels, natural crises, cultural symbols, the pending atmospheric catastrophe, or terrorist threats. Therefore, it is the reflexivity of the world risk society that breaks the silence of words and allows globality to become painfully aware of itself in its own context and builds new approaches to conflicts and alliances. What has been shown for the modern nation-states is that they can only keep their vulnerability in check through constant communication—this has proved true even for the world risk society. This brings me to my second question: How do the meanings of "terrorism" and "war" change in the context of the world risk society?

TERRORISM AND WAR

Even the notion of "terrorist" is misleading in the end when talking about the novelty of the threat because it creates the illusion of a familiarity with motifs of national liberation movements that do not apply at all to the perpetrators of suicide and mass murder. What is simply inexplicable to the Western observer is namely the way in which fanatical antimodernism, antiglobalism, *and* modern global thinking and acting are interrelated.

Hannah Arendt coined the term "banality of evil" with the fascist mass murderer Adolf Eichmann in mind. In this vein, we can imagine absolutely evil technocrats who are family oriented, but not terrorists in the name of God, who marry in the West, earn engineering degrees in Germany, bear a fondness for vodka, and quietly plan years in advance technically perfect group suicide murders as mass murders and execute them in cold blood. How is this at all rooted in modernity and to be simultaneously understood as the archaic selflessness of evil?

If up until now the military focused its attention on itself and other national military organizations and their defenses, now it is transnational threats from underground perpetrators and networks that challenge world governments. Just as earlier in the cultural realm, it is possible to experience the *death of distance* in the military realm as well, that is, the end of the state monopoly on violence in a civilized world, in which everything can turn into weapons in the hands of a few decisive fanatics. The peaceful symbols of the civilized society could be converted into instruments of hell. In principle, this is nothing new but, rather, it is a critical experience that is omnipresent.

With the horrific scenes from New York, terrorist groups have established themselves as new global actors in competition with states, economies, and civil societies in one swoop. The terrorist networks are similar to "violence NGOs." They act like nongovernmental organizations (NGOs) in a nonterritorially bound, decentered fashion—acting locally on the one hand, and transnationally on the other. They use the Internet. While Greenpeace, for example, uses environmental crises, and Amnesty International, human rights causes, against national governments, terrorist NGOs increase their monopoly on violence. This means that on the one hand, this type of transnational terrorism is not limited to *Islamic* terrorism. Rather, it can align itself with any possible goal, ideology, and fundamentalism. On the other hand, a distinction has to be made between the terrorism of national freedom movements that are nationally and territorially bound and that of the new, transnational terrorist networks that act without any territorial affiliations and across national boundaries and manage, as a consequence, to cancel the national language of war and the military with one strike. Previous terrorists tried to save their lives after committing terrorist acts. Suicide terrorists create a monstrous destructive force through their intended surrendering of their lives. The suicide bomber is the most radical contrast to the *homo oeconomicus*. He is both economically and morally uninhibited and, for this reason, a bearer of absolute cruelty. In a strict sense, the act and the suicide bomber are one. A suicide bomber can neither commit a suicide attack more than once, nor can state authorities convict him. This singularity is marked by the simultaneity of act, confession, and self-extinguishment.

To be exact, governments did not even have to search for suicide bombers in order to find them guilty of their crimes. The culprits have confessed to their crimes and turned their weapons on themselves. For this reason, the antiterrorism alliance does not want to capture the culprits of New York and Washington (these have pulverized themselves); rather, it seeks the alleged people behind them: the puppet masters or the state patrons. Whereas the culprits turn the weapons on themselves, the causalities dissipate and get lost. This means that states are indispensable for building transnational terrorist networks. But perhaps it is precisely this lack of government identification, this lack of functional government structures, that offers the humus for terrorist activities. Perhaps the placing of responsibility on governments and on those behind the scenes who give the orders stems from military thinking, and we are on the threshold of an *individualization of war*, a type of warfare in which wars are no longer conducted state against state, rather, individuals against states.

The power of terrorist actions rises with a series of conditions: with the vulnerability of a civilization; with the global, mass media–informed presence of terrorist risk; with the U.S. president's assessment that "civilization" is under threat because of these culprits; and with their readiness to extinguish themselves. Finally, the risks of terrorism exponentially multiply with technological advancement. With the technologies of the future—genetic engineering, nanotechnology, and robotics—we are opening what Bill Joy termed "a new Pandora's box." Genetic manipulation, communication technologies, and artificial intelligence are all interconnected ways that can get around the government monopoly of violence and will wind up opening, if no international bar is placed in front of this, the door and gate to an individualization of war.

Thus a genetically engineered menace with long periods of incubation that threatens and targets specific populations—in other words, a genetically engineered miniature bomb—can be built by anyone without any tremendous effort. This is just to cite one of many examples. The difference between atomic and biological weapons is notable. It is founded on scientifically based technological developments that can be easily expanded and are capable of revolutionizing themselves again and again, so much so that the possibility of government controls and monopolies fails, as with atomic and biochemical weapons when they were given as specific materials and resources (weapon-convertible uranium, costly laboratories). *Politically*, this empowerment of individuals against governments could open a Pandora's box. Not only were the recent boundaries between the military and civil society torn down, but also the boundaries between innocent and guilty, between suspects and nonsuspects, where jurisdiction up until now made sharp distinctions. If the individualization of war should continue to be a threat, then the citizen will have to *prove* that he or she is not dangerous, because under these circumstances every individual could come under suspicion of being a potential terrorist. Everyone has to put up with the fact that he or she, in the absence of any concrete reason, has to be checked "for security reasons." This indicates that in the end, the individualization of war can translate into the death of democracy. Governments would have to ally themselves with other governments against citizens in order to avert the dangers with which their citizens threatened them.

When thought through fully, a world premise in the present discussion on terrorism, namely, the distinction between "good" and "bad" terrorists, crumbles. Nationalists are to be respected and fundamentalists are to be abhorred. If one wants to find justifications for such value judgments and distinctions in the age of the nationalistic modernity, they will become a moral and political perversion in the terroristic world risk society as well as in consideration of the possibility of an individualization of war.

Is a political response to this challenge at all possible? I would like to name one principle, and it is that of the *law*. In a nationalist context, that which infringes upon the legal sensibilities of the civilized world is the fact that the victims of the attempts assume the roles of prosecutor, judge, and executive

power at once. This type of "self-justice" must also be overcome in international relations. Even if relations between the states are not fully ripe for it, the
global alliance against terrorism has to be based on the law. Thus it follows
that an international convention against terrorism must be discussed and ratified. It must be a convention that not only clarifies certain notions but also
provides a legal basis for the intergovernmental prosecution of terrorists—in
other words, this convention has to create a unified, universal space for the law
to be executed. This, among other things, requires that the statutes of the international courts of all nations, even those of the United States, have to be
ratified.[3] The goal would be that terrorism would be punished as a crime
against humanity worldwide. States that refused to adopt this convention
would have to face combined sanctions from all states. Would this not be an
interest that Europe and Russia, based on their historical backgrounds, could
espouse as their own in order to sharpen their political profile in the global
alliance—to help in the battle against terrorism by building its own opposing
military momentum to success? This brings me to my third question: How do
the meanings of the concepts "economic globalization" and "neoliberalism"
shift in the context of the world risk society?

ECONOMIC GLOBALIZATION AND NEOLIBERALISM

Allow me to start with an anecdote. When I hear the word "globalization," the
following political caricature appears before my eyes: The Spanish con-
querors. The conquistadores appear in the New World in their shiny armor
with horses and weapons. The speech bubble reads, "We have come to you to
talk to you about God, civilization, and the truth." And a group of bewildered
native onlookers responds, "Of course. What would you like to know?"

This scenario can easily be transported into the present. Economic experts
from the World Bank and the International Monetary Foundation, corporate
managers, lawyers, and diplomats step off of intercontinental flights in post-
Soviet Moscow. A speech bubble reads, "We have come to you to talk to you
about democracy, human rights, and the free market economy." A delegation
of readers responds, "But of course. How else do the Germans go around
spreading open violence against foreigners on their streets?"

Perhaps this caricature gives an idea about yesterday's situation, which is no
longer valid today. The terrorist attacks and the anthrax scare raise a question
that can no longer be swept under the rug: Is the triumph of the economy already over? Will the primacy of politics be rediscovered? Has neoliberalism's

apparently unstoppable victory suddenly been broken? In fact, the outbreak of global terrorism resembles a Chernobyl of globalization. If with Chernobyl it was about taking the exaltation of nuclear energy to its grave, with September 11 it is about bidding farewell to the beatification of neoliberalism. The suicide bombers have not only uncovered the vulnerability of Western civilization but have also at the same time given a taste of the sorts of conflicts that are generated by economic globalization. In the world of global risks the mark of neoliberalism rapidly loses its credibility to substitute the state and politics with economics.

The privatization of airline security in the United States is particularly emblematic of the above point. Until now there has been quite a bit of reluctance to discuss this because the tragedy of September 11 was homemade, in part. Moreover, the United States' vulnerability certainly has something to do with its political philosophy. America is a neoliberal nation through and through and is thus unwilling to pay the price for public safety. When all is said and done, it was long known that the United States was a target for terrorist attacks. But unlike in Europe, flight security was privatized and taken over by miracle-working, highly flexible part-time workers whose wages are lower than those of fast-food workers, meaning approximately six dollars an hour. Persons who go through very few hours of training and practice this profession for no more than six months occupy these important security positions. Before restricting the basic rights of all citizens to guard against terrorism and endangering democracy and an under-rule-of-law state, the United States should make efforts toward making flight security government run and more professional. This is just one example of the many other improvements that could be made.

It is America's neoliberal concept of itself—its government penny-pinching on the one hand, and the triad of deregulation, liberalization, and privatization on the other—that contributes to America's vulnerability to terrorism. The measure to which this realization catches on will break the hegemonic power that neoliberalism has gained in shaping its philosophy and actions in the past. In this sense the horrific pictures of New York contain a message that has yet to be deciphered: a state, a country, can become neoliberal to the point of death.

The economic commentators of the big daily newspapers worldwide suspect this and insist that what was true before September 11 cannot after September 11 be false. In other words, the neoliberal model will persist even after the terrorist attacks because there are no other alternatives to it. But this is precisely what is wrong. This reveals a lack of alternative thinking. Neoliberalism has always been frowned upon for being a good-weather philosophy that only works when blatant conflicts or crises arise. The neoliberal imperative insists that too much government and politics and the regulating hand of bureaucracy are the real causes of world problems like unemployment, global poverty, and economic breakdowns. The success of neoliberalism relied on the promise that a free economy and a globalization of markets would solve the problems of humanity. It championed the belief that if free rein were given to egoism, inequality could be battled against in accordance with global standards and global justice could prevail. Instead, this belief of capitalist fundamentalists in the magic power of the market has recently proven itself to be a dangerous illusion.

In times of crisis, neoliberalism is left standing without a single political response. The approach of increasing the dosage of bitter economic medicine even more radically when a breakdown is pending or comes full circle in order to rectify the problematic consequences of globalization is an illusionary theory that only now begins to pay the price. On the contrary, terrorist threats make the simple truths that the neoliberal triumph had suppressed known again: The separation of the world economy from politics is illusionary. There is no security without the state and public service. Without taxation there is no government. Without taxation there is no education, no affordable health care, no social security. Without taxation there is no democracy. Without the public, democracy and civil society have no legitimacy. And without legitimacy there is also no security. Thus it follows that without the shape and form of a legally regulated (meaning recognized and not violent) national settlement of conflict in the future and above all on the global level, there will also be no world economy in any form.

Wherein lies, then, the alternative to neoliberalism? Certainly not in national protectionism. We need an expanded concept of politics that is capable of appropriately regulating the potential of crises and conflicts. The Tobin Tax—being demanded more and more by political parties in Europe and worldwide—on the unbridled flow of capital is only a first programmatic step. Neoliberalism insisted upon the economy breaking out of its nationalistic dwelling and building transnational rules for itself. At the same time it assumed that the government would keep on playing its old game and keep its national boundaries. After the terrorist attack, even the States recognized the power and possibilities of transnational cooperation, even if only for the scope of internal security. All of a sudden the opposite of neoliberalism, the importance of the state, becomes once again omnipresent and in its oldest Hobbesian variant: that of guaranteeing security. What was unthinkable up until recently—a European warrant of arrest that disregards the sacred national sovereignty of matters of the law and the police—is now within reach. But perhaps soon we will also experience a similar joining of forces in light of the possible world economic crises. The economy has to prepare itself for new rules and new circumstances. The times of "everyone to the best of their abilities and will" are certainly over.

The terrorist resistance to globalization has achieved in this sense the exact opposite of what it sought to achieve. It introduced a new era of globalization of politics and of the states—the transnational invention of the political through cooperation and networking. In this way the not yet publicly noticed strange natural law that to resist globalization—whether you like it or not— only accelerates its engine has proven itself. This paradox is enough to grasp that globalization is the name for a strange process, which gets realized on two opposite tracks: either one is for it or against it. All of those who oppose globalization not only share global communications media with those in favor of it, but they also operate on the foundation of global rights, global markets, global mobility, and global networks. They also think and act in global categories that they create through their acts of global openness and global attention. One need only to think of the precision with which the terrorists of September 11 staged their acts in New York as a television-worthy *live* catastrophe and *live* mass murder. They were able to count on the destruction of the second tower through a passenger aircraft transformed into a missile being transmitted *live* throughout the entire world through omnipresent television cameras.

Does globalization have to be the cause for terrorist attacks? Is it perhaps about an understandable reaction to a neoliberal steamroller that, as critics state it, seeks to flatten out every corner of this world? No, that is nonsense. No cause, no abstract idea, no God can justify or excuse these attacks. Globalization is an ambivalent process that cannot be reversed. Precisely smaller and weak states give up their politics of self-sufficiency and rush to join the world market. How did one of the big daily newspapers title the news about the German chancellor's visit to the Ukraine? "We forgive the crusaders and await the investors." In fact, there is just one thing that is worse than being steamrolled by foreign investors and that is *not* being steamrolled by foreign investors. It is necessary, however, to link economic globalization with a policy of cosmopolitan understanding. The dignity of people, their cultural identities, the otherness of others must be taken more seriously in the future. Wouldn't it make sense to build a new pillar in the alliance against terrorism? To build a cultural bridge, so to speak, and foster a dialogue between the cultures on the inside and outside in relation to the countries in the Islamic world and also to the countries of the so-called Third and Fourth Worlds, which view themselves as victims of globalization? And couldn't a culturally extroverted Europe, and in particular a culturally extroverted Germany, play a leading role since it is less plagued by a colonial past, but still cognizant of its obligation because of the Holocaust?

This brings me to the fourth and final question: How and to what extent do the concepts of "state" and "sovereignty" change in the eyes of the world risk society?

STATE AND SOVEREIGNTY

To get right to it, terrorist attacks reinforce the state, but cancel its central historical form, the nation-state. National security is, in the borderless age of risks, no longer national security. This is the biggest lesson from the terrorist attacks. Certainly, there were always alliances. The deciding difference is that today, global alliances are necessary not only for external but also for *internal* security. In the past it was accurate to say that foreign policy was a question of choice, not of necessity. Today, on the contrary, a new principle of this as well as that governs the scene; national security and international cooperation are directly linked with one another. The only way to have national security in the face of the threat of globalized terrorism (but also of financial risks, the downfall of organized crime) is transnational cooperation. The paradoxical principle is valid here: states need to *de*nationalize and *trans*nationalize themselves. This means that they need to sacrifice certain aspects of their autonomy in order to overcome their *national* problems in a globalized world. The acquisition of a new space for action and leeway, that is, the expansion of political sovereignty and control, has to be paid for with "self-denationalization." The dismantling of national autonomy and the growth of national sovereignty do not by any means logically cancel each other out. Rather they can reciprocally reinforce and expedite each other. The logic of the zero-sum game that was valid for empires, superpowers, colonialism, economic and cultural imperialism, independent nation-states, and military blocs loses its power of justification.

In this sense it is crucial to introduce the difference between sovereignty and autonomy. The nation-state was based on the equation of sovereignty with autonomy. Viewed in this light, economic independence, cultural diversification, and military, legal, and technological cooperation between states automatically lead to loss of autonomy and sovereignty. Though if one measures sovereignty by political creative power and fixes it on the question of to what extent a state succeeds at gaining power and influence on the stage of world politics and increases its citizens' security and prosperity, it follows that an increasing interconnection and cooperation leads to a loss of autonomy and to a *gain* in sovereignty. In other words, the worth of a state like Russia in the world is no longer measured by its potential for confrontation, as it was during the Cold War, but by its *cooperative* potential and art, that is, by its ranking in the networked states of the world and the world market as well as by its presence in supranational organizations. That is, separated and united sovereignty does not reduce this; on the contrary, it increases the potential for single-state sovereignty. In this sense, not only the global terrorist threats but also the world risk society in its entirety opens a new era of transnational and multilateral cooperation.

The disintegration of the Soviet Union, Yugoslavia, and Czechoslovakia notably led to a large number of nationally defined successor states in which ethnic, national, and civic identities in part find conflictual overlap with one another and in part exclude one another. This newly awakened national consciousness in the countries and states of central and eastern Europe seems at first glance to be in conflict with the discovery and development of cooperative transnational states in the face of the challenges placed by the world risk society. The opposite is true. These challenges can contribute toward taming the borderless national and ethnic tensions in the post-Soviet states. If these countries concur in defining their position such that they can be confronted with common historical challenges, then it will be possible and necessary to find political frames and coordinates to vote on national solutions and demands on sovereignty under transnational conditions. This is now being experienced and spelled out in geopolitical questions of borderless "internal security" of states that overlap one another both ethnically and nationally. In any case, this can be transferred onto questions regarding regional world economic cooperation, the curbing of global financial crises, the impending atmospheric catastrophes and environmental dangers, poverty, and, last but not least, human rights. In other words, in the recognized and acknowledged threats of the future there may even be a key to lessen the historical experiences of violence cooperatively.

Two ideal types of transnational cooperation among states emerge: "surveillance" states and "open world" states, in which national autonomy gets reduced in order to renew and expand national sovereignty in the world risk society. Surveillance states with their cooperative power threaten to become fortress states in which security and the military will be writ large and freedom and democracy writ small. The word is already out that Western societies accustomed to peace and prosperity lack the necessary measure of friend-or-foe thinking and the readiness, the advantage that the marvel of human rights had up until now, to give up the now necessary measures of resistance. This attempt to build a Western fortress against the cultural others is omnipresent and will surely increase in the coming years. A policy of state authoritarianism that behaved adaptively in foreign relations and authoritarian in domestic affairs could stem from this. For the winners of globalization, neoliberalism is appropriate; for the losers of globalization, it stirs up terrorism and xenophobia and administers doses of the poison of racism. This would resemble a victory of the terrorists because the nations of modernity would rob themselves precisely of that which makes them attractive and superior: freedom and democracy.

In the future, it will mostly come to posing the following question: What are you fighting for, what are we fighting for, if it is about fighting transnational terrorism? An open world state system based on the recognition of the otherness of others holds the answers to this.

Nation-states, whether their borders are internal or external, can possess ethnic and national identities that overlap and exclude one another or have not grown together peaceably. Open world states, on the other hand, emphasize the necessity of self-determination with the responsibility toward others and uniting foreigners within and beyond national borders. It is not about denying self-determination or damming it in—on the contrary, it is about freeing it from national tunnel vision and connecting it with an openness toward world interests. Open world states not only fight against terrorism, but also against the *causes* of terrorism in the world. They gain and renew the powers of creation and persuasion of the political by solving pressing global problems and problems that seem insolvable by single national initiative.

Open world states are founded on the principle of the state's national indifference. Similar to the Westphalian peace that was able to end the sixteenth-century religious civil war through separation of church and state—which is the crux of the argument here—the world national (civil) wars of the twentieth and early twenty-first centuries are also addressed with a separation of church and state. As the irreligious state renders the practice of different religions possible, open world states have to provide this for border-crossing closeness of ethnic, national, and religious identities through the principle of constitutional tolerance.

I am coming to my conclusion. It is almost superfluous to pronounce it, but I am hopelessly rooted in the tradition of the Enlightenment, even if self-critically applied. With this in mind I have attempted inadequately and provisionally to trace how a political handbook, which is seemingly composed for perpetuity, gets dissolved and reshaped. Perhaps it has astounded you as much as it has me that the fear of danger that paralyzes us also succeeds in obstructing our view of the very broad political perspectives that are opening up. I have hinted at three of these only seemingly paradoxical opportunities that the world risk society has to offer.

First, it seems possible and necessary to me to create an *international legal foundation* for the alliance against terrorism. It would entail an antiterror regime that regulated issues like tax investigation as well as the extradition of perpetrators, the authorization of armed forces, the jurisdiction of courts, and so forth; only in this way can the long-term challenge in shifting historical and political contexts really be met.

Second, it would be necessary to base the promise of the alliance not only on military means but also on a credible *policy of dialogue*—first of all with regard to the Islamic world, but also toward other cultures who see their worth as threatened through globalization. Only in this way can what military actions provoke in helping terrorists to succeed in allying themselves worldwide with the Islamic populations be prevented. Perhaps the more culturally experienced and, in foreign policy, more dialogue-experienced Europe is better equipped to do this than the culturally introverted America?

Third, the dangers of the world risk society could be transformed into opportunities in order to create regional structures of cooperation between *open world multinational states*. Let me end with a quote from Immanuel Kant: "To think of oneself as a member of a cosmopolitan society in compliance with state laws is the most sublime idea that man can have about his predicament and which cannot be thought of without enthusiasm."

NOTES

This article is based on a talk given to the Russian Duma in November 2001 and was translated from the German by Elena Mancini.

1. Hugo von Hofmannsthal, *Der Brief des Lord Chandos* (Stuttgart, 2000), pp. 51–52.

2. See Gregory Benford, *Deep Time: How Humanity Communicates across Millenia* (New York: Avon, 1999), as well as Frank Schirrmacher, "Ten Thousand Years of Isolation," *Frankfurter Allgemeine Zeitung*, no. 209, September 2000, p. 49, whom I have to thank for this example.

3. Baltasar Garzón, "Die einzige Antwort auf den Terror" ("The only answer to terror"), *Die Zeit*, no. 44, October 25, 2001, p. 11.

2

Globalism and the Selling of Globalization

Manfred B. Steger

In his celebrated address to a joint session of Congress nine days after the terrorist attacks on September 11, President George W. Bush made it abundantly clear that the deep sources of the new conflict between "the civilized world" and terrorism were to be found neither in religion nor culture, but in political ideology. Referring to the radical network of terrorists and the governments that support them as "heirs of all the murderous ideologies of the twentieth century," Bush described the sinister motives of the terrorists: "By sacrificing human life to serve their radical visions, by abandoning every value except the will to power, they [the terrorists] follow the path of fascism, Nazism and totalitarianism. And they will follow that path all the way to where it ends in history's unmarked grave of discarded lies."

There are two remarkable pieces of information that stand out in this passage of the president's speech. First, by omitting any reference to Communist ideology, the president chose to put political expediency over ethical principle, presumably not to alienate China. In other words, his silence on the horrors of Communism makes sense within the administration's overall strategic framework of putting together the broadest possible alliance against terrorism. Second and more importantly, Bush's reference to the birth of a new totalitarian ideology runs counter to the idea of a "de-ideologized world" that dominated the post-Soviet intellectual landscape in the West. Advanced by social theorists such as Francis Fukuyama more than a decade ago, the "end of ideology" thesis postulated that the passing of Marxism-Leninism marked nothing less than the "end point of mankind's ideological evolution," evident in the total exhaustion of viable ideological alternatives to Western liberalism. Fukuyama explicitly downplayed the significance of rising religious fundamentalism and ethnic nationalism in the "New World Order" of the 1990s, predicting that the global triumph of the "Western idea" would be irreversible and that the spread of its consumerist culture to all corners of the earth would prove to be unstoppable.

Bush's emphasis on the continuing significance of ideology also runs counter to the popular thesis of the "clash of civilizations" suggested by Harvard political scientist Samuel Huntington in the mid-1990s. Arguing that the fundamental source of conflict in the New World Order would be neither ideological nor economic but "cultural," Huntington identified seven or eight self-contained "civilizations," of which the conflict between "Islam" and "the West" receives most attention. While seemingly pertinent to the current situation, it is precisely this large-scale scenario of clashing cultures and religions that the president rejected when he insisted that America's new enemy was not Islam per se, but "those who commit evil in the name of Allah" and thus "blaspheme the name of Allah." Indeed, in a recent newspaper interview, Huntington himself admitted that the current crisis does not fit his model since the former appears not to be based upon a wholesale civilizational paradigm but on extremist political ideas within Islam. In short, ideology is alive and well.

Given the resilience of ideas, values, and beliefs as the source of major conflicts, I submit that we are currently witnessing the beginning of a new ideological struggle over the meaning and the direction of globalization. If global terrorism constitutes one extreme protagonist in this struggle, then neoliberal globalism represents the other. It is my purpose here to explore the main features of the latter position.

At the outset of the new century, it has already become a cliché to observe that we live in an age of globalization. Although it may not be an entirely new phenomenon, globalization in its current phase has been described as an unprecedented compression of time and space reflected in the tremendous intensification of social, political, economic, and cultural interconnections and interdependencies on a global scale. But not everybody experiences globalization in the same way. In fact, people living in various parts of the world are affected very differently by this gigantic transformation of social structures and cultural zones. Globalization seems to generate enormous wealth and opportunity for the few while relegating the many to conditions of abject poverty and hopelessness.

The public interpretation of the origin, direction, and meaning of the profound social changes that go by the name of globalization has fallen disproportionately to a powerful phalanx of social forces located mainly in the global North. Corporate managers, executives of large transnational corporations, corporate lobbyists, journalists and public relations specialists, intellectuals writing for a large public audience, state bureaucrats, and politicians serve as the chief advocates of globalism, the dominant ideology of our time. Saturating the public with idealized images of a consumerist, free market world, globalists simultaneously distort social reality, legitimate and advance their power interests, and shape collective and personal identities. In order to analyze these ideological maneuvers, it is important to distinguish between *globalism*, a neoliberal market ideology of Anglo-American origin that endows globalization with certain norms, values, and meanings, and *globalization*, a set of social processes defined and described by various commentators in different, often contradictory ways.

Globalists have marshaled their considerable resources to sell to the public the alleged benefits of market liberalization: rising global living standards, economic efficiency, individual freedom and democracy, and unprecedented technological progress. Globalists promise to "liberate" the economy from social constraints by privatizing public enterprises, deregulating trade and industry, providing massive tax cuts, reducing public expenditures, and maintaining strict control of organized labor. Inspired by the liberal utopia of the "self-regulating market," neoliberal globalists have linked their quaint nineteenth-century ideals to fashionable "globalization talk." Thus, globalism represents a gigantic repackaging enterprise—the pouring of old philosophical wine into new ideological bottles.

Dozens of magazines, journals, newspapers, and electronic media feed their readers a steady diet of globalist claims. For example, *Business Week* recently featured a cover story on globalization that contained the following statement: "For nearly a decade, political and business leaders have struggled to persuade the American public of the virtues of globalization." Citing the results of a national poll on globalization conducted in April 2000, the author of the article goes on to report that about 65 percent of the respondents consider globalization to be a "good thing." At the same time, however, nearly 70 percent of those polled believe that free trade agreements with low-wage countries are responsible for driving down wages in the United States. Ending on a rather combative note, the author issues a stern warning to American politicians and business leaders that they should be more effective in high-lighting the benefits of globalization. He claims that rising public fears over globalization might result in a violent backlash, jeopardizing the health of the international economy and "the cause of free trade."[1]

Note the author's open admission that political and business leaders are, in fact, peddling their preferred version of globalization to the public. In fact, the discourse of globalization itself has turned into an extremely important commodity destined for public consumption. Neoliberal decision makers have become expert designers of an attractive ideological container for their political agenda. Indeed, the realization of a global market order depends on the construction of arguments and images that portray market globalization in a positive light. Analyzing countless utterances, speeches, and writings of globalism's most influential advocates, I have identified five ideological claims that recur with great regularity throughout the globalist discourse.

CLAIM #1: GLOBALIZATION IS ABOUT THE LIBERALIZATION AND GLOBAL INTEGRATION OF MARKETS

This claim is anchored in the neoliberal ideal of the self-regulating market as the normative basis for a future global order. One can find in major newspapers and magazines countless statements that celebrate the "liberalization" of markets. Consider the following statement in a recent issue of *Business Week*: "Globalization is about the triumph of markets over governments. Both proponents and opponents of globalization agree that the driving force today is markets, which are subordinating the role of government. The truth is that the size of government has been shrinking relative to the economy almost everywhere." Joan Spiro, former U.S. under secretary of state in the Clinton administration, echoes this assessment: "One role [of government] is to get out of the way—to remove barriers to the free flow of goods, services, and capital." British journalist Peter Martin concurs: "The liberal market economy is by its very nature global. It is the summit of human endeavor. We should be proud that by our work and by our votes we have—collectively and individually—contributed to building it."[2]

Most importantly, these globalist voices present the liberalization and integration of global markets as "natural" phenomena that further individual liberty and material progress in the world. Presenting as "fact" what is actually a contingent political initiative, globalists seek to persuade the public that their neoliberal account of globalization represents an objective or at least a neutral diagnosis. To be sure, neoliberals offer some empirical evidence for the occurring liberalization of markets. But do market principles spread because of some intrinsic connection between globalization and the expansion of markets? Or do they expand because globalist discourse contributes to the emergence of the very conditions it purports to analyze? In most instances, globalists hold the political and discursive power to shape the world largely according to their ideological formula: LIBERALIZATION + INTEGRATION OF MARKETS = GLOBALIZATION.

CLAIM #2: GLOBALIZATION IS INEVITABLE AND IRREVERSIBLE

At first glance, the idea of the historical inevitability of globalization seems to be a poor fit for an ideology based on neoliberal principles. After all, throughout the twentieth century, liberals and conservatives have consistently criticized Marxists for their determinist claims that devalue human free agency and downplay the ability of noneconomic factors to shape social reality. Yet globalists rely on a similar monocausal, economistic narrative of historical inevitability. According to the globalist interpretation, globalization reflects the spread of irreversible market forces driven by technological innovations that make the integration of national economies inevitable. The multiple voices of globalism convey to the public their message of inevitability with a practiced consistency.

Former president Bill Clinton, for example, argued on many occasions that "today we must embrace the inexorable logic of globalization—that everything from the strength of our economy to the safety of our cities, to the health of our people, depends on events not only within our borders, but half a world away. . . . Globalization is irreversible. Protectionism will only make things worse." Likewise, Frederick W. Smith, chairman and CEO of FedEx Corporation, insists that "globalization is inevitable and inexorable and it is accelerating. . . . It does not matter whether you like it or not, it's happening, it's going to happen." *New York Times* correspondent Thomas Friedman comes to a similar conclusion: "Globalization is very difficult to reverse because it is driven both by powerful human aspiration for higher standards of living and by enormously powerful technologies which are integrating us more and more every day, whether we like it or not." Neoliberal elites in non-Western countries faithfully echo this globalist language of inevitability. For example, Rahul Bajaj, a leading Indian industrialist, insists that "we need much more liberalization and deregulation of the Indian economy. No sensible Indian businessman disagrees with this. . . . Globalization is inevitable. There is no better alternative." Manuel Villar, the Philippines' Speaker of the House of Representatives, agrees: "Of course, we cannot simply wish away the process of globalization. It is a reality of a modern world. The process is irreversible."[3]

The portrayal of globalization as some sort of natural force, like the weather or gravity, makes it easier for globalists to convince people that they must adapt to the discipline of the market if they are to survive and prosper. Hence, the claim of its inevitability depoliticizes the public discourse about globalization. Neoliberal policies are above politics, because they simply carry out what is ordained by nature. This implies that instead of acting according to a set of choices, people merely fulfill world-market laws that demand the elimination of government controls. There is nothing that can be done about the natural movement of economic and technological forces; political groups ought to acquiesce and make the best of an unalterable situation. Resistance would be unnatural, irrational, and dangerous.

The idea of inevitability also makes it easier to convince the general public to "share the burdens of globalization," thus supporting an excuse often utilized by neoliberal politicians: "It is the market that made us cut social programs." As German president Roman Herzog put it in a nationally televised appeal, the "irresistible pressure of global forces" demands that "everyone will have to make sacrifices."[4] To be sure, President Herzog never spells out what kinds of sacrifices will await large shareholders and corporate executives. Recent examples suggest that it is much more likely that sacrifices will have to be borne disproportionately by those workers and employees who lose their jobs or social benefits as a result of neoliberal trade policies or profit-maximizing practices of "corporate downsizing."

Finally, the claim that globalization is inevitable and irresistible is inscribed within a larger evolutionary discourse that assigns a privileged position to certain countries at the forefront of "liberating" markets from political control. Political scientist Francis Fukuyama, for example, insists that globalization is a euphemism that stands for the irreversible Americanization of the world: "I think it has to be Americanization because, in some respects, America is the most advanced capitalist society in the world today, and so its institutions represent the logical development of market forces. Therefore, if market forces are what drives globalization, it is inevitable that Americanization will accompany globalization."[5]

And so it appears that globalist forces have been resurrecting the nineteenth-century paradigm of Anglo-American vanguardism propagated by the likes of Herbert Spencer and William Graham Sumner. The main ingredients of classical market liberalism are all present in globalism. We find inexorable laws of nature favoring Western civilization, the self-regulating economic model of perfect competition, the virtues of free enterprise, the vices of state interference, the principle of laissez-faire, and the irreversible, evolutionary process leading up to the survival of the fittest.

CLAIM #3: NOBODY IS IN CHARGE OF GLOBALIZATION

Globalism's deterministic language offers yet another rhetorical advantage. If the natural laws of the market have indeed preordained a neoliberal course of history, then globalization does not reflect the arbitrary agenda of a particular social class or group. In that case, globalists merely carry out the unalterable imperatives of a transcendental force. People aren't in charge of globalization; markets and technology are. Certain human actions might accelerate or retard globalization, but in the last instance (to quote none other than Friedrich Engels), the invisible hand of the market will always assert its superior wisdom.

As economist Paul Krugman puts it, "Many on the Left dislike the global marketplace because it epitomizes what they dislike about markets in general: the fact that nobody is in charge. The truth is that the invisible hand rules most domestic markets, too, a reality that most Americans seem to accept as a fact of life." Robert Hormats, vice chairman of Goldman Sachs International, agrees: "The great beauty of globalization is that no one is in control. The great beauty of globalization is that it is not controlled by any individual, any government, any institution."[6]

But Hormats is right only in a formal sense. While there is no conscious conspiracy orchestrated by a single, evil force, that does not mean that nobody is in charge of globalization. The liberalization and integration of global markets do not proceed outside the realm of human choice. The globalist initiative to integrate and deregulate markets around the world both creates and sustains asymmetrical power relations. Backed by the powerful countries of the northern hemisphere, international institutions like the WTO, the IMF, and the World Bank enjoy the privileged position of making and enforcing the rules of the global economy. In return for supplying much-needed loans to developing countries, the IMF and the World Bank demand from their creditors the implementation of neoliberal policies that further the material interests of the First World.

Moreover, if nobody is in control of globalization, why do globalists like former U.S. national security adviser Samuel Berger try so hard to convince their audiences that the United States ought to become a "more active participant in an effort to shape globalization"?[7] The obvious answer is that the claim of a leaderless globalization process does not reflect reality. Rather, it serves the neoliberal political agenda of defending and expanding the hegemony of the global North. Like the rhetoric of historical inevitability, the idea that nobody is in charge seeks to depoliticize the public debate on the subject and thus demobilize antiglobalist movements. The deterministic language of a technological progress driven by uncontrollable market laws turns political issues into scientific problems of mere administration. Once large segments of the population have accepted the globalist image of a self-directed juggernaut that simply runs its course, it becomes extremely difficult to challenge neoliberal policies. As ordinary people cease to believe in the possibility of choosing alternative social arrangements, globalism gains even more strength in its ability to construct passive consumer identities.

CLAIM #4: GLOBALIZATION BENEFITS EVERYONE

This claim lies at the very core of globalism because it provides an affirmative answer to the crucial normative question of whether globalization should be considered a "good" or a "bad" thing. For example, former U.S. secretary of the treasury Robert Rubin asserts that free trade and open markets provide "the best prospect for creating jobs, spurring economic growth, and raising living standards in the U.S. and around the world." Denise Froning, trade policy analyst at both the Center for International Trade and Economics and the Heritage Foundation, suggests that "societies that promote economic freedom create their own dynamism and foster a wellspring of prosperity that benefits every citizen." Alan Greenspan, chairman of the U.S. Federal Reserve Board, insists that "there can be little doubt that the extraordinary changes in global finance on balance have been beneficial in facilitating significant improvements in economic structures and living standards throughout the world."[8]

But what about the solid evidence suggesting that income disparities between nations are actually widening at a quicker pace than ever before in recent history? The global hunt for profits actually makes it more difficult for poor people to enjoy the benefits of technology and scientific innovations. Consider the following example. A group of scientists in the United States recently warned the public that economic globalization may now be the greatest threat to preventing the spread of parasitic diseases in sub-Saharan Africa. They pointed out that U.S.-based pharmaceutical companies are stopping production of many antiparasitic drugs because developing countries cannot afford to buy them. The U.S. manufacturer for a drug to treat bilharzia, a parasitic disease that causes severe liver damage, has stopped production because of declining profits—even though the disease is thought to affect more than 200 million people worldwide. Another drug used to combat damage caused by liver flukes has not been produced since 1979 because the "customer base" in the Third World does not wield enough "buying power."[9]

While globalists typically acknowledge the existence of unequal global distribution patterns, they nonetheless insist that the market itself will eventually correct these "irregularities." According to John Meehan, chairman of the U.S. Public Securities Association, such "episodic dislocations" are "necessary" in the short run, but they will eventually give way to "quantum leaps in productivity."[10] Globalists who deviate from the official portrayal of globalization as benefiting everyone must bear the consequences of their criticism. For example, Joseph Stiglitz, the Nobel Prize–winning former chief economist of the World Bank, was severely attacked for publicly criticizing the neoliberal economic policies created by his institution. He argued that the structural adjustment programs imposed on developing countries by both the World Bank and the IMF often lead to disastrous results. He also noted that "market ideologues" had used the 1997–1998 Asian economic crisis to discredit state intervention and to promote more market liberalization. At the end of 1999, Stiglitz was pressured into resigning from his position. Five months later, his consulting contract with the World Bank was terminated.[11]

CLAIM #5: GLOBALIZATION FURTHERS
THE SPREAD OF DEMOCRACY IN THE WORLD

This globalist claim is rooted in the neoliberal assertion that free markets and democracy are synonymous terms. Persistently affirmed as "common sense," the actual compatibility of these concepts often goes unchallenged in the public discourse. The most obvious strategy by which neoliberals generate popular support for the equation of democracy and the market is through a discrediting of "socialism." As late as the 1970s, socialists provided a powerful critique of the elitist, class-based character of liberal democracy, which, in their view, revealed that a substantive form of democracy had not been achieved in capitalist societies. Since the 1989 collapse of Communism in

eastern Europe, however, the ideological edge has shifted decisively to the defenders of a neoliberal perspective who emphasize the relationship between
economic liberalization and the emergence of democratic political regimes.

Francis Fukuyama, for example, asserts that there exists a clear correlation
between a country's level of economic development and successful democracy. While globalization and capital development do not automatically produce democracies, "the level of economic development resulting from
globalization is conducive to the creation of complex civil societies with a
powerful middle class. It is this class and societal structure that facilitates democracy." Praising the economic transitions toward capitalism in eastern Europe, U.S. Senator Hillary Rodham Clinton argued that the emergence of new
businesses and shopping centers in former Communist countries should be
seen as the "backbone of democracy."[12]

Such arguments hinge on a conception of democracy that emphasizes formal procedures such as voting at the expense of the direct participation of
broad majorities in political and economic decision making. This "thin" definition of democracy is part of what William I. Robinson has identified as the
U.S.-backed political project of "promoting polyarchy" in the global South.
"Polyarchy" refers to an elitist and regimented model of "low intensity" market democracy that typically limits democratic participation to voting in elections. This ensures that those elected remain insulated from popular pressures
and thus can govern "effectively."[13]

In addition, the globalist claim that globalization furthers the spread of
democracy in the world must contend with evidence that points in the opposite direction. Even media outlets that spread faithfully the gospel of globalism occasionally concede that large transnational corporations often invest
in developing countries that are not considered "free" according to generally
accepted political rights and civil liberties standards. The conservative
Chicago Tribune recently cited a report released by the New Economic Information Service suggesting that democratic countries are losing out in the
race for American export markets and American foreign investments. In
1989, democratic countries accounted for more than half of all U.S. imports
from the global South. Ten years later, with more democracies to choose
from, democratic countries supplied barely one-third of U.S. imports from
developing countries: "And the trend is growing. As more of the world's
countries adopt democracy, more American businesses appear to prefer dictatorships."[14]

Why are powerful investors in the global North making these business decisions? For one, wages tend to be lower in authoritarian regimes than in democracies, giving businesses in dictatorships a monetary advantage in selling exports abroad. In addition, lower wages, bans on labor unions, and relaxed environmental laws give authoritarian regimes an edge in attracting foreign investment.

CONCLUDING REMARKS

The five central claims of globalism constitute the foundation of a dominant discursive regime that bestows public meaning on the process of globalization. Yet, as both the terrorist attacks of September 11 and the massive antiglobalist protests from Seattle to Genoa have shown, the expansion of this market narrative has encountered considerable resistance. Ideological challengers both on the political left (internationalist-egalitarians) and the political right (nationalist-protectionists) have already begun to flex their conceptual and political muscles. Far from condemning people to intellectual boredom in a world without ideology, the opening decade of the twenty-first century is quickly becoming a teeming battlefield of clashing ideologies. It appears that globalist forces will continue to struggle with their antiglobalist opponents as each side tries to impress its agenda on the public mind.

Yet it is important to remember that globalization is an incipient process, slowly giving rise to a new condition of globality whose eventual qualities and properties are far from being determined. Globalization does not necessarily have to mean or to be what globalists say it means or is. However, such a skeptical posture toward globalism should not be interpreted as a blanket rejection of globalization. One should take comfort in the fact that the world is becoming a more interdependent place. One should welcome the progressive transformation of social structures, provided that modernity and the development of science and technology go hand in hand with greater forms of freedom and equality for all people, as well as with a more effective protection of our global environment. The task for critical theorists of globalization is not to denounce *globalization*, but to offer a thoughtful analysis and critique of *globalism*.

Indeed, it is insufficient to analyze globalization as if it were simply the outcome of objective material processes "out there." Globalization has also important normative and ideological dimensions that are always part of social and economic processes. Hence, we must understand the dynamics of our age, in part at least, as the result of intricately interacting ideas, values, and beliefs. As the events of September 11 have shown, academic observers of the phenomenon can hardly remain untouched by the ongoing ideological battle over the meaning and direction of globalization.

In my view, globalism is ethically unsustainable because it routinely privileges self-interested market relations over other-regarding social relations. Indeed, as extreme market policies impose conditions of inequality on billions of people around the globe, globalism will eventually inflict enough damage to global social relations and the environment to cause ever more severe reactions against those countries and regions that are identified with extreme neoliberalism. Such a violent backlash harbors the potential to unleash armies of religious fundamentalism and irrational hatred that could dwarf even the most sinister forces of the recent past: fascism and Stalinism.

Guided by a vision of an egalitarian global order that may involve the creation of a gigantic "Marshall Plan" for the global South, critical theorists of globalization ought to uncover the ways in which unfettered market forces undermine the capacity of human beings to participate in shaping their own destinies. Once globalism and its corresponding neoliberal power base begin to lose their grip on the construction of meaning, alternative interpretations of globalization centered on the political demands for global citizenship and a redistribution of the world's economic resources will circulate more freely in public discourse. As a result, more and more people will realize that positive change is possible. Indeed, there is nothing "inevitable" or "irreversible" about globalism.

NOTES

1. Aaron Bernstein, "Backlash: Behind the Anxiety over Globalization," *Business Week*, April 24, 2000, p. 44. This *Business Week*–Harris poll on globalization was conducted by Harris Interactive between April 7 and 10, 2000. A total of 1,024 interviews were conducted.

2. *Business Week*, December 13, 1999, p. 212; Joan E. Spiro, "The Challenges of Globalization," speech at the World Economic Development Congress in Washington, D.C., September 26, 1996, http://www.state.gov/www/issues/economic/960926.html; and Peter Martin, "The Moral Case for Globalization," in *The Globalization Reader*, ed. Frank J. Lechner and John Boli (Malden, MA: Blackwell, 2000), pp. 12–13.

3. Bill Clinton, "Remarks by the President on Foreign Policy," San Francisco, CA, February 26, 1999, http://www.pub.whitehouse.gov/urires/12R?urn:pdi://oma.eop.gove.us/1999/3/1/3.text .1html; President Clinton cited in Sonya Ross, "Clinton Talks of Better Living," Associated Press,

October 15, 1997; "International Finance Experts Preview Upcoming Global Economic Forum," April 1, 1999, http://www.econstrat.org/pctranscript.html; Thomas Friedman, *The Lexus and the Olive Tree: Understanding Globalization* (New York: Anchor Books, 2000), p. 407; Rahul Bajaj, "Interview with *The Rediff Business Interview*," February 2, 1999, http://rediff.com/business/1999/feb/02bajaj.html. See also http://www.ascihyd.org/asci701.html; and Manuel Villar Jr., "High-Level Dialogue on the Theme of the Social and Economic Impact of Globalization and Interdependence and their Policy Implications," New York, September 17, 1998, http://www.un.int/philippines/villar.html.

4. Roman Herzog cited in Hans-Peter Martin and Harald Schumann, *The Global Trap: Globalization and the Assault on Democracy and Prosperity* (London: Zed Books, 1997), p. 6.

5. "Economic Globalization and Culture: A Discussion with Dr. Francis Fukuyama," http://www.ml.com/woml/forum/global2.html.

6. Paul Krugman, "We Are Not the World," in *The Accidental Theorist* (New York: W. W. Norton, 1998), p. 78; Robert Hormats, "PBS Interview with Danny Schechter," February 1998, http://pbs.org/globalization/hormats1.html.

7. Remarks by Samuel R. Berger, Columbia University, New York City, May 2, 2000, http://www.usis.it/file2000_05/alia/a0050415.html.

8. Robert Rubin, "Reform of the International Financial Architecture," *Vital Speeches* 65, no. 15 (1999): 455; Denise Froning, "Why Spurn Free Trade?" *Washington Times*, September 15, 2000; and Alan Greenspan, "The Globalization of Finance," October 14, 1997, http://cato.org/pubs/journal/cj17n3-1.html.

9. "Tropical Disease Drugs Withdrawn," *BBC News*, October 31, 2000.

10. John J. Meehan, "Globalization and Technology at Work in the Bond Markets," speech given in Phoenix, Arizona, March 1, 1997, http://www.bondmarkets.com/news/Meehanspeechfinal.shtml.

11. Doug Henwood, "Stiglitz and the Limits of 'Reform,'" *Nation*, October 2, 2000, p. 20.

12. "Economic Globalization and Culture: A Discussion with Dr. Francis Fukuyama," http://www.ml.com/woml/forum/global2.html; and Hillary Rodham Clinton, "Growth of Democracy in Eastern Europe," Warsaw, Poland, October 5, 1999, http://www.whitehouse.gov/WH/EOP/FirstLady/html/generalspeeches/1999/19991005.html.

13. William I. Robinson, *Promoting Polyarchy: Globalization, US Intervention, and Hegemony* (Cambridge: Cambridge University Press, 1996), pp. 56–62.

14. R. C. Longworth, "Democracies Are Paying the Price," *Chicago Tribune*, November 19, 1999.

3

National Culture, the Globalization of Communications, and the Bounded Political Community

Davis Held

The globalization of culture has a long history. The formation and expansion of the great world religions are profound examples of the capacity of ideas and beliefs to cross great distances with decisive social impacts. No less important are the vast premodern empires such as the Roman Empire, which, in the absence of direct military and political control, held its domains together through a shared and extensive ruling class culture (Millar et al. 1967; Mann 1986). For most of human history, these extensive ruling cultures passed through a fragmented mosaic of local cultures and particularisms; little stood between the political center and the village. It was only with the emergence of nation-states and national cultures that a form of cultural identity coalesced between these two poles.

With the rise of nation-states and nationalist projects, the spatial organization of culture was transformed. Nation-states took control of educational practices, linguistic policies, postal systems, and so on. However, from the eighteenth century, as European empires expanded and as a series of technological innovations began to have far-reaching practical effects (regularized mechanical transport and the telegraph most notably), new forms of cultural globalization crystallized. The most important ideas and arguments to emerge from the West during this era were science, liberalism, and socialism (Held et al. 1999, chap. 7). Each of these modes of thought—and the practices that went with them—transformed the ruling cultures of almost every society on the planet. They have certainly had a more considerable impact on national and local cultures than Nike, Coca-Cola, McDonald's, and a host of pop music groups.

However, in the period since World War II, the extensity, intensity, speed, and sheer volume of cultural communication are unsurpassed at a global level (UNESCO 1950, 1986, 1989; OECD 1997). The global diffusion of radio, television, the Internet, and satellite and digital technologies has made instantaneous communication possible, rendered many border checks and controls over information ineffective, and exposed an enormous constituency to diverse cultural outputs and values (Silverstone 2001, pp. 15–17). A telling example is the viewing figures for *Baywatch*; more than two billion people are estimated to have seen each episode! While linguistic differences continue to be a barrier to these processes, the global dominance of English (especially in business, politics, administration, science, academia, and computing) provides a linguistic infrastructure that parallels the technological infrastructures of the era. In contrast to earlier periods in which states and theocracies were central to cultural globalization, the current era is one in which corporations are the central producers and distributors of cultural products. Private international institutions are not new but their mass impact is. News agencies and publishing houses in previous eras had a much more limited reach than the consumer goods and cultural output of the global corporations today.

Though the vast majority of these cultural products come from the United States, this does not amount to a simple case of "cultural imperialism." One of the surprising features of our global age is how robust national and local cultures have proved to be (Appadurai 1990). National institutions remain central to public life, while national audiences constantly reinterpret foreign products in novel ways (see Thompson 1995). The central question is the future impact of communication and cultural flows on local and national cultures, and on our sense of personal identity, national identity, and politics. It is to this debate that the next section turns.

NATIONAL CULTURE AND ITS PRESUPPOSITIONS

The rise of the modern nation-state and nationalist movements altered the landscape of political identity. The conditions involved in the creation of the modern state often helped generate a sense of nationhood. In particular, the military and administrative requirements of the modern state "politicized" social relations and day-to-day activities (Giddens 1985; Mann 1986). Gradually, people became aware of their membership in a shared political community, with a common fate. Although the nature of this emergent identity was often initially vague, it grew more definite and precise over time (Therborn 1977; Turner 1986; Mann 1987).

The consolidation of the ideas and narratives of the nation and nationhood has been linked to many factors, including: the attempt by ruling elites and governments to create a new identity that would legitimize the enhancement of state power and the coordination of policy (Breuilly 1982); the creation, via a mass education system, of a common framework of understanding—ideas, meanings, practices—to enhance the process of state-coordinated modernization (Gellner 1983); the emergence of new communication systems—particularly new media (such as printing and the telegraph), independent publishers, and a free market for printed material—which facilitated interclass communication and the diffusion of national histories, myths, and rituals, that is, a new imagined community (Anderson 1983); and, building on a historical sense of homeland and deeply rooted memories, the consolidation of ethnic communities via a common public culture, shared legal rights and duties, and an economy creating mobility for its members within a bounded territory (Smith 1986, 1995).

Even where the establishment of a national identity was an explicit political project pursued by elites, it was rarely their complete invention. That nationalist elites actively sought to generate a sense of nationality and a commitment to the nation—a "national community of fate"—is well documented. But "it does not follow," as one observer aptly notes, that such elites "invented nations where none existed" (Smith 1990, pp. 180–81). The "nation-to-be" was not any large social or cultural entity; rather, it was a "community of history and culture," occupying a particular territory, and often laying claim to a distinctive tradition of common rights and duties for its members. Accordingly, many nations were "built up on the basis of pre-modern 'ethnic cores' whose myths and memories, values and symbols shaped the culture and boundaries of the nation that modern élites managed to forge" (Smith 1990, p. 180; and see Smith 1986). The identity that nationalists strove to uphold depended, in significant part, on uncovering and exploiting a community's "ethnohistory" and on highlighting its distinctiveness in the world of competing political and cultural values (Hall 1992).

Of course, the construction of nations, national identities, and nation-states has always been harshly contested, and the conditions for the successful development of each never fully overlapped with that of the others (see Held et al. 1999, pp. 48–49, 336–40). The fixed borders of the modern state have generally embraced a diversity of ethnic, cultural, and linguistic groups with mixed leanings and allegiances. The relationships between these groups, and between these groups and states, have been checkered and often a source of bitter conflict. In the late nineteenth and twentieth centuries, nationalism became a force that supported and buttressed state formation in certain places (for example, in France) and challenged or refashioned it elsewhere (for instance, in multiethnic states such as Spain or the United Kingdom; see Held et al. 1999, pp. 337–38; Appadurai 1990).

However, despite the diversity of nationalisms and their political aims, and the fact that most national cultures are less than two hundred years old, these "new" political forces created fundamentally novel terms of political reference in the modern world—terms of reference that appear so well rooted today that many peoples, if not the overwhelming majority of them, take them as given and practically natural (see Barry 1998). In fact, advocates of the primacy of national identity juxtapose its enduring qualities and the deep appeal of national cultures with the ephemeral and ersatz qualities of the products of the transnational media corporations (see Smith 1990; and Brown 1995). Since national cultures have been centrally concerned with consolidating the relationships between political identity, self-determination, and the powers of the state, they are, and will remain, so the argument runs, formidably important sources of ethical and political direction.

The political significance of nationalism, along with the development and consolidation of the state, has been at the heart of modern political theory. Political theory, by and large, has taken the nation-state as a fixed point of reference and has sought to place the state at the center of interpretations of the nature and proper form of the political good (Dunn 1990, pp. 142–60). The theory and practice of liberal democracy have added important nuances to this position. For within the framework of liberal democracy, while territorial boundaries and the nation-state demarcate the proper spatial limits of the political good, the articulation of the political good is directly linked to the national citizenry. The political good inheres in, and is to be specified by, a process of political participation in which the collective will is determined through the medium of elected representatives (Bobbio 1989, p. 144).

The theory of the political good in the modern territorial polity rests on a number of assumptions that repay an effort of clarification (see Miller 1995, 1999; Held 1995, chap. 10). These are that a political community is properly constituted and bounded when:

1. its members have a common sociocultural identity; that is, they share an understanding, explicit or implicit, of a distinctive culture, tradition, language, and homeland, which binds them together as a group and forms a (if not the) basis (acknowledged or unacknowledged) of their activities

2. there is a common framework of "prejudices," purposes, and objectives that generates a common political ethos, that is, an imagined "community of fate" that connects its envoys directly to a common political project—the notion that they form a people who should govern itself

3. an institutional structure exists—or is in the process of development—that protects and represents the community, acts on its behalf, and promotes the collective interest

4. "congruence" and "symmetry" prevail between a community's "governors" and "governed," between political decision makers and decision takers; that is to say, national communities "program" the actions, decisions, and policies of their governments, and governments determine what is right or appropriate for their citizens

5. members enjoy, because of the presence of conditions 1–4, a common structure of rights and duties; that is, they can lay claim to, and can reasonably expect, certain kinds of equal treatment, that is, certain types of egalitarian principles of justice and political participation

According to this account, appropriate conceptions of what is right for the political community and its citizens follow from its cultural, political, and institutional roots, traditions, and boundaries. These generate the resources—conceptual and organizational—for the determination of its fate and fortunes. Underpinning this understanding of the bounded community is a principle of justification that involves a significant communitarian thought: ethical discourse cannot be detached from the "form of life" of a community; the categories of political discourse are integral to a particular tradition; and the values of such a community take precedence over or trump global requirements (Walzer 1983; Miller 1988, 1995; MacIntyre 1981, 1988).

THE GLOBALIZATION OF COMMUNICATIONS AND CULTURE

Globalists take issue with each of these propositions, and they mount a sustained critique of them. First, shared identity in political communities historically has been the result of intensive efforts of political construction; it has never been a given (cf. Gellner 1983; Anderson 1983; Smith 1995). Even within the boundaries of old-established communities, cultural and political identity is often disputed by and across social classes, gender divisions, local allegiances, ethnic groupings, and the generations. The existence of a shared political identity cannot simply be derived from vociferously proclaimed symbols of national identity. The meaning of such symbols is contested and the "ethos" of a community frequently debated. The common values of a community may be subject to intense dispute. Justice, accountability, and the rule of law are just a few terms around which there may appear to be a shared language, and yet fiercely different conceptions of these may be present. In fact, if by "political consensus" normative integration within a community is meant, then it is all too rare (Held 1996, pt. 2; and see below). Political identity is only by exception, for instance during wars; it is a singular, unitary phenomenon. Moreover, contemporary "reflexive" political agents, subject to an extraordinary diversity of information and communication, can be influenced by images, concepts, lifestyles, and ideas from well beyond their immediate communities and can come to identify with groups beyond their borders—ethnic, religious, social, and political (Thompson 1998; Held et al. 1999, chap. 8; Keck and Sikkink 1998). Further, while there is no reason to suppose that they will uncritically identify with any one of these, self-chosen ideas, commitments, or relations may well be more important for some people's identity than "membership in a community of birth" (Thompson 1998, p. 190; cf. Giddens 1991; Tamir 1993). Cultural and political identity today is constantly under review and reconstruction at both individual and collective levels.

Second, the argument that locates cultural value and the political good firmly within the terrain of the nation-state fails to consider or properly appreciate the diversity of political communities individuals can appreciate; and the fact that individuals can involve themselves coherently in different associations or collectivities at different levels and for different purposes (Thompson 1998). It is perfectly possible, for example, to enjoy membership and voting rights in Scotland, the United Kingdom, and Europe without necessarily threatening one's identification or allegiances to any one of these three political entities (see Archibugi, Held, and Köhler 1998). It is perfectly possible, in addition, to identify closely with the aims and ambitions of a transnational social movement—whether concerned with environmental, gender, or human rights issues—without compromising other more local political commitments. Such a pluralization of political orientations and allegiances can be linked to the erosion of the state's capacity to sustain a singular political identity in the face of migration, the movement of labor, and the globalization of communications. Increasingly, successful political communities have to work with, not against, a multiplicity of identities, cultures, and ethnic groupings.

Multiculturalism, not national culture, is increasingly the norm (Parekh 2000).

Third, globalization is "hollowing out" states, eroding their sovereignty and autonomy. State institutions and political agents are, globalists contend, increasingly like "zombies" (Beck 1992; Giddens 1999b). Contemporary political strategies involve easing adaptation to world markets and transnational economic flows. Adjustment to the international economy—above all, to global financial markets—becomes a fixed point of orientation in economic and social policy. The "decision signals" of these markets, and of their leading agents and forces, become a, if not the, standard of rational decision making. States no longer have the capacity and policy instruments they require to contest the imperatives of global economic change; instead, they must help individual citizens go where they want to go via provision of social, cultural, and educational resources (Giddens 1999a). Accordingly, the roles of the state as protector and representative of the territorial community, as a collector and (re)allocator of resources among its members, and as a promoter of an independent, deliberatively tested shared good are all in decline.

Fourth, the fate of a national community is no longer in its own hands. Regional and global economic, environmental, and political processes profoundly redefine the content of national decision making. In addition, decisions made by quasi-regional or quasi-supranational organizations such as the EU, WTO, IMF, or the North Atlantic Treaty Organization (NATO) diminish the range of political options open to given national "majorities." In a similar vein, decisions by particular states—not just the most economically or militarily powerful nations—can have ramifications across borders, circumscribing and reshaping the political terrain. Political communities are, thus, embedded in a substantial range of processes that connect them in complex configurations, making them all too often decision takers, not decision makers.

Fifth, national communities are locked into webs of regional and global governance that alter and compromise their capacity to provide a common structure of rights, duties, and welfare to their citizens. From human rights to trade regimes, political power is being rearticulated and reconfigured. Increasingly, contemporary patterns of globalization are associated with a multilayered system of governance. Locked into an array of geographically diverse forces, national governments are having to reconsider their roles and functions. Although the intensification of regional and global political relations has diminished the powers of national governments, it is recognized ever more that the nurturing and enhancement of the political good requires coordinated multilateral action, for instance, to prevent global recession and enhance sustainable growth, to protect human rights and intercede where they are grossly violated, and to act to avoid environmental catastrophes such as ozone depletion or global warming. A shift is taking place from government to multilevel global governance. Accordingly, the institutional nexus of the political good is being reconfigured.

Each of the five propositions set forth by the theorists of national culture and of the modern national state can be contrasted with positions held by the globalists. Thus, the political community and the political good need, in the globalists' account, to be understood as follows:

1. Individuals increasingly have complex loyalties and multilayered identities, corresponding to the globalization of economic and cultural forces and the reconfiguration of political power.
2. The continuing development of regional, international, and global flows of resources and networks of interaction, along with the recognition by growing numbers of people of the increasing interconnectedness of political communities—in domains as diverse as the social, cultural, economic, and environmental—generates an awareness of overlapping "collective fortunes" that require collective solutions. Political community begins to be reimagined in regional and global terms.
3. An institutional structure exists comprising elements of local, national, regional, and global governance. At different levels, individual communities (albeit often imperfectly) are protected and represented; their collective interests require both multilateral advancement and domestic (local and national) adjustment if they are to be sustained and promoted.
4. Complex economic, social, and environmental processes, shifting networks of regional and international agencies, and the decision outcomes of many states cut across spatially delimited national locales with determinate consequences for their agendas and policy options. Globalization alters decisively what it is that a national community can ask of its government, what politicians can promise and deliver, and the range of people(s) affected by government outputs. Political communities are "reprogrammed."
5. The rights, duties, and welfare of individuals can only be adequately entrenched if they are underwritten by regional and global regimes, laws, and

institutions. The promotion of the political good and of egalitarian principles of justice and political participation are rightly pursued at regional and global levels. Their conditions of possibility are inextricably linked to the establishment of transnational organizations and institutions of governance. In a global age, transnational organizations and institutions are the basis of cooperative relations and just conduct.

Accordingly, what is right for the individual political community and its citizens, in the globalists' account, must follow from reflection on the processes that generate an intermingling of national fortunes. The contemporary world "is not a world of closed communities with mutually impenetrable ways of thought, self-sufficient economies and ideally sovereign states" (O'Neill 1991, p. 282). Not only is ethical discourse separable from forms of life in a national community, but it is developing today at the intersection and interstices of overlapping communities, traditions, and languages. Its categories are increasingly the result of the mediation of different cultures, communication processes, and modes of understanding. There are not enough good reasons for allowing, in principle, the values of individual political communities to trump or take precedence over global principles of justice and political participation. While for the traditionalists, ethical discourse is, and remains, firmly rooted in the bounded political community, for the globalists it belongs squarely to the world of "breached boundaries"—the "world community" or global order.

COSMOPOLITAN ALTERNATIVES

There is insufficient space here to appraise all the claims of these two positions. But by way of a conclusion, I would like to make a number of additional points and indicate the plausibility of a third position—neither traditionalist, nor globalist, but cosmopolitan.

The leading claims of the globalists are at their strongest when focused on institutional and process change in the domains of economics, politics, and the environment, but they are at their most vulnerable when considering the movements of people, their attachments, and their cultural and moral identities. The available evidence suggests that national (and local) cultures remain robust; national institutions continue in many states to have a central impact on public life; national television and radio broadcasting continue to enjoy substantial audiences; the organization of the press and news coverage retain strong national roots; and imported foreign products are constantly read and reinterpreted in novel ways by national audiences; that is, they become rapidly indigenized (Miller 1992; Liebes and Katz 1993; Thompson 1995). Moreover, the evidence indicates that there is no simple, common global pool of memories; no common global way of thinking; and no "universal history" in and through which people can unite. There is only a manifold set of political meanings and systems through which any new global awareness, or multicultural politics, or human rights discourse must struggle for influence (see Bozeman 1984; Silverstone 2001). Given the deep roots of national cultures and ethnohistories, and the many ways they are often refashioned, this can hardly be a surprise. Despite the vast flows of information, imagery, and people around the world, there are only a few signs, at best, of a universal or global history in the making, and few signs of a decline in the importance of nationalism.

There has been a shift from government to multilevel governance, from the modern state to a multilayered system of power and authority, from relatively discrete national communication and economic systems to their more complex and diverse enmeshment at regional and global levels. Yet there are few grounds for thinking that a concomitant widespread pluralization of political identities has taken place. One exception to this is to be found among the elites of the global order—the networks of experts and specialists, senior administrative personnel, and transnational business executives—and those who track and contest their activities, the loose constellation of social movements, trade unionists, and (a few) politicians and intellectuals. However, even the latter groups have a significant diversity of interest and purpose, a diversity clearly manifest in the "antiglobalization" protests of Seattle, Genoa, and elsewhere. The globalists' emphasis on the transformation of political identities is overstated. What one commentator writes about the European Union can be adapted to apply, in many respects, to the rest of the world: the central paradox is that governance is becoming increasingly a multilevel, intricately institutionalized, and spatially dispersed activity, while representation, loyalty, and identity remain stubbornly rooted in traditional ethnic, regional, and national communities (Wallace 1999, p. 521).

One important qualification needs to be added to the above arguments, one which focuses on generational change. While those who have some commitment to the global order as a whole, and to the institutions of global governance, constitute a distinct minority, a generational divide is evident.

Compared to the generations brought up in the years prior to 1939, those born after World War II are more likely to see themselves as cosmopolitans, to support the UN system, and to be in favor of the free movement of migrants and trade. Examining Eurobarometer data and findings from the World Values Survey (involving over seventy countries), Norris concludes that "cohort analysis suggests that in the long term public opinion is moving in a more international direction" (2000, p. 175). Generations brought up with Yahoo!, MTV, and CNN affirm this trend and are more likely to have some sense of global identification, although it remains to be seen whether this tendency crystallizes into a majority position and whether it generates a clearly focused political orientation.

Hence, the shift from government to governance is a potentially unstable shift, capable of reversal in some respects, and certainly capable of engendering a fierce reaction—a reaction drawing on nostalgia, romanticized conceptions of political community, hostility to outsiders (immigrants and refugees), and a search for a pure national state (e.g., in the politics of Haider in Austria). But this reaction itself is likely to be highly unstable, and a relatively short- or medium-term phenomenon. To understand why this is so, nationalism has to be desegregated. As "cultural nationalism" it is, and in all likelihood will remain, central to people's identity; however, as political nationalism—the assertion of the exclusive political priority of national identity and the national interest—it cannot deliver many sought-after public goods and values without seeking an accommodation with others, in and through regional and global collaboration. In this respect, only a cosmopolitan outlook can, ultimately, accommodate itself to the political challenges of a more global era, marked by overlapping communities of fate and multilayered politics. Unlike political nationalism, cosmopolitanism registers and reflects the multiplicity of issues, questions, processes, and problems that affect and bind people together, irrespective of where they were born or reside.

Cosmopolitanism is concerned with disclosing the cultural, ethical, and legal basis of political order in a world where political communities and states matter, but not exclusively. It dates at least to the Stoics' description of themselves as cosmopolitans—"human beings living in a world of human beings and only incidentally members of polities" (Barry 1999, p. 35). The Stoic emphasis on the morally contingent nature of membership in a political community seems anachronistic after two hundred years of nationalism. But what is neither anachronistic nor misplaced is the recognition of the partiality, one-sidedness, and limitedness of "reasons of political community" or "reasons of state" when judged from the perspective of a world of "overlapping communities of fate"—where the trajectories of each and every country are tightly entwined. States can be conceived of as vehicles to aid the delivery of effective public regulation and equal justice and rights, but they should not be thought of as ontologically privileged. Cosmopolitanism today must take this as a starting point, and build a robust conception of the proper basis of political community and the relations among communities. The Kantian understanding of this, based on a model of human interaction anchored in copresence, cannot be an adequate basis of this (Held 1995, chap. 10). Cosmopolitanism needs to be reworked for another age.

What would such a cosmopolitanism amount to? In the little space available here, I cannot unpack what I take to be the multidimensional nature of cosmopolitanism (see Held 2002). But I would like to end on a few words about cultural cosmopolitanism. Cultural cosmopolitanism is not at loggerheads with national culture; it does not deny cultural difference or the enduring significance of national tradition. It is not against cultural diversity. Few, if any, contemporary cosmopolitans hold such views (see, for example, Waldron 1999; Barry 2000). Rather, cultural cosmopolitanism should be understood as the capacity to mediate between national cultures, communities of fate, and alternative styles of life. It encompasses the possibility of dialogue with the traditions and discourses of others with the aim of expanding the horizons of one's own framework of meaning and prejudice (Gadamer 1975). Political agents who can "reason from the point of view of others" are better equipped to resolve, and resolve fairly, the challenging transboundary issues that create overlapping communities of fate. The development of this kind of cultural cosmopolitanism depends on the recognition by growing numbers of peoples of the increasing interconnectedness of political communities in diverse domains, and the development of an understanding of overlapping "collective fortunes" that require collective solutions—locally, nationally, regionally, and globally.

Cultural cosmopolitanism emphasizes the possible fluidity of individual identity—"people's remarkable capacity to forge new identities using materials from diverse cultural sources, and to flourish while so doing" (Scheffler 1999, p. 257). It celebrates, as Rushdie put it, "hybridity, impurity, intermingling, the transformation that comes of new and unexpected combinations of human beings, cultures, ideas, politics, movies, songs" (quoted in Waldron

1992, p. 751). But it is *the ability to stand outside of a singular location (the location of one's birth, land, upbringing, conversion), and to mediate traditions,* that lies at its core. However, there are no guarantees about the extent to which such an outlook will prevail. For it has to survive and jostle for recognition alongside deeply held national, ethnic, and religious traditions (see Held and McGrew 2000, pp. 13–18 and pt. 3). It is a cultural and cognitive orientation, not an inevitability of history.

The core requirements of cultural cosmopolitanism include:

- recognition of the increasing interconnectedness of political communities in diverse domains including the social, economic, and environmental
- development of an understanding of overlapping "collective fortunes" that require collective solutions—locally, nationally, regionally, and globally
- the celebration of difference, diversity, and hybridity while learning how to "reason from the point of view of others" and mediate traditions

Like national culture, cultural cosmopolitanism is a cultural project, but with one difference: it is better adapted and suited to our regional and global age.

REFERENCES

Anderson, B. 1983. *Imagined Communities: Reflections on the Origins and Spread of Nationalism.* London: Verso.

Appadurai, A. 1990. "Disjuncture and Difference in the Global Cultural Economy." *Public Culture* 2 (2).

Archibugi, D., D. Held, and M. Köhler, eds. 1998. *Re-imagining Political Community: Studies in Cosmopolitan Democracy.* Cambridge: Polity Press.

Barry, B. 1998. "The Limits of Cultural Politics." *Review of International Studies* 24 (3).

———. 1999. "Statism and Nationalism: A Cosmopolitan Critique." In *Global Justice,* ed. I. Shapiro and L. Brilmayer. New York: New York University Press.

———. 2000. *Culture and Equality.* Cambridge: Polity Press.

Beck, U. 1992. *Risk Society: Towards a New Modernity.* London: Sage.

Bobbio, N. 1989. *Democracy and Dictatorship.* Cambridge: Polity Press.

Bozeman, A. B. 1984. "The International Order in a Multicultural World." In *The Expansion of International Society,* ed. H. Bull and A. Watson. Oxford: Oxford University Press.

Breuilly, J. 1982. *Nationalism and the State.* Manchester: Manchester University Press.

Brown, C. 1995. "International Political Theory and the Idea of World Community." In *International Relations Theory Today*, ed. K. Booth and S. Smith. Cambridge: Polity Press.

Cohen, R. 1997. *Global Diasporas*. London: UCL Press.

Dunn, J. 1990. *Interpreting Political Responsibility*. Cambridge: Polity Press.

Ekins, P. 1992. *A New World Order: Grassroots Movements for Global Change*. London: Routledge.

Fernández-Armesto, F. 1995. *Millennium*. London: Bantam.

Gadamer, H.-G. 1975. *Truth and Method*. London: Sheed and Ward.

Gellner, E. 1983. *Nations and Nationalism*. Oxford: Blackwell.

Giddens, A. 1985. *The Nation-State and Violence*. Vol. 2 of *A Contemporary Critique of Historical Materialism*. Cambridge: Polity Press.

———. 1990. *The Consequences of Modernity*. Cambridge: Polity Press.

———. 1991. *Modernity and Self-Identity*. Cambridge: Polity Press.

———. 1999a. *The Third Way*. Cambridge: Polity Press.

———. 1999b. *Runaway World*. London: Profile Books.

Hall, S. 1992. "The Question of Cultural Identity." In *Modernity and its Futures*, ed. S. Hall, D. Held, and A. McGrew. Cambridge: Polity Press.

Held, D. 1995. *Democracy and the Global Order: From the Modern State to Cosmopolitan Governance*. Cambridge: Polity Press.

———. 1996. *Models of Democracy*. 2nd ed. Cambridge: Polity Press.

———. 2002. "Law of States, Law of Peoples: Three Models of Sovereignty." *Legal Theory* 8 (2).

Held, D., and A. McGrew, eds. 2000. *The Global Transformation Reader*. Cambridge: Polity Press.

Held, D., A. McGrew, D. Goldblatt, and J. Perraton. 1999. *Global Transformations: Politics, Economics and Culture*. Cambridge: Polity Press.

Keck, M., and K. Sikkink. 1998. *Activists beyond Borders*. New York: Cornell University Press.

Liebes, T., and E. Katz. 1993. *The Export of Meaning: Cross-Cultural Readings of "Dallas."* Cambridge: Polity Press.

MacIntyre, A. 1981. *After Virtue*. London: Duckworth.

———. 1988. *Whose Justice? Which Rationality?* London: Duckworth.

Mann, M. 1986. *The Sources of Social Power*. Vol. 1, *A History of Power from the Beginning to AD 1760*. Cambridge: Cambridge University Press.

———. 1987. "Ruling Strategies and Citizenship." *Sociology* 21 (3).

Massey, D., and P. Jess, eds. 1995. *A Place in the World? Culture, Places and Globalization.* Oxford: Oxford University Press.

Meyrowitz, J. 1985. *No Sense of Place.* Oxford: Oxford University Press.

Millar, F., et al. 1967. *The Roman Empire and its Neighbours.* London: Weidenfeld and Nicholson.

Miller, D. 1988. "The Ethical Significance of Nationality." *Ethics* 98.

———. 1992. "The Young and the Restless in Trinidad: A case of the Local and the Global in Mass Consumption." In *Consuming Technology*, ed. R. Silverstone and E. Hirsch. London: Routledge.

———. 1995. *On Nationality.* Oxford: Oxford University Press.

———. 1999. "Justice and Inequality." In *Inequality, Globalization and World Politics*, ed. A. Hurrell and N. Woods. Oxford: Oxford University Press.

Norris, P. 2000. "Global Governance and Cosmopolitan Citizens." In *Governance in a Globalizing World*, ed. J. S. Nye and J. D. Donahue. Washington, DC: Brookings Institution Press.

OECD. 1997. *Communications Outlook.* Paris: Organization for Economic Co-operation and Development.

O'Neill, O. 1991. "Transnational Justice." In *Political Theory Today*, ed. D. Held. Cambridge: Polity Press.

Parekh, B. 2000. *Rethinking Multiculturalism.* Cambridge, MA: Harvard University Press.

Rheingold, H. 1995. *The Virtual Community.* London: Mandarin.

Robins, K. 1991. "Tradition and Translation." In *Enterprise and Heritage: Crosscurrents of National Politics*, ed. J. Corner and S. Harvey. London: Routledge.

Scheffler, S. 1999. "Conceptions of Cosmopolitanism." *Utilitas* 11 (3).

Silverstone, R. 2001. "Finding a Voice: Minorities, Media and the Global Commons." *Emergences* 11 (1).

Smith, A. D. 1986. *The Ethnic Origins of Nations.* Oxford: Blackwell.

———. 1990. "Towards a Global Culture?" In *Global Culture: Nationalism, Globalization and Modernity*, ed. M. Featherstone. London: Sage.

———. 1995. *Nations and Nationalism in a Global Era.* Cambridge: Polity Press.

Tamir, Y. 1993. *Liberal Nationalism.* Princeton: Princeton University Press.

Therborn, G. 1977. "The Rule of Capital and the Rise of Democracy." *New Left Review* 13.

Thompson, J. 1998. "Community Identity and World Citizenship." In Archibugi, Held, and Köhler 1998.

Thompson, J. B. 1995. *The Media and Modernity*. Cambridge: Polity Press.

Turner, B. S. 1986. *Citizenship and Capitalism*. London: Allen and Unwin.

UNESCO. 1950. *World Communications Report*. Paris: United Nations Educational, Scientific and Cultural Organization.

———. 1986. *International Flows of Selected Cultural Goods*. Paris: United Nations Educational, Scientific and Cultural Organization.

———. 1989. *World Communications Report*. Paris: United Nations Educational, Scientific and Cultural Organization.

Waldron, J. 1992. "Minority Cultures and the Cosmopolitan Alternative." *University of Michigan Journal of Law Reform* 25.

Waldron, J. 1999. "What Is Cosmopolitan?" *Journal of Political Philosophy* 8 (2).

Wallace, W. 1999. "The Sharing of Sovereignty: The European Paradox." Special issue, *Political Studies* 47 (3).

Walzer, M. 1983. *Spheres of Justice: A Defence of Pluralism and Equality*. Oxford: Martin Robertson.

4

Globalization: A Contested Terrain

Douglas Kellner

"Is globalization only for the powerful? Does it offer nothing to the men, women and children who are ravaged by the violence of poverty?"

—*Former South African president Nelson Mandela*

As the new millennium opened, there was no clear answer to Mandela's question. In the early years of this century, there have been ritual proclamations of the need to make globalization work for the developing nations at all major meetings of global institutions like the WTO or G-8 convenings. For instance, at the September 2003 WTO meeting at Cancun, organizers claimed that its goal was to fashion a new trade agreement that would reduce poverty and boost development in poorer nations. But critics pointed out that in the past years the richer nations of the United States, Japan, and Europe continued to enforce trade tariffs and provide subsidies for national producers of goods such as agriculture, while forcing poorer nations to open their markets to "free trade," thus bankrupting agricultural sectors in these countries that could not compete. Significantly, the September 2003 WTO trade talks in Cancun collapsed as leaders of the developing world concurred with protesters and blocked expansion of a "free trade zone" that would mainly benefit the United States and overdeveloped countries. Likewise, in Miami in November 2003 the "Free-Trade Summit" collapsed without an agreement as the police violently suppressed protesters.[1]

Moreover, major economists like Joseph Stiglitz (2002), as well as anticorporate globalization protesters and critics, argued that the developing countries were not adequately developing under current corporate globalization policies and that divisions between the rich and poor nations were growing. Under these conditions, critics of globalization were calling for radically new policies that would help the developing countries, regulate the rich and overdeveloped countries, and provide more power to working people and local groups.

THE GLOBAL MOVEMENT AGAINST CAPITALIST GLOBALIZATION

With the global economic recession and the terror war erupting in 2001, the situation of many developing countries has worsened. As part of the backlash against globalization in recent years, a wide range of theorists have argued that the proliferation of difference and the shift to more local discourses and practices best define the contemporary scene. In this view, theory and politics should shift from the level of globalization (and its accompanying often totalizing and macro dimensions) in order to focus on the local, the specific, the particular, the heterogeneous, and the micro level of everyday experience. An array of theories associated with poststructuralism, postmodernism, feminism, and multiculturalism focus on difference, otherness, marginality, the personal, the particular, and the concrete in contrast to more general theory and politics that aim at more global or universal conditions.[2] Likewise, a broad spectrum of subcultures of resistance have focused their attention on the local level, organizing struggles around identity issues such as gender, race, sexual preference, or youth subculture (see Kahn and Kellner 2003).

It can be argued that such dichotomies as those between the global and the local express contradictions and tensions between crucial constitutive forces on the present scene. It may be a mistake to focus on one side in favor of exclusive concern with the other (Cvetkovitch and Kellner 1997). Hence, an important challenge for a critical theory of globalization is to think through the relationships between the global and the local by observing how global forces influence and even structure an increasing number of local situations. This requires analysis as well of how local forces mediate the global, inflecting global forces to diverse ends and conditions, and producing unique configurations of the local and the global as the matrix for thought and action in today's world (see Luke and Luke 2000).

Globalization is thus necessarily complex and challenging to both critical theories and radical democratic politics. But many people these days operate with binary concepts of the global and the local, and promote one or the other side of the equation as the solution to the world's problems. For globalists, globalization is the solution while underdevelopment, backwardness, and provincialism are the problems. For localists, globalization is the problem and localization is the solution. But politics is frequently contextual and pragmatic, and whether global or local solutions are most fitting depends on the conditions in the distinctive context that one is addressing and the specific solutions and policies being proposed.[3]

For instance, the Internet can be used to promote capitalist globalization or struggles against it. One of the more instructive examples of the use of the Internet to foster movements against the excesses of corporate capitalism occurred in the protests in Seattle and throughout the world against the World Trade Organization (WTO) meeting in December 1999. Behind these actions was a global protest movement using the Internet to organize resistance to the WTO and capitalist globalization, while championing democratization. Many websites contained anti-WTO material, and numerous mailing lists used the Internet to distribute critical material and to organize the protest. The result was the mobilization of caravans from throughout the United States to take protesters, many of whom had never met before and were Internet recruits, to Seattle. There were also significant numbers of international participants in Seattle who exhibited labor, environmentalist, feminist, anticapitalist, animal rights, anarchist, and other protests against aspects of globalization while forming new alliances and solidarities for future struggles. In addition, protests occurred throughout the world, and a proliferation of anti-WTO material against the extremely secret group spread throughout the Internet.[4]

Furthermore, the Internet provided critical coverage of the event, documentation of the various groups' protests, and debate over the WTO and globalization. Whereas the mainstream media presented the protests as "antitrade," featured the incidents of anarchist violence against property, and minimized police violence against demonstrators, the Internet provided pictures, eyewitness accounts, and reports of police brutality and the generally peaceful and nonviolent nature of the protests. Mainstream media framed the protests negatively and privileged suspect spokespersons like Patrick Buchanan, an extreme right-wing and authoritarian critic of globalization, whereas the Internet provided multiple representations of the demonstrations, advanced reflective discussion of the WTO and globalization, and presented a diversity of critical perspectives.

Initially, the incipient antiglobalization movement was precisely that—an *anti*globalization movement. The movement, itself, however, became increasingly global, linking a diversity of movements into global solidarity networks and using the Internet and instruments of globalization to advance its struggles. Moreover, many opponents of capitalist globalization recognized the need for a global movement to have a positive vision and be for such things as social justice, a democratized globalization, equality, labor, civil liberties and human rights, and a sustainable environmentalism. Accordingly, the anticapitalist and pro–social justice and democracy globalization movement began advocating common values and visions.

In particular, the movement against capitalist globalization used the Internet to organize mass demonstrations and to disseminate information to the world concerning the policies of the institutions of capitalist globalization. The events made clear that protesters were not against globalization per se, but were against neoliberal and capitalist globalization, opposing specific policies and institutions that produce intensified exploitation of labor, environmental devastation, growing divisions among the social classes, and the undermining of democracy. The emerging anticorporate globalization movements are contesting the neoliberal model of market capitalism that extols maximum profit with zero accountability and have made clear the need for democratization, regulation, rules, and globalization in the interests of people, not just profit.

The emergent movements against capitalist globalization have thus placed the issues of global justice, human rights, and environmental destruction squarely in the center of important political concerns of our time. Hence, whereas the mainstream media had failed to vigorously debate or even report on globalization until the eruption of a vigorous antiglobalization movement, and rarely, if ever, critically discussed the activities of the WTO, World Bank, and IMF, there is now a widely circulating critical discourse and controversy over these institutions. Stung by criticisms, representatives of the World Bank, in particular, are pledging reform, and pressures are mounting concerning proper and improper roles for the major global institutions, highlighting their limitations and deficiencies and the need for reforms such as debt relief for overburdened developing countries to solve some of their fiscal and social problems.

Against capital's globalization from above, cyber activists and a multitude of groups have thus been attempting to carry out globalization from below, developing networks of solidarity and propagating oppositional ideas and movements throughout the planet. To counter the capitalist international of transnational corporate-led globalization, a Fifth International, to use Waterman's phrase (1992), of computer-mediated activism is emerging, and it is qualitatively different from the party-based Socialist and Communist internationals. Such networking links labor, feminist, ecological, peace, and other anticapitalist groups, providing the basis for a new politics of alliance and solidarity to overcome the limitations of postmodern identity politics (see Dyer-Witheford 1999; Hardt and Negri 2000; Burbach 2001; and Best and Kellner 2001).

Of course, right-wing and reactionary forces can and have used the Internet to promote their political agendas as well. In a short time, one can easily access an exotic witch's brew of websites maintained by the Ku Klux Klan and myriad neo-Nazi assemblages, including the Aryan Nation and various militia groups. Internet discussion lists also disperse these views, and right-wing extremists are aggressively active in many computer forums, as well as radio programs and stations, public access television programs, fax campaigns, and video and even rock music productions. These organizations are hardly harmless, having carried out terrorism of various sorts extending from church burnings to the bombings of public buildings. Adopting quasi-Leninist discourse and tactics for ultraright causes, these groups have been successful in recruiting working-class members devastated by the developments of global capitalism, which have resulted in widespread unemployment for traditional forms of industrial, agricultural, and unskilled labor. Moreover, extremist websites have influenced alienated middle-class youth as well (a 1999 HBO documentary called *Hate on the Internet* provides a disturbing number of examples of how extremist websites influenced disaffected youth to commit hate crimes).

A recent twist in the saga of technopolitics, in fact, seems to be that allegedly "terrorist" groups are now increasingly using the Internet and websites to promote their causes. An article in the *Los Angeles Times* (February 8, 2001, pp. A1 and A14) reports that Hamas, for example, uses its website to post reports of acts of terror against Israel, rather than calling newspapers or broadcasting outlets. A wide range of groups labeled as "terrorist," causes including Hizbullah and Hamas, the Maoist group Shining Path in Peru, and a variety of other groups in Asia and elsewhere, reportedly use e-mail, Listservs, and websites to further their struggles. The Tamil Tigers, for instance, a liberation movement in Sri Lanka, offers position papers, daily news, and free e-mail service. According to the *Los Angeles Times* story cited above, experts are still unclear "whether the ability to communicate online worldwide is prompting an increase or a decrease in terrorist acts."

There have been widespread discussions of how the bin Laden al Qaeda network used the Internet to plan the September 11 terrorist attacks on the United States, how the group communicated with each other, got funds and purchased airline tickets via the Internet, and used flight simulations to practice their hijacking (see Kellner 2003a). In the contemporary era, the Internet can thus be used for a diversity of political projects and goals ranging from education, to business, to political organization and debate, to terrorism.

Moreover, different political groups are engaging in cyberwar as an adjunct of their political battles. Israeli hackers have repeatedly attacked the websites of Hamas and Hizbullah, while pro-Palestine hackers have reportedly placed militant demands and slogans on the websites of Israel's army, foreign ministry, and parliament. Likewise, Pakistani and Indian computer hackers have waged similar cyberbattles against opposing nations' websites in the bloody struggle over Kashmir, while rebel forces in the Philippines taunt government troops with cell-phone calls and messages and attack government websites.

The examples in this section suggest how technopolitics makes possible a refiguring of politics, a refocusing of politics on everyday life, and the use of the tools and techniques of new computer and communication technology to expand the field and domain of politics. In this conjuncture, the ideas of Guy Debord and the Situationist International are especially relevant with their stress on the construction of situations—the use of technology, media of communication, and cultural forms to promote a revolution of everyday life, and to increase the realm of freedom, community, and empowerment.[5] To some extent, the new technologies are revolutionary, and they do constitute a revolution of everyday life, but they also promote and disseminate the capitalist consumer society and involve new modes of fetishism, enslavement, and domination, yet to be clearly perceived and theorized.

The Internet and emerging forms of technopolitics also point to the connection between politics and pedagogy. Paulo Freire has long argued that all pedagogy is political and politics contains a pedagogical dimension (which could be manipulative or emancipatory). Critical educators need to devise strategies to use the Internet and information and communication technologies to enhance education and to produce more active democratic and global citizens.

The Internet is thus a contested terrain, used by Left, Right, and Center to promote their own agendas and interests. The political battles of the future may well be fought in the streets, factories, parliaments, and other sites of past struggle, but politics is already mediated by broadcast, computer, and information technologies and will increasingly be so in the future. Those interested in the politics and culture of the future should, therefore, be clear on the important role of the new public spheres and intervene accordingly, while critical pedagogues have the responsibility of teaching students the skills that will enable them to participate in the politics and struggles of the present and future.

GLOBALIZATION AND PLANETARY POLITICS

And so, to paraphrase Foucault, wherever there is globalization from above, globalization as the imposition of capitalist logic, there can be resistance and struggle. The possibilities of globalization from below result from transnational alliances between groups fighting for better wages and working conditions, social and political justice, environmental protection, and more democracy and freedom worldwide. In addition, a renewed emphasis on local and grassroots movements has put dominant economic forces on the defensive in their own backyard. Often, the broadcasting media or the Internet has called attention to oppressive and destructive corporate policies on the local level, putting national and even transnational pressure upon major corporations for reform. Moreover, proliferating media and the Internet make possible a greater circulation of struggles and the formation of new alliances and solidarities that can connect resistant forces who oppose capitalist and corporate-state elite forms of globalization from above (Dyer-Witheford 1999).

Globalization should thus be seen as a contested terrain with opposing forces attempting to use its institutions, technologies, media, and forms for their own purposes. A critical theory of globalization should be normative, specifying positive values and potentials of globalization such as human rights, rights for labor, women, children, and oppressed groups; ecological protection and enhancement of the environment; and the promotion of democracy and social justice. Yet it should also critique negative aspects of globalization that strengthen elite economic and political forces over and against the underlying population, and specify in detail bad aspects of globalization such as destructive IMF policies, unfair policies within the WTO, and environmental, human rights, and labor abuse throughout the world.

Consequently, a dialectic of globalization seeks positive potential while criticizing negative and destructive aspects. Other beneficial openings include the opportunity for greater democratization, increased education and health care, and new opportunities within the global economy that open entry to members of races, regions, and classes previously excluded from mainstream economics, politics, and culture within the modern corporate order. In the light of the neoliberal projects to dismantle the welfare state, colonize the public sphere, and control globalization, it is up to citizens, activists, and educators to create alternative public spheres, politics, and pedagogies. In these spaces, which could include progressive classrooms, students and citizens could learn to use information and multimedia technologies to discuss what kinds of society people today want and to oppose the society against which people resist and struggle. This involves, minimally, demands for more education, health care, welfare, and benefits from the state, and the struggle to create a more democratic and egalitarian society. But one cannot expect that generous corporations and a beneficent state are going to make available to citizens the bounties and benefits of the globalized information economy. Rather, it is up to individuals and groups to promote democratization and progressive social change.

Thus, in opposition to the globalization of corporate and state capitalism, I would advocate an oppositional democratic, pedagogical, and cosmopolitan globalization, which supports individuals and groups using information and multimedia technologies to create a more multicultural, egalitarian, democratic, and ecological globalization. Of course, the new technologies might exacerbate existing inequalities in the current class, gender, race, and regional configurations of power and give dominant corporate forces powerful tools to advance their interests. In this situation, it is up to people of goodwill to devise strategies to use emergent technologies to promote democratization and social justice on a planetary scale. For as the proliferating technologies become ever more central to everyday life, developing an oppositional technopolitics in alternative public spheres and pedagogical sites will become increasingly important. Changes in the economy, politics, and social life demand a constant rethinking of politics and social change in the light of globalization and the technological revolution, requiring new thinking as a response to ever-changing historical conditions.

NOTES

This study is part of a larger theoretical project. For my perspectives on globalization and technopolitics that inform this study, see Best and Kellner 2001; Kellner 2002; and Kellner 2003a. On 9/11 and the subsequent terror war, see Kellner 2003b.

1. On the Cancun meetings, see Chris Kraul, "WTO Meeting Finds Protests Inside and Out," *Los Angeles Times*, September 11, 2003, p. A3; Patricia Hewitt, "Making Trade Fairer," *Guardian*, September 12, 2003; and Naomi Klein, "Activists Must Follow the Money," *Guardian*, September 12, 2003. On the collapse of the so-called Free-Trade Summit, see Carol J. Williams and Hohn-Thor Dahlberg, "Free-Trade Summit Ends without Pact," *Los Angeles Times*, November 21, 2003. On the growing division between rich and poor, see Benjamin M. Friedman, "Globalization: Stiglitz's Case," *New York Review of Books*, August 15, 2002; George Monbiot, "The Worst of Times," *Guardian*, September 12, 2003; and James K. Galbraith, "Debunking the Economist—Again," *Salon*, March 22, 2004.

2. Such positions are associated with the postmodern theories of Foucault, Lyotard, and Rorty and have been taken up by a wide range of feminists, multiculturalists, and others. On these theorists and postmodern politics, see Best and Kellner 1991, 1997, and 2001, and the valorization and critique of postmodern politics in Hardt and Negri 2000 and Burbach 2001.

3. In a report on the 2002 World Social Forum event in Porto Alegre, Michael Hardt suggests that protesters divided into antiglobalization groups that promoted national sovereignty as a bulwark against globalization and local groups connected into networks affirming an alternative democratic globalization. See "Today's Bandung?" *New Left Review* 14 (March–April 2002): 112–18. Not all countries or regions that oppose specific forms of globalization should be labeled "antiglobalization." Moreover, one might also delineate a category of localists who simply focus on local problems and issues and do not engage globalization. There is accordingly a growing complexity of positions on globalization and alternative political strategies.

4. As a December 1 abcnews.com story titled "Networked Protests" put it:

> disparate groups from the Direct Action Network to the AFL-CIO to various environmental and human rights groups have organized rallies and protests online, allowing for a global reach that would have been unthinkable just five years ago. As early as March, activists were hitting the news groups and list-serves—strings of e-mail messages people use as a kind of long-term chat—to organize protests and rallies.

In addition, while the organizers demanded that the protesters agree not to engage in violent action, there was one website that urged WTO protesters to help tie up the WTO's Web servers, and another group produced an anti-WTO website that replicated the look of the official site (see RTMark's website, http://gatt.org/; the same group had produced a replica of George W. Bush's site with satirical and critical material, winning the wrath of the Bush campaign). For compelling accounts of the anti-WTO demonstrations in Seattle and an acute analysis of the issues involved, see Paul Hawkens, "What Really Happened at the Battle of Seattle," http://www.purefood.org/Corp/PaulHawken.cfm; and Naomi Klein, "Were the DC and Seattle Protests Unfocused, or Are Critics Missing the Point?" www.shell.ihug.co.nz/~stu/fair.

5. On the importance of the ideas of Debord and the Situationist International to make sense of the present conjuncture, see Best and Kellner 1997, chapter 3, and on the new forms of the interactive consumer society and Debordian critique, see Best and Kellner 2001 and Kellner 2003a.

REFERENCES

Best, S., and D. Kellner. 1991. *Postmodern Theory: Critical Interrogations*. London and New York: Macmillan and Guilford.

———. 1997. *The Postmodern Turn*. London and New York: Routledge and Guilford.

———. 2001. *The Postmodern Adventure*. London and New York: Routledge and Guilford.

Burbach, R. 2001. *Globalization and Postmodern Politics: From Zapatistas to Hi-Tech Robber Barons*. London: Pluto Press.

Cvetkovich, A., and D. Kellner. 1997. *Articulating the Global and the Local: Globalization and Cultural Studies*. Boulder, CO: Westview.

Dyer-Witheford, N. 1999. *Cyber-Marx: Cycles and Circuits of Struggle in Hi-Technology Capitalism*. Urbana and Chicago: University of Illinois Press.

Hardt, M., and A. Negri. 2000. *Empire*. Cambridge, MA: Harvard University Press.

Kahn, R., and D. Kellner. 2003. "Internet Subcultures and Oppositional Politics." In *The Post-subcultures Reader*, ed. D. Muggleton. London: Berg.

Kellner, D. 2002. "Theorizing Globalization." *Sociological Theory* 20 (3): 285–305.

———. 2003a. *From September 11 to Terror War: The Dangers of the Bush Legacy*. Lanham, MD: Rowman and Littlefield.

———. 2003b. "Postmodern Military and Permanent War." In *Masters of War: Militarism and Blowback in the Era of the American Empire*, ed. Carl Boggs, pp. 229–44. New York and London: Routledge.

Luke, A., and C. Luke. 2000. "A Situated Perspective on Cultural Globalization." In *Globalization and Education*, ed. N. Burbules and C. Torres, pp. 275–98. London and New York: Routledge.

Stiglitz, J. 2002. *Globalization and Its Discontents*. New York: Norton.

Waterman, P. 1992. "International Labour Communication by Computer: The Fifth International?" Working Paper Series, no. 129. The Hague: Institute of Social Studies.

Watson, J., ed. 1998. *Golden Arches East: McDonald's in East Asia*. Palo Alto, CA: Stanford University Press.

II

PLANETARY PERILS

5

Terror and Politics

NADIA URBINATI

The events that the "war on terrorism" has put in motion are succeeding one another so quickly that the spontaneous desire to suspend comments and reflections follows as well. The fronts of this war are too varied, heterogeneous, and new to allow a genuinely systematic theory to take form. From September 11, and particularly from the beginning of the bombardments in Afghanistan, the exception has become the norm. The *politics of the exception* dominates every domain.

The principal objective of terrorism is to create fear, and this is an age of fear. In light of the success that European states scored against terrorism in the 1970s and 1980s, some European commentators have argued that terrorism is a sign of weakness in those who perpetrate it, not of strength. Yet it is a sign of weakness that has the power to create a real state of fear in its victims. If it has no future, terrorism has, nonetheless, the power to dominate and shape the present. And the present, for those who have experienced terrorist violence closely and directly, is immersed in brooding fear. If we turn our attention to American domestic politics, the schizophrenia of normality/emergency is barely veiled. There is only one theme and one preoccupation that dominates the public debate: how to guarantee the safety of citizens now and in the future. To cope with this palpable condition of fear and uncertainty, the media and political leaders have taken great pains to repeat that everything is under control: that bin Laden will be brought to justice very soon; that the reserves of anthrax antibiotics are more than enough; that airports and airplanes are safe; that New York is safe and still the financial capital of the world; that life continues as before. In fact, there is more determination than before to do, to work, to produce *as if* things were normal. In the meantime, it is clear to all of us that in reality everything is very uncertain, and nothing is normal. Finding and capturing bin Laden will require time. Seeing justice prevail will prove a difficult task, for no court will be able to try him without passion or prejudged opinions (bin Laden is not indictable because he is already guilty). The health care system (with some local exceptions where something resembling a social welfare state exists) seems unprepared to deal with this kind of crisis, which would require something we do not have: a national health care system. The private companies in charge of airport security are not fond of the idea of being replaced by federal and state security forces, and the tug-of-war between economic interests and citizens' security is despicable and disgraceful. The headquarters of financial corporations are moving away from New York and its skyscrapers and prefer smaller buildings in New Jersey. New York is laboring to reclaim its usual role as financial capital of the world. Unemployment is becoming less a dreaded possibility and more a reality. The laissez-faire politics with which George W. Bush won the elections is buried under the ruins of the Twin Towers.

The rift between words and things is so obvious that even the most naive city dweller knows how unconvincing the assurances of those who inform and govern it are. It is the daily news that testifies to this rift. We all have received instructions and warnings to use certain precautions when opening the mail, to check what we eat, to not think twice about going in for a checkup. We all know, from our instinctual wisdom of survival, that it would be better to avoid crowded places, that cabs are safer than the subway. In this climate of palpable fear and real crisis, what certainties do we have?

It seems to me that for the time being what we mostly do have are negative certainties. We know what is wrong and unacceptable, but we do not have a clear, positive response for how better to handle the situation. Or if we do, we know how difficult and long term our efforts would be, and how uncertain the outcomes would be. The same category of terrorism is completely unclear. There are those who have tried to compare this terrorism with the terrorism Europe knew in past decades and with secessionist terrorism of Ireland and the Basque region. Although there are similarities in the psychological effects of fear the terror creates, the European terrorism spoke the language of its victims—a political language. It made an instrumental use of violence to reach ends that were political: questionable and absurd but not obscure. The terrorists stayed in the shadows, but they publicly justified, with a grand profusion of printed paper, their ideas and ends. The declarations of the Red Brigades in Italy and Germany were ideological and political analyses, interpretations of a revolutionary idea that everyone knew well, even if the majority were opposed to it. Our disagreement with them was both a disagreement over the relationship between means and ends and a disagreement over the interpretation of texts and languages we all knew.

The terrorism is completely different because it is "theirs" and not "ours." It has the determination of religious faith, even if its deeper reasons are economic and political. There is, furthermore, an ulterior aspect disturbing and new. These terrorists have not stated in detail what it is they want (except the complete destruction of Western civilization, which is so far-fetched it cannot be taken seriously or mentally represented). They assign us the burden of deciphering, interpreting, and understanding their motives. This is a tremendous power they have, and one of the reasons (the least apparent but the most insidious) that drives our fear and makes us the authors of the narrative of our own fear. They have the power of making us turn against ourselves because when we try to rationally explain or make sense of this terrorism we put ourselves in a condition that is contrary to the democratic values we hold so dear. The terrorists celebrate their loyalty to their own beliefs while instigating us to betray our own: we close our borders, we hunt down the witches, we celebrate how different we are from them, and we declare them an absolute evil. These are the reactions that the terrorists expect of us, and, unfortunately for us, the ones they are able to instigate. The result is that they turn us into their doppelganger.

This is the new power of this breed of terrorism: a power that derives from the absence of political language and objectives and that forces its victims to adopt the same language. And in the tradition of the victims there is, unfortunately, a vast range of religious dogmatism and fundamentalism. It's a phenomenon that resembles cannibalism: to destroy our enemies we assimilate their characteristics in the conviction that this will allow us to surpass them in strength and, hence, annihilate them. The strength of this terrorism lies in its ability to translate human and social phenomena into religious language: justice becomes the Good; wrong becomes Evil; the political adversary becomes the Infidel. On this side of the fence we are doing the same thing—in Europe as well as the United States. Everyone suddenly makes himself or herself an "expert" in the religion of Islam because in this part of the world it is "expertise" that grants authority—words are the sacred object of a secularized society. In the West, social and political action must be founded on justifications that are supposedly grounded in reason. This gives us the expertise to make an argument for intolerance. But in this case, the search for reasonable arguments induces an elaboration of explanations that are most of the time unreasonable, indefensible, imprudent, and the origins of new uncertainties. Reason and civility beget irrationality and barbarism. In the West this story has been repeating for thousands of years: Athenian citizens democratically voted for a Sicilian military expedition without even knowing how large or distant Sicily was. And yet they discussed and deliberated using sensible arguments. As for us, in the name of reason and civility we fall into the trap of absolute, ultimate, and total righteousness—West versus East, Christianity versus Islam, Capitalism versus Barbarism, Modernity versus Feudalism. It is an old song, but one that is still audible.

Terrorism, this terrorism, is bringing politics back into the arms of religion and is renewing the kind of language to which half a century of cold war made us accustomed: two conflicting worlds, each one of which is represented as a compact and homogeneous universe in and of itself—the dogmatism of good versus the dogmatism of evil. It's an easy habit of mind that rewards mental laziness. It doesn't require the effort of making distinctions. It doesn't impose on us the moral and intellectual obligation to try a different road from the mainstream one: the stigmatization and rejection of anything that seems not to belong to or resemble our world, and its subsequent banishment and expulsion. The problem is that, like the dualism of the two sides of the fence I mentioned above, this dualism presumes something that is exactly what one of the protagonists (the West) cannot reasonably sustain without contradicting its own principles: the fantasy that a democratic and liberal society can and must have a cultural and religious homogeneity.

Dogmatism is the anthem of mental sloth and for this reason it is tyrannical. When we take refuge in the East/West dichotomy we reward our atavistic mental laziness and the easy generalization. An individual, a group of individuals, a country become examples of an entire world, a world we hardly know and which is now revealing itself to us extraordinarily clearly. One of the leaders of the xenophobic Northern League Party, Francesco Speroni, reports the *New York Times* of Saturday, October 20, 2001, announced that Italy is ready to adopt a policy of "kicking out the Muslims" and tried to ennoble this policy by comparing it to that of the United States toward the American residents and citizens of Japanese origin after the attack on Pearl Harbor. Perhaps Speroni doesn't know that today the United States is ashamed of that racist policy and has agreed to ask for forgiveness and make reparations. Articles like this one are an insult to our intelligence and the aesthetic sense of a culture of moderation. Those who fuel a politics of cultural cleansing should be cognizant, especially in moments so delicate as these, of the binding responsibility of words, particularly when words are no longer private opinions but cover the pages of newspapers.

The simplicity of the generalizations is wrong because human things and human society are not simple. The East and the West are not simple or homogeneous, and moreover they don't exist in places that are far away or easily identifiable and circumscribed. They coexist together in our cities and neighborhoods. They make up part of our world and they change the supposed character of our world. Homogeneous and conflicting universes are a religious construction, and in this case a true opiate for the masses, which serves perhaps to satisfy our desire to silence our uncertainties, not our need for knowledge and freedom. Here we have a certainty that this terrorism gives us: the certainty of doubt against the simplification of emphatic truth, and the certainty that it is necessary that our reason does not capitulate in the effort to resist simplification. Dogmatism and Terror speak the same language, which is absolute, irrefutable and hostile to the complexity of the world of things and opinions, of societies and human life.

Another certainty that comes to us from this terrorism concerns the relation between religion and politics, and consequently the specificity and strength of liberalism. Religions are supposed to exclude in order to protect the basic nucleus of fundamental beliefs that distinguish them from one another. One should not turn to them for the source of toleration. One should ask religions for negotiation. It is politics that must worry about religions coexisting, and make this possible. Dialogue comes from a nondogmatic outlook, and no religion can exist without a body more or less filled with dogmatic axioms and arguments. The fall of the empire that today's Islamic fundamentalists preach was preached by early Christianity about the Roman Empire. Those old fundamentalists, no less than today's, rather liked and desired the decadence of what they thought to be a materialistic, immoral, epicurean world. The infidel (the Pagan) was—they believed—the real cause of the decline of Roman civilization, not the believer (the Christian), who, like a

midwife, helped the birth of the new world and the manifestation of an outcome that was already written. Augustine's *The City of God* is intriguing and
surprisingly timely.

Liberalism—or rather democratic rules—can set the coordinates of the
strategy of dialogue on the condition that it is perceived as a frame in which
the puzzle of our experiences and cultures can find a peaceful coexistence, not
as another faith. Liberalism is faced with a formidable challenge, because it
creates a system of security that protects and also nurtures pluralism and diversity, and, at the same time, has to deal with the risks that diversity and pluralism can entail. Liberalism is indeed an art of pluralism and tolerance but it
is also an art of the limits of pluralism and tolerance. To find the right limits,
and especially to find the right rationale for these limits, is the most arduous
challenge of today. It is an arduous challenge because liberalism, in order to be
an art of limitation, must know how to limit itself so as not to become like its
own opposite. It must know how to give prominence to procedures, to rules,
to rights, to cohabitation: or rather, to those instruments that, since John
Locke and Baruch Spinoza, have defended the individual from the domineer-
ing attitude of both the powerful state and the dogmatism of the believers.
Liberalism must resist the temptation to pose itself as the all-encompassing
philosophy of the free world and thus put up high requirements for reception
and inclusion.

The distinction between different forms of liberalism becomes indispensable at this point, and it must be made with great accuracy. Disarticulating liberalism in order to protect it from religious contamination: this is a further
lesson coming from September 11. There can be a fundamentalist nucleus in
liberalism. Liberalism can present itself in the guise of religion, secular but no
less canonized and intolerant: a religion of Darwinian social struggle for supremacy and of an ontological individualism, the gospel of the naturelike entities such as the market, the spontaneity of rational calculation, and the
one-dimensional free rider—a pack of truthful, undisputed (and undis-
putable) metahistorical foundations, the object of a cult by which those who
don't accept them can be judged as "false" liberal and "infidel." This form of
liberalism is illiberal because it has a theological essence. Its followers are no
less devotees and believers than those who believe in a god, and no less free
from the credulity and the temptation to exclude those who dissent.

The need to de-theologize politics and to depoliticize religion is another
certainty that comes to us from this terrorism. The religious rebirth of the

new millennium was welcomed by some as a reawakening from the ideological torpor of the sixties and seventies. In the last two decades, communities of identity have celebrated themselves against the materialistic wave of the age of civil rights, and proclaimed that the good of the individual is identical with that of the community to which she belongs. They have declared their enmity against the universalism of the theory of justice because it would erode any identity—religious, national, or ethnic. Justice, communitarians have claimed, prescribes that groups should govern themselves according to and in order to protect their own traditions. Theorists have employed communitarianism to criticize the role of the state in distributive justice; politicians and parties have used it to dismantle the welfare state; both of them have claimed that social goods should be distributed by those and among those who belong to a given faith, or a given ethnic group or nation, that each community should create its own schools and take care of the needs of its members. This is what the slogan "less state, more civil society" means for many critics of liberalism: a mortal embrace between libertarianism and communitarianism, with the consequence that religions have expanded well beyond the sphere of beliefs to become social glue, a vehicle of violence and of exclusion together. Today we are faced with the extreme effects of the perniciousness of identity segregation.

We read sometimes that there are faiths more reasonable than others. This is not a very good argument. One mustn't pretend that religions negotiate, for reasonableness is a word that does not find fertile ground in the world of faith. It may seem that some religions are friendlier to liberal society and individual autonomy than others. If this is so, however, it is because the liberal politics of the modern state have barred religions from political power, forcing them to limit their range of action. Christian religions have not become more liberal. They were defeated in the fight against the liberal state and where the liberal state won, religion was forced to accept the rule of limitation. It was politics that limited the dominion of religions, not religions' own reasonability. And it was the defeat by politics that made room for the excesses of religions, for their ideal of homogeneity with the result of either exclusion (Judaism) or proselytism (Christianity and Islam). Fundamentalism and terrorism are the extreme results of the victory of religion over politics, of the religious language over all other languages. Religious extremism is moreover functional to autocratic regimes that the West has unfortunately considered expedient to sustain in the Middle East for quite a number of reasons, but never for reasons favorable to the people living in the Middle East. It is functional because it justifies autocracy and, therefore, doesn't offer their people reasons to consider the West as a symbol of liberty and justice.

The most important positive certainty that this terrorism has made us consider is this: the need to restore negotiation and help promote decent living conditions beyond the strongholds of the West. Peace in the Middle East is a diplomatic task, as is the implementation of a project for the reconstruction of economic and civil society in Islamic nations. The American strategy of protecting oil resources (in the name of national interests) has sustained antiliberal and antidemocratic regimes. This strategy is wrong and ultimately harmful to the very interests the United States wants to protect. We are told by human rights theorists that the issues of democracy and social justice have become both global and pressing, that we cannot be passive viewers of injustice and despotic regimes but must actively promote freedom and justice. From now on, disagreements will concern the means. The issue of the means to help the growth of democracy in Middle Eastern countries will be the challenge that faces us after September 11, the most demanding and risky trench of contemporary politics. The first step to make in order for this task not to be a debacle is that we move away from the simplicity of Good versus Evil language and the myopic conviction that we live in a fortress and the barbarians are outside.

NOTE

Translated by Greg Tuculescu from Italian. This is a broadly revised version of the English edition that was published in the first issue of the electronic journal *Logos*.

6

The New Militarism: Imperial Overreach

CARL BOGGS

The new militarism refers to far-reaching changes in the U.S. armed forces and their role in the world: high-tech innovations, weaponization of space, new global flexibility, overall growth of the war economy, a bolstering of empire through economic globalization. More crucially, it is the product of a specific conjuncture in the post–Cold War era where the United States has emerged as the lone superpower and the Pentagon has forged more aggressive strategies in the context of international terrorism, 9/11 and its aftermath, a flexible nuclear doctrine, the concept of preemptive strike, and the urgency of resource wars presently focused on the Middle East and central Asia. U.S. willingness to subvert or bypass international treaties, conventions, and laws including those embedded in the UN Charter, though hardly novel, when taken together also corresponds to a new phase of militarism. The increasing American obsession with military power as a means of asserting national interests, taken to new levels with President George Bush II, has opened up a potentially ominous new era of world politics. A question that needs to be posed here is: Can the United States sustain long-term global domination mainly on the basis of deployment of overwhelming force? Are there modes of ideological legitimation available to American ruling elites that could help solidify their supremacy in the face of mounting contradictions and dispersed forms of resistance, both domestic and worldwide?

The contemporary resurgence of militarism in the service of U.S. global domination hangs over the world like a horrific nightmare that promises never to go away. Over a period spanning many decades American superiority has been reached through a combination of economic, political, diplomatic, and cultural as well as military power, but in the post–Cold War period the *military* dimension has taken on new significance. Of course there is little that is absolutely novel about an aggressive U.S. foreign and military policy: it has been central to the imperial legacy from the very outset. As a result of a variety of domestic and international trends at work, however, we are witnessing something of a historic turn in the scope, intensity, and probable long-term consequences of Pentagon interventionism. Old limits and restraints are superseded by intensified growth of the war economy, mounting resource pressures, the information revolution, and the plain hubris of imperial power. The result could be new levels of barbarism that the planet will not be able to withstand.

The fusion of capitalism, racism, and imperial expansion is deeply rooted in U.S. history. With recent developments we have not so much a loss of national innocence or betrayal of democracy, much less any departure from "American values," as an intensification of old patterns in a profoundly changed historical matrix. Traditions and ideals frequently associated with the American experience—democracy, freedom, rights, and so forth—appear at the start of the twenty-first century in largely truncated, distorted, partial form, eroded by the harsh effects of corporate, government, and military power swollen by the dictates of empire. Such traditions and ideals, assimilated by large sectors of the population, can be viewed as sources of legitimation that help sustain unprecedented concentrations of wealth and power. As in the past, empire cannot long survive without mass belief systems (nationalism, religion, political ideologies) that justify burdensome adventures and deflect public attention away from the terrible costs, pain, and material hardships that inescapably accompany militarism. For most of U.S. history, in fact, widespread acceptance of hegemonic discourses and practices—involving an organic linkage between elites and masses—has endowed the imperial project with popular energies. In foreign policy more than other realms, U.S. political leaders have enjoyed a great measure of autonomy, latitude, and credibility even in the face of costly failures such as Vietnam.

An urgent question for the fate of the planet is whether U.S. ruling elites can for long sustain their drive toward global domination—that is, whether they can prevail in an arena where military force and political coercion have become the chosen methods of supremacy. We know that what governing regimes may require for popular support *domestically* may not readily extend to the sphere of world politics, where Hobbesian chaos tends to block the normal mechanisms of legitimacy and order. U.S. efforts to impose corporate and geopolitical agendas through military power, which of course it has in great abundance, will depend upon conditions of effective popular mobilization— needed to justify the costs and sacrifices of empire—but those very conditions (e.g., patriotism) quickly lose their ideological rationale beyond the national territory. Such conditions are in fact more likely to breed opposition and resistance to empire, including diverse expressions of blowback. Signs of expanding opposition to empire have become increasingly visible: global terrorism and the events of 9/11, flourishing of an international antiwar movement during 2002 and 2003, growth of antisystem forces such as the World Social Forum, diffusion of anti-American sentiment in Europe, the Muslim world, Asia, and elsewhere. To the degree that those ideological factors generating legitimacy for a new *American* militarism are bound to be counterproductive *globally*, imperial stability will more likely be reinforced by "postmodern" conditions involving widespread depoliticization, mass apathy, and privatized retreat ensuring greater elite autonomy.[1] No doubt the rulers of empire would prefer a quieter, more atomized, depoliticized universe smoothly governed by routine economic transactions, the market, and consumerism, the ideal of an American-managed neoliberal hegemony grounded in a peaceful, more or less consensual imperial order. The problems here are twofold—the neoliberal model itself generates massive social contradictions while globalized, aggressive U.S. military power works against the trajectory of orderly corporate globalization. As the United States consolidates its status as single world hegemon, hoping to extend its rule over the entire planet, these contradictions are bound to significantly worsen.

The global system, shaped by U.S. economic and military supremacy, requires a strong modicum of ideological hegemony to reproduce the conditions of that supremacy: "automatic" mechanisms of corporate globalization, a relatively open network of communications and trade, "free markets," consumerism, sufficiently popular apathy to permit elite flexibility. Widespread chaos and disorder endemic to the ongoing cycle of militarism and terrorism, while possibly favorable to the power aspirations of specific elites, works against a smoothly functioning new world order, including any system of consensual governance. Alternatives to a Hobbesian scenario look bleak in the post-9/11 setting, in the wake of U.S. military interventions in Afghanistan and Iraq, the prospect of new military ventures, and what promises to be an endless war on terrorism. As noted, moreover, hegemonic discourses readily available to elites on the home front (nationalism, consumerism, etc.) are likely to be ineffective outside American borders; they will more likely *subvert* hegemony as the United States mobilizes its resources to shore up its global supremacy. In the postwar years the United States has enjoyed something of a precarious hegemony, built upon liberal democracy, economic successes, consumerism, and diffusion of its cultural products, but in recent years these sources have begun to atrophy. At the same time, to ensure world *domination* today the United States retains a wide repertoire of ruling devices—not only its military superiority but its corporate and financial power and capacity to manipulate international structures like the United Nations, World Trade Organization, World Bank, and the International Monetary Fund. The predicament today derives from the fact that such *domination* does not inevitably translate into *hegemony*.

The concept of ideological hegemony does not exclude reliance of a power structure on force, but rather indicates that two elements—force and consent—develop within some measure of equilibrium. The issue is not military power as such but the degree to which its exercise can be legitimated by various social and political arrangements and through popular support. Hegemony is reproduced across multiple venues: education, religion, laws, the political system, mass media, culture. Effective power is established largely within the political arena, where legitimating mechanisms are typically formed and crystallized. Such mechanisms can scarcely be anticipated on the global terrain, however, insofar as distinctly political structures are weak or absent, lacking in effective universality. For Antonio Gramsci, as for Machiavelli before him, dynamic leadership was always emphatically *political* in character since it was politics that had the special capacity to mobilize popular consent behind generalized ideals and objectives, as in the process of Italian unification, which transcended the limits of social fragmentation and cultural provincialism while creating the foundations of a cohesive, stable nation-state. Here visionary leadership resorts to force only where consensual supports are already widespread, where political goals have been assimilated by large (or at least strategically central) sectors of the population. Where such conditions are absent, reliance on military force exhibits weakness, not strength, which means that the *political* agenda is doomed. For both Machiavelli and Gramsci, viable military operations demand a strong ideological bond between leaders and led, rulers and masses, the state and popular strata. Gramsci's schema in the *Prison Notebooks* indicated formation of a powerful "moral-intellectual" leadership grounded in widely shared beliefs and values associated with an *emergent* hegemony. Even the most awesome military machine requires such consensual support to forge its own brand of order and discipline and carry out battlefield victories—a case in point being the rise and consolidation of Italian fascism that in the 1920s and 1930s legitimated hierarchical rule through its capacity to mobilize a powerful ensemble of nationalist, religious, and political beliefs.[2]

In the tracks of Machiavelli and Benedetto Croce, Gramsci wrote that power structures need a supportive "ethico-political" element to sustain effective governance. Coercive methods can work in the short term, but *durable* order necessitates a shift to popular, consensual footing, an equilibrium of force and consent. As for Machiavelli, "politics" for Gramsci involved the winning of popular support that would endow leaders with two crucial resources: stability and flexibility. Thus: "But to fix one's mind on the military model is the mark of a fool: politics here too must have priority over the military aspect, for only politics creates the possibility for maneuver and movement."[3] Such resources were never available to military power alone, whatever its might and scope, because it can never establish firm hegemony. At the same time, to build legitimacy, a power structure must achieve not only consensual but "national-popular" presence, sinking roots in particular (that is, national) traditions, myths, and ways of life. Thus only *politics*, here regarded as the distinct sphere of creative action, historical vision, and legitimation, could organize and manage the various complex expressions of social life—the "ensemble of relations." It follows that in matters of governance military power is usually trapped within limits of its own authoritarian rigidity, its deep attachment to discipline and rules, its penchant for violent solutions. The eclipse of hegemony means a severe crisis of authority, an erosion of governing capacity that no amount of coercive power or bureaucratic controls can reverse. Imposition of dictatorial or military rule in the absence of consensual supports—Gramsci refers at different points to "Caesarism," "Bonapartism," and "Cadornism"—is sure to be counterproductive, leading to dysfunctions, breakdowns, and resistance.[4] In the case of present-day capitalism, hegemony serves to compensate for systemic contradictions in the economy: nationalism, religion, and Fordism, for example, furnish ideological cohesion in a world where people face terrible material hardships, dislocations, and a sense of powerlessness. A strong consensual base, moreover, reduces the need for political coercion and military violence, precisely what Machiavelli had anticipated—contrary to the common misconceptions about his work.

Gramsci argued that military leadership must be subordinated to politics, a maxim that Napoleon, among others, failed to recognize to his great undoing. Of course, the military always has the capacity to impose a regime of order and discipline within its own domain—perhaps even briefly outside it—but it lacks resources to generate ideological or cultural unity over broad expanses of time; it can win "battles" but rarely "wars" in the larger historical sense. The temptation of leaders to seek military solutions at moments of crisis is grievously mistaken insofar as "only a very skillful political leadership, capable of taking into account the deepest aspirations and feelings of the human masses, can prevent disintegration and defeat."[5] Put differently, as power arrangements require integration and coordination, they also demand *legitimation* based in an "organic relationship between leaders and led," beyond the rigid, hierarchical, instrumental outlook of military elites.

While Gramsci never systematically brought the concept of hegemony into the realm of international politics, insights can be gleaned from several passages in the *Prison Notebooks*, including those referred to above. Of course, the global terrain with its vast mélange of competing nation-states, expansive scope, and virtual absence of governing mechanisms differs radically from the state system that commanded most of Gramsci's attention. Yet it is not too difficult to see how the unique conditions of *domestic* support for U.S. worldwide economic and military power might run counter to requirements for *global* hegemony. Strong elements of "national-popular" consent underlying U.S. empire, rooted in a strong patriotism, will naturally conflict with the multiplicity of competing interests and wills across the globe—interests and wills leading often to anti-imperial resistance and opposition just as predictably as any law of physics. A system of global domination resting largely upon military force, or threat of force, cannot in the scheme of things consolidate its rule on a foundation of legitimating beliefs and values, nor can it smooth over the harsh dysfunctions and conflicts endemic to the corporate world economy by mobilizing forms of hegemony such as nationalism and consumerism that work so fluidly in domestic politics. As the lone superpower with a huge, seemingly invincible military apparatus, and dedicated to ruling the globe by force, the United States has already lost much of its room to maneuver even as it wins immediate victories by means of economic and diplomatic leverage combined with military power—the same power that may soon become a double-edged sword.

The long history of empires aspiring to tyrannical rule over mass populations, hoping to expand their domain by overwhelming political coercion and military force, has been saturated with fierce resistance, deep quagmires, and humiliating failure: Rome, Spain, France under Napoleon, England, the brief twentieth-century global ventures of Nazi Germany and Imperial Japan. All at some point combined an unshakable political hubris with faith in armed violence as a means for building empire—and all had dazzling periods of success before disintegrating or being vanquished. Previous imperial regimes violated the basic Machiavellian premise that power without broad popular consent is destined to either implode or be overthrown. A corollary is that imperial domination by its very logic cannot easily secure much popular legitimacy, if any. By the 1950s the very idea of imperial control based upon foreign occupation had become historically obsolete, swept away by a series of postwar (and earlier) anticolonial struggles. The French colonial wars intended to retain control of Indochina and parts of Africa amounted to a final desperate reliance on brute force as the famous European "civilizing" mechanisms of religion, culture, and legal codes met with increasingly violent resistance. Dien Bien Phu and the Battle of Algiers symbolized the final eclipse of a colonial era in which European powers had recognized few limits to the use of military violence, much of it directed against civilian populations. The very *ideology* of imperial domination had been assaulted and destroyed in the name of ideals mainly imported from Europe itself—national self-determination, cultural autonomy, democracy.

If there had been an overriding logic to European colonization, there was an equally powerful logic underlying its demise, identified by such diverse theorists as J. A. Hobson, Rosa Luxemburg, V. I. Lenin, Albert Camus, and Frantz Fanon. As a general statement one could say that the more militarized the system of rule, the more coercive and bloody the foreign domination, the more widespread and successful the resistance—leading to a pattern of deep-seated nationalist mobilization against the presence of a foreign power. This dynamic produced the major Communist and radical-nationalist revolutions of the twentieth century: Mexico, Russia, China, Algeria, Yugoslavia, Vietnam, Cuba, Nicaragua. Eric Wolf points to the vast political turbulence, social dislocations, and armed violence experienced by mostly peasant local populations that were essentially *forced* to oppose the foreign presence and its local clients.

Large-scale military operations gave rise to a multitude of antisystem movements, community organizations, and political parties with enough structural
and ideological cohesion to win state power in a setting where the imperial
forces could never win much popular legitimacy.[6] Valiant attempts by the
leading powers to dismantle indigenous social structures, community networks, and political groups, while often all too successful, were eventually
counterproductive, owing precisely to their lack of legitimacy. As the old control systems broke down or were destroyed, new, more oppositional ones generally emerged in their place.

It was in such circumstances that mass-based revolutionary movements,
armed in the fight against a militarily superior colonial force, achieved sufficient legitimacy and then power to overthrow the imperial regime. The
greater and more bloody the militarism of the dominant power, the more generalized and militant the resistance. In Russia, prerevolutionary colonialism
was largely a matter of European (mostly French) economic penetration, but
it was the protracted and costly military encounters of World War I, followed
by armed interventions of several capitalist powers, that set the stage for the
Bolshevik Revolution. The Yugoslav partisans mobilized popular insurgency
against a brutal Nazi military occupation in the early 1940s—a pattern of resistance duplicated in France, Italy, Greece, and Czechoslovakia—leading to
consolidation of a Communist regime after the war. The Algerian Revolution
of 1962 marked the culmination of decades of opposition to militarized
French rule. In Vietnam, the struggle for national independence mixed with
radical goals produced a mass-based guerrilla insurgency against a series of
occupiers—Japan, Britain, France, the United States—that had for decades
brought unspeakable devastation to the country. The Cuban situation de-
parted somewhat from this pattern: U.S. domination was primarily economic
and political, but the ceaseless authoritarian controls as well as Cuba's close
proximity to the United States could be said to have approximated militarized
rule.

The Chinese Revolution offers perhaps the best historical evidence of the
dynamic play of harsh contradictions resulting from military-driven imperial
domination. Japanese invasion and occupation, beginning in 1937, wrought
terrible destruction and hundreds of thousands of casualties across several
Chinese provinces, much of it the result of scorched-earth policies deliber-
ately carried out to subdue the peasant population. The Japanese army laid
waste to vast areas, in the process brutalizing the local inhabitants. Rather

than being subdued and defeated, however, great masses of people rebelled and joined the anti-imperialist insurgency, which included Mao's Communist Party, as their hatred of the brutal occupier intensified; barbaric levels of military violence brought unprecedented chaos and breakdown, out of which popular struggles mushroomed. According to Chalmers Johnson, it was precisely Japanese militarism that stimulated a merger of nationalist and Communist rebellion leading to the 1949 Maoist triumph. Johnson writes that

> prior to 1937, the peasants were a passive element in politics; even the earlier Communist bid for power, based on an appeal to peasant economic interests, was a conspicuous failure. The prewar peasant was absorbed in local matters and had only the dimmest sense of 'China.' Japan's invasion changed this condition by heightening the peasant's interest in such concepts as national defense, citizenship, treason, legitimacy of government, and the long-range betterment of the Chinese state. . . . Although the peasantry, on the eve of war, was no more opposed to the Japanese than it was to other authorities, it acquired anti-Japanese attitudes as a result of the behavior of Japanese troops and the failure of Japanese leaders to offer a better alternative than resistance or slavery.[7]

Where does U.S. militarism today fit into this historical picture? We have seen how earlier forms of American global domination—economic, political, cultural—have become increasingly fragile, while the military dimension has grown in importance. Assuming continuation of this trend, fueled by the war on terrorism, mounting resource pressures, and simple geopolitical ambitions, crucial questions arise about the precise *modalities* of American power—namely, the degree to which military solutions might be compatible with the requisites of global domination. Viewed from another angle, in what manner would it make sense to apply Gramscian discourses of ideological hegemony to a global scene that appears more Hobbesian with each passing day? So long as U.S. ruling elites seem determined to solidify their global supremacy at all costs, will existing international conditions ensure a trajectory of militarization and, if so, is the United States destined to follow the historical pattern of crumbled, failed imperial projects? Is a consensual empire even possible?

One possible answer is that American power will sooner or later disintegrate from the weight of its own contradictions—so long as in decline or defeat it does not initiate a nuclear holocaust that would render discussion of future empire meaningless. The U.S. imperial domain, despite appearances of insurmountable strength, is in many ways fragile and vulnerable. If prescriptions for consensual power set forth by Machiavelli and Gramsci cannot be automatically extended from national to global politics, the theoretical insight remains compelling, especially when brazen U.S. resort to military force has become a more durable feature of international relations. The severe consequences of this epochal shift in both imperial capabilities and designs are increasingly visible: upsurge in worldwide military conflict, growth of civic violence, greater blowback, eclipse of legitimating mechanisms, elevated challenges to the neoliberal economy.

A potentially explosive contradiction of empire is the built-in conflict between global dimensions of power associated with the world hegemon and a range of distinctly *national* interests and agendas that elites want to pursue—a predicament embedded in the Middle East cauldron today. A strong patriotic mobilization that feeds into domestic legitimation needs quickly evaporates beyond American borders, where it breeds contempt, hostility, and resistance; nationalism by its very logic cannot serve *general* interests on the global terrain, even as it seeks universal justification. The single hegemon predictably works against diversity, independent centers of power, and peaceful balance, favoring coercive methods in support of a single neoliberal order, enforced along lines of an American-style fundamentalism. Empire rests on a logic of perpetual expansion: the global managers can never accrue sufficient power or enough mastery of the universe, just as billionaires can never accumulate enough wealth. Despite the onset of a supposedly postnational globalization, distinctly *national* agendas lie behind U.S. pursuit of international global double standards: breaking treaties, violations of the UN Charter and international law, refusal to accept inclusive disarmament processes, rejection of the World Criminal Court, seizing hold of space militarization for itself, launching of preemptive wars, hectoring of other nations for human rights abuses the United States itself commits on an even larger scale (and more regularly) around the globe. Further, to even speak of globalization as some kind of objective, abstract, benign historical process is mystified nonsense, largely a cover for American corporate, geopolitical, and military interests that have little in common with a balanced, multipolar globalism in which single-power domination becomes obsolete.

As the cycle of militarism and terrorism intensifies—as the world moves ever closer to barbarism—the very premise of warfare as a method for advancing national goals has become bankrupt and irrational, for reasons having less to do with democracy or worldwide diffusion of liberal values than with the brutal nature of contemporary warfare itself. The proliferation of WMDs—and the growing prospect that such horrific weapons will be used—only underscores the insanity of militarism in a world where deep social polarization is the norm and *universal* disarmament seems a distant fantasy. Put differently, American designs for implementing "full-spectrum dominance" across a global system where anti-U.S. sentiment flourishes are bound to jeopardize planetary survival. We stand at a juncture where large-scale military action tends to aggravate national, religious, and other conflicts, a point doubly applicable to the lone superpower as it takes measures to secure global domination. The classic strategic view that war unfolds as an extension of politics thus makes no sense for twenty-first-century realities. As the Iraq disaster shows, war (and its aftermath) is the vehicle of senseless death and destruction, destroying civilian infrastructures, violating established rules of engagement, and destabilizing entire countries and regions. Civilian populations are deeply and irrevocably drawn into the horrors of modern warfare. As Istvan Meszaros argues, if the efforts of the only superpower to maintain total armed supremacy persist long into the future, the result is sure to be a "recipe for military suicide."[8]

As the militarization of society proceeds, the confluence of the domestic war economy and global empire generates popular attitudes inconsistent with a vibrant, democratic public sphere: fear, hatred, jingoism, racism, and aggression. We have arrived at a bizarre mixture of imperial arrogance and collective paranoia, violent impulses and retreat from norms of civic engagement and obligation that patriotic energies furnish only falsely and ephemerally. Further: the celebration of guns and violence in American society, cavalier attitudes toward war and military escapades abroad, and widespread indifference to established moral and legal codes give elites wider autonomy to pursue their global schemes. As war becomes more acceptable, often the preferred instrument to fight ubiquitous enemies, we can expect further erosion of the domestic infrastructure and culture. For elites this could well be tolerable, but the long-term consequences for U.S. imperial hegemony—both domestically and globally—are certain to be disastrous.

Corruption of the public sphere, hastened along by militarism and imperial overreach, can be detected across the political landscape, perhaps nowhere more than in the remarkable deceits and criminal conduct of the Bush presidency itself. Bush's long parade of lies and schemes used to justify an illegal and immoral war against Iraq has brought political discourse to a new low, the reflection of a corrosive leadership with few parallels in U.S. history. Lies have become a recurrent feature of Bush officialdom, carried out with sheer contempt for public opinion. Such behavior in high places serves to devalue citizenship and public life, undermining government and further delegitimating U.S. international power already compromised by the hubris of an aggressive empire.

We have seen how one anticipated outgrowth of imperial power is blowback, which has many points of origin and takes many forms. At work here is a sort of Newtonian law of motion: power begets opposition, force generates counterforce. Blowback involves pervasive anger and hatred that self-interested U.S. economic and military actions breed over many decades, resulting not just in terrorism but in local resistance, popular movements, guerrilla insurgency, and rival national alliances. As Johnson puts it, "blowback is simply another way of saying that a nation reaps what it sows." Invincible as U.S. empire might now appear, it cannot effectively control the long-term effects of its policies and actions, so that "future blowback possibilities are seeded into the world" where "blowback itself can lead to more blowback, in a spiral of destructive behavior."[9] This logic is exacerbated the more U.S. leaders continue along a militaristic path, justified by the omnipresent terrorist menace. Recent moves to "remap" the Middle East provide a case in point—the perfect recipe for new cycles of terrorism and other modes of opposition. As the superpower behemoth extends its global reach, blowback correspondingly spreads, precisely as the Japanese and Germans learned from their military overextension in World War II. Ironically, militarism thus renders the imperial power somewhat *weaker*, more vulnerable to delegitimation and counterforce as it relies upon force to assert geopolitical interests, as in Vietnam, the Balkans, Central America, and the Middle East. Insofar as global terrorism constitutes a uniquely threatening instance of blowback, one can also speak of *political* blowback, as with the international backlash against U.S. military action in Iraq, Bush's subversion of the UN, repeated U.S. violations of international treaties, and stepped-up American development of nuclear weapons and Star Wars. It follows that the very conditions needed to maintain imperial power could simultaneously militate against its legitimation.

The very idea of global hegemony exercised by a lone superpower turns out to be problematic given the inherent conflict between general and particular interests along with severe dysfunctions of neoliberal globalization itself: class

polarization, growing world poverty, decline of public services, coercive practices of international agencies, recurrent financial crises. The absence of governing or planning mechanisms, usually available to national elites, permits
these contradictions in the global system to veer out of control. Elites may be
tempted to "resolve" conflict through military force, a frequent modus
operandi of post–Cold War U.S. foreign policy. In this milieu, U.S. attempts to
contain anarchic features of the world system are likely to aggravate the dialectic of militarism and terrorism, as the increasing superpower reliance on
force simultaneously reflects and intensifies the superpower *weakness* in other
spheres. As Giovanni Arrighi and Beverly Silver write: "The declining hegemon is thus left in the anomalous situation that it faces no credible military
challenge, but it does not have the financial means needed to solve system-
level problems that require system-level solutions."[10] One might add that the
deficit involves not only financial but political and ideological resources as
well. Meanwhile, militarization itself breeds chaos and disruption that helps
destabilize a global economy dependent on the smooth flow of capital, materials, and information. It follows that the Bush II foreign policy, with its emphasis on patriotic mobilization and U.S. exceptionalism, could subvert its
own global agendas, weakening the very international system over which it
rules, or presumes to rule.

The *domestic* harm that can be attributed to empire, the Pentagon having
consumed up to fifteen trillion dollars in public revenues during the postwar
years, has left a declining social infrastructure, decaying cities, and depleted
government resources. Contrary to myth, war and preparations for war have
not elevated industrial growth or living standards, as Seymour Melman among
others has shown.[11] Enormous human, technical, and natural resources continue to flow into the war economy, as the Pentagon remains the biggest exception in a period when politicians argue for cutbacks in public spending; the
huge and efficient military lobby exerts almost mystical influence within Congress, and will do so as long as the war on terrorism continues. With aug-
mented U.S. military deployments around the globe, with bases in some 120
countries, future operations and weapons programs will be far more costly,
boosting Pentagon revenue to well over $500 billion yearly by 2006. The occu-
pation of Iraq, which Bush seeks to "internationalize," could amount to more
than $200 billion alone and far more if the quagmire deepens. The war on ter-
rorism likewise figures to run into hundreds of billions. The pressing question
here is: To what degree, and for how long, will American citizens be willing to

make these kinds of sacrifices, both human and material, on behalf of an empire that satisfies mainly elite interests? Can the power structure adequately legitimate such demands? At issue here is not merely costs alone but the entire ideological paradigm through which costs and sacrifices are perceived and filtered by the general population. Cracks in the ideological edifice were starkly visible during the large antiwar mobilizations that preceded the war against Iraq, surpassing even those of the Vietnam era. If future military interventions give rise to larger, more sustained movements against the war machine, more severe legitimation crises (both global and domestic) can be expected.

As the new militarism reshapes the contours of imperial strategy, the American political system and media offer more glowing celebratory images of modern warfare that have the effect of loosening restraints on U.S. global behavior. By the 1990s the United States had indeed become a rogue nation, a status already in place before Bush II, and it continues to trample on arrangements and rules that keep the fragile international order from unraveling. The invasion and occupation of Iraq demonstrates this paradox in all its clarity: anxious to secure U.S. geopolitical and economic interests in the Middle East, the Bush administration worked overtime to bribe and coerce UN members, lied and forged documents to contrive a pretext for military action, violated the UN Charter, broke international law, dismissed the court of public opinion, and seemed blissful of any long-term consequences of its policies. For many years the United States has paid little heed to global arrangements and treaties it views to be in conflict with its national interests. Even the famous U.S. "crusade" against WMDs is hypocritical in the extreme, reinforcing the very trend (proliferation) it claims to oppose while reserving for itself the right to manufacture and deploy far more WMDs than all other nations in the world combined. Invoking the rhetoric of democracy and human rights, U.S. leaders have made a mockery of international order, helping reinforce a Hobbesian state of nature fully at odds with all their stated intentions. The longer such conditions persist, the more the United States relies on military force to ensure its global domination, the more precarious becomes its legitimacy within the world system.

As the war machine strengthens its hold over American society, political elites face increased global hostility, trapped in a predicament where massive power begets equally massive countervailing forces: terrorism and sabotage, guerrilla insurgencies as in Iraq and Afghanistan, nation-state rivalries, hostile groups or nations laying hold of WMDs, popular movements against corporate globalization and U.S. imperialism. These developments, taken together, will eventually work against U.S. efforts to maintain global supremacy, all the more so with each resort to military action. Moreover, hopes for sustaining hegemony by means of economic success and cultural influence—historically a strong suit for U.S. leaders—will flounder in the world of neoliberal excesses, U.S. militarization, and imperial overreach.

The U.S. "preemptive" move into Iraq has ironically shown the entire world just how fragile the military juggernaut can be. The historical record is clear: armed force can achieve a string of military victories but it cannot sustain *legitimacy* in the form of popular support for imperial ambitions. Technowar, moreover, cannot serve as a viable tool of occupation. When the Soviet Union invaded Czechoslovakia in 1968, hoping to quell unrest and an upsurge of anti-Communist ferment—in other words, to maintain its great-power control—the aggression backfired terribly, doing egregious damage to Soviet interests. The superpower could impose its coercive rule briefly, but the action was internationally condemned, the Brezhnev regime emerged from the crisis as a pariah state, and the USSR suffered a loss of legitimacy across Eastern Europe from which it would never recover. In the 1980s the Afghanistan quagmire turned out to be the final blow against Soviet bloc hegemony. As with the French in Algeria, the Japanese in China, the Nazis in Russia, and the Americans in Vietnam, national chauvinism combined with militarism and imperial overreach turned out to be brutally self-defeating. Of course, the American political and media systems work indefatigably to convince the nation and the world that the U.S. brand of imperial and military power is fundamentally *different* from anything in the past, embracing the most noble, democratic ends possible. As Edward Said writes:

> Every empire tells itself and the world that it is unlike all other empires, that its mission is not to plunder and control but to liberate. These ideas are by no means shared by the people who inhabit that empire, but that hasn't prevented the U.S. propaganda and policy apparatus from imposing its imperial perspective on Americans, whose sources of information about Arabs and Islam are woefully inadequate.[12]

Such an apparatus, however, will never be enough to guarantee the kind of ideological hegemony the United States will require to sustain its global domination over the coming decades.

NOTES

1. Perry Anderson, "Force and Consent," *New Left Review*, September–October 2002, p. 12.

2. Antonio Gramsci, "State and Civil Society," in *Selections from the Prison Notebooks*, ed. Quintin Hoare and Geoffrey Nowell Smith (New York: International Publishers, 1971), p. 218.

3. Gramsci, "State and Civil Society," p. 232.

4. For Gramsci's discussion of "Caesarism" and "Bonapartism," see Gramsci, "State and Civil Society," pp. 219–23.

5. Gramsci, "Notes on Italian History," in *Selections from the Prison Notebooks*, ed. Quintin Hoare and Geoffrey Nowell Smith (New York: International Publishers, 1971), p. 88.

6. See Eric Wolf, *Peasant Wars in the Twentieth Century* (New York: Harper and Row, 1969), chap. 1.

7. Chalmers A. Johnson, *Peasant Nationalism and Communist Power* (Stanford: Stanford University Press, 1962), p. 69.

8. Istvan Meszaros, "Militarism and Coming Wars," *Monthly Review*, June 2003, p. 23.

9. Chalmers Johnson, *Blowback: The Costs and Consequences of American Empire* (New York: Metropolitan Books, 2000).

10. Giovanni Arrighi and Beverly J. Silver, *Chaos and Governance in the Modern World System* (Minneapolis: University of Minnesota Press, 1999), p. 278.

11. Seymour Melman, *The Demilitarized Society* (Montreal: Harvest House, 1988), chap. 1.

12. Edward Said, Commentary, *Los Angeles Times*, July 20, 2003.

Unconcealed Empire: "The Awesome Thing America Is Becoming"

Leo Panitch and Sam Gindin

"American imperialism . . . has been made plausible and attractive in part by the insistence that it is not imperialistic."

—*Harold Innis, 1948*

"What word but "empire" describes the awesome thing that America is becoming? . . . Being an imperial power . . . means enforcing such order as there is in the world and doing so in the American interest."

—*Michel Ignatieff, 2003*

As the American empire becomes ever more unconcealed, the term "imperialism" not only makes its way onto the front cover of the *New York Times Magazine* to feature liberal human rights apologetics for the invasion of Iraq (the new white man's burden), but it also has led to the revival of Marxist conceptions of imperialism understood as interimperial rivalry. These trace current developments to overaccumulation and excess competition whose roots go back to the unresolved crisis of the 1970s. We cannot understand imperialism today in these terms.

The differences between today and the 1970s begin with the fact that while the earlier period was characterized by the relative economic strength of Europe and Japan, the current moment underlines their relative *weakness*. Concern with the American trade deficit seems to overlap both periods, but the context and content of that concern has radically changed. Earlier, the American deficit was just emerging, was generally seen as unsustainable even in the short run, and was characterized by foreign central bankers as exporting American inflation abroad. Today, the global economy has not only come to live with American trade deficits for a period approaching a quarter of a century, but global stability has come to depend on these deficits, and it is the passage to their "correction" that is the threat—this time a deflationary threat. In the earlier period, global financial markets were just emerging; the issue this raised at the time was their impact in undermining existing forms of national and international macromanagement, including the international role of the American dollar. The consequent explosive development of financial markets has resulted in financial structures and flows that have now, however, made "finance" itself a focal point of global macromanagement—whether it be enforcing the discipline of accumulation, reallocating capital across sectors and regions, providing the investor/consumer credit to sustain even the modest levels of growth that have occurred, or supporting the capacity of the U.S. economy to attract the global savings essential to reproducing the American empire.

In this context, the extent of the theoretically unself-conscious use of the term "rivalry" to label the economic competition between the EU, Japan (or East Asia more broadly), and the United States is remarkable. The distinctive meaning the concept had in the pre–World War I context, when economic competition among European states was indeed imbricated with comparable military capacities, as V. I. Lenin said in his preface to the French and German editions of *Imperialism*, "imperialist wars are absolutely inevitable," is clearly lacking in the contemporary context of overwhelming American military dominance. But beyond this, the meaning it had in the past is contradicted by the distinctive economic as well as military integration that exists between the leading capitalist powers today.

The term "rivalry" inflates economic competition between states far beyond what it signifies in the real world. While the conception of a transnational capitalist class, loosened from any state moorings or about to spawn a supranational global state, is clearly exceedingly extravagant,[1] so too is any conception of a return to rival national bourgeoisies. The asymmetrical power relationships that emerged out of the penetration and integration among the leading capitalist countries under the aegis of informal American empire were not dissolved in the wake of the crisis of the Golden Age, and the greater trade competitiveness and capital mobility that accompanied it; rather, they were refashioned and reconstituted through the era of neoliberal globalization.

None of this means, of course, that state and economic structures have become homogeneous or that there is no divergence in many policy areas, or that contradiction and conflict are absent from the imperial order. But these contradictions and conflicts are located not so much in the relationships between the advanced capitalist states, as *within* these states, as they try to manage their internal processes of accumulation, legitimation, and class struggle. This is no less true of the American state as it tries to manage and cope with the complexities of neoimperial globalization.

Nor does the evolution of the European Union make the theory of inter-imperial rivalry relevant for our time.[2] Encouraged at its origins by the American state, its recent development through economic and monetary union, up to and including the launching of the Euro and the European Central Bank, has never been opposed by American capital within Europe, or by the American state. What it has accomplished in terms of free trade and capital mobility within its own region has fitted, rather than challenged, the American-led "new form of social rule" that neoliberalism represents. And what it has accomplished in terms of the integration of European capital markets has not only involved the greater penetration of American investment banking and its principle of "shareholder value" inside Europe but has, as John Grahl has shown, been "based on the deregulation and internationalization of the US financial system."[3]

The halting steps toward an independent European military posture, entirely apart from the staggering economic cost this would involve (all the more so in the context of relatively slow growth), were quickly put in perspective by the war on the former Yugoslavia over Kosovo—supported by every European government—through which the United States made it very clear that NATO would remain the ultimate policeman of Europe.[4] But this only drove home a point over which pragmatic European politicians had never entertained any illusions. Dependence on American military technology and intelligence would still be such that the United States itself sees "an EU force that serves as an effective, if unofficial, extension of NATO rather than a substitute [as] well worth the trouble."[5] And on the European side, Joschka Fischer, Germany's foreign minister, has similarly acknowledged that "the transatlantic relationship is indispensable. The power of the United States is a decisive factor for peace and stability in the world. I don't believe Europe will ever be strong enough to look after its security alone."[6] Indeed, it is likely the very appreciation of this reality within European elite circles that lies at the heart of their oft-expressed frustrations with the current American leadership's tendency to treat them explicitly as merely "junior" partners. Though it has been argued that the end of the Cold War left Europe less dependent on the American military umbrella and therefore freer to pursue its own interests, this same development also left the United States freer to ignore European sensitivities.

As for East Asia, where Japan's highly centralized state might be thought to give it the imperial potential that the relatively loosely knit EU lacks, it has shown even less capacity for regional let alone global leadership independent of the United States. Japan's ability to penetrate East Asia economically, moreover, has been and remains mediated by the American imperial relationship.[7] This was particularly rudely underlined by the actions of the American Treasury (especially through the direct intervention of Rubin and Summers) in the East Asian crisis of 1997–1998, when it dictated a harsh conditionality right in Japan's backyard.[8] Those who interpreted Japan's trade penetration of American markets and its massive direct foreign investments in the United States through the 1980s in terms of interimperial rivalry betrayed a misleadingly economistic perspective. Japan remains dependent on American markets and on the security of its investments within the United States, and its central bank is anxious to buy dollars so as to limit the fall of the dollar and its impact on the yen. And while China may perhaps emerge eventually as a pole of interimperial power, it will obviously be very far from reaching such a status for a good many decades. The fact that certain elements in the American state are concerned to ensure that its "unipolar" power today is used to prevent the possible emergence of imperial rivals tomorrow can hardly be used as evidence that such rivals already exist.

During the 1990s, not only the literal deflation of the Japanese economy but also the slow growth and high unemployment in Europe stood in stark contrast with the American boom. So much was this the case that if Donald Sassoon was right to say that "how to achieve the European version of the American society was the real political issue of the 1950s,"[9] so it once again seemed to be the case in the 1990s, at least in terms of emulation of U.S. economic policies and shareholder values. Now, with the end of that boom, and the growing U.S. trade and fiscal deficit, new predictions of American decline and interimperial rivalry have become commonplace. But the question of the sustainability of the American empire cannot be answered with such short-term and economistic measures.

This is not to say that the current economic conjuncture does not reveal genuine economic problems for every state in global capitalism, including the

American. These problems reflect not the continuation of the crisis of the 1970s but, rather, new contradictions that the dynamic global capitalism ushered in by neoliberalism has itself generated, including the synchronization of recessions, the threat of deflation, the dependence of the world on American markets, and the dependence of the United States on capital inflows to cover its trade deficit. There is indeed a systemic complexity in today's global capitalism that includes, even at its core, instabilities and even crises. Yet this needs to be seen not so much in terms of the old structural crisis tendencies and their outcomes but as quotidian dimensions of contemporary capitalism's functioning, and, indeed, the way these crises are resolved is sometimes the basis for the spread of neoliberal globalization.

The issue for capitalist states is not preventing episodic crises—they will inevitably occur—but containing them. The American imperial state has, to date, demonstrated a remarkable ability to limit the duration, depth, and contagion of crises. And there is as yet little reason to expect that even the pressure on the value of the dollar today has become unmanageable. This is what lies behind the confidence of Andrew Crockett, general manager of the Bank for International Settlements and chairman of the Financial Stability Forum (comprising central bankers, finance ministry officials, and market regulators from the G7 states), that "they have the network of contacts, [and] the contingency plans, to deal with shocks to the markets."[10] Of course, such confidence does not itself guarantee that the U.S. Treasury and Federal Reserve, which worked closely with their counterparts in the other core capitalist states during the war on Iraq (whatever their governments' disagreements over that war) just as they had immediately after the disruption of Wall Street caused by the terrorist attacks of September 11,[11] will always have the capacity to cope with all contingencies. We would, however, argue that the future development of such capacities is not ruled out by any inherent *economic* contradictions alone.

The crisis that has produced an unconcealed American empire today lies, then, not in overaccumulation leading back to anything like interimperial rivalry, but in the limits that an informal empire based on ruling through other states sets for a strategy of coordinated economic growth, even among the advanced capitalist countries. In these liberal democratic states, the strength of domestic social forces—in spite of, and sometimes because of, the internationalization of domestic capital and the national state—has limited the adoption of neoliberalism (as seen, for example, in the difficulties experienced by the German state in introducing flexible labor markets, or the inertia of the Japanese state in restructuring its banking system). This has frustrated the "reforms" that capital sees as necessary, along the lines of the American state's own earlier restructuring, to revive economic growth in these countries so as to allow them to share the burden of absorbing global imports and relieve pressure on the American trade deficit. It is also by no means obvious, despite the energy that capitalists in each country have invested in securing these "reforms," that they would, by themselves, prove to be the magic bullets that would produce renewed growth. And their full introduction could in any case generate far more intense class struggles from below—though it must be said that these would need to generate something approaching a fundamental transformation in class and state structures to generate a new alternative to neoliberalism and break the links with the American empire.

The most serious problems for imperialism as a whole today arise in relation to the states outside the capitalist core. Where these states are—as in much of the Third World and the former Soviet bloc—relatively undeveloped capitalist states, yet increasingly located within the orbit of global capital, the international financial institutions, as well as the core capitalist states acting either in concert or on their own, have intervened to impose "economically correct" neoliberal structural "reforms." In the context of financial liberalization, this has meant a steady stream of economic crises. Some of these could be seen as a functionally necessary part of neoliberalism's success (as may perhaps be said of South Korea after the Asian crisis of 1997–1998), but all too often these interventions have aggravated rather than solved the problem because of the abstract universalism of the remedy. Whatever neoliberalism's successes in relation to strengthening an already developed capitalist economy, it increasingly appears as a misguided strategy for capitalist development itself. As for so-called "rogue states"—those which are not within the orbit of global capitalism so that neither penetrating external economic forces nor international institutions can effectively restructure them—direct unilateral intervention on the part of the American state has become increasingly tempting. It is this that has brought the term "empire" back into mainstream currency, and it is fraught with all kinds of unpredictable ramifications.

In this context, the collapse of the Communist world that stood outside the sphere of American empire and global capitalism for so much of the postwar era has become particularly important. On the one hand, the rapid penetration and integration by global capital and the institutions of informal American empire (such as NATO) of so much of what had been the Soviet bloc, and the opening of China, Vietnam, and even Cuba to foreign capital and their integration in world markets (even if under the aegis of Communist elites), has been remarkable. It has also removed the danger that direct U.S. intervention in states outside the American hemisphere would lead to World War III and nuclear Armageddon. The fact that even liberal human rights advocates and institutions through the 1990s repeatedly called for the United States to act as an international police power reflected the new conjuncture. But, on the other hand, both the hubris and sense of burden that came with the now evident unique power of the American state led it to question whether even the limited compromises it had to make in operating through multilateral institutions were unnecessarily constraining its strategic options, especially in relation to "rogue states" outside the orbit of the informal empire.

The "loneliness of power" was increasingly involved here. The felt burden of ultimate responsibility (and since 9/11 the much greater sensitivity to U.S. vulnerability as a target of terrorism at home as well as abroad) promotes the desire to retain full "sovereignty" to act as needed. This is what underlies the increasingly unconcealed nature of American imperialism. The problem it now faces in terms of "conjugating its particular power with the general task of coordination" (in Perry Anderson's incisive phrase)[12] can clearly be seen not only in relation to the economic contradictions of neoliberalism discussed above but also in the growing contradictions between nature and capitalism (as revealed, for example, not only in the severe problems of carbon emissions that the Kyoto Accord is supposed to address, but also in the problem of oil reserves addressed by the Cheney Report).

These issues are multiplied all the more by the role the American imperial state now has come to play (and often is to be expected to play) in maintaining social order around the whole globe. From the perspective of creating a "world environment in which the American system can survive and flourish," the understanding of the 1950 National Security Council document NSC-68 that "even if there were no Soviet Union we would face the great problem . . . [that] the absence of order among nations is becoming less and less tolerable" anticipated what has finally become fully clear to those who run the American empire. George W. Bush's own National Security Strategy document of September 2002 (intimations of which were surfacing inside the American state as soon as the Soviet bloc collapsed)[13] had a long pedigree.

In this context, just as neoliberalism at home did not mean a smaller or weaker state but rather one in which coercive apparatuses flourished (as welfare offices emptied out, the prisons filled up), so has neoliberalism led to the enhancement of the coercive apparatus the imperial state needs to police social order around the world. The transformation of the American military and security apparatus through the 1990s in such a way as to facilitate this can only be understood in this light. (U.S. unilateralism in the use of this apparatus internationally is hardly surprising if we consider how the activities of the coercive apparatuses of states at a domestic level are protected from extensive scrutiny from legislatures, and from having to negotiate what they do with noncoercive state apparatuses.)

All this was already apparent in the responses to "rogue states" under the Bush I and Clinton administrations. The United States did work hard to win the UN's support for the 1990–1991 Gulf War, and the UN oversaw the long regime of sanctions against Iraq that the American state insisted on through the 1990s. But other governments sensed a growing unilateralism on the part of the United States that made them increasingly nervous, if only in terms of maintaining their own states' legitimacy. The Gulf War had shown that the United Nations could be made to serve "as an imprimatur for a policy that the United States wanted to follow and either persuaded or coerced everybody else to support," as the Canadian ambassador to the UN put it at the time. And thus playing "fast and loose with the provisions of the UN Charter" unnerved "a lot of developing countries, which were privately outraged by what was going on but felt utterly impotent to do anything—a demonstration of the enormous US power and influence when it is unleashed."[14]

Yet at the very same time, it also made American strategists aware just how little they could rely on the UN if they had to go to such trouble to get their way. The United Nations, by its very nature as a quasi-parliamentary and diplomatic body made up of all the world's states, could not be as easily restructured as were the Bretton Woods institutions after the crisis of the 1970s. This, as evidenced in the repeated use of the American veto in the Security Council since that time, was a constant irritant. And while NATO could be relied on as a far more reliable vehicle for the American war on the former Yugoslavia over Kosovo (with the added benefit of making clear to the Europeans exactly who would continue to wield the international police power in their own backyard), even here the effort entailed in having to keep each and every NATO member onside was visibly resented within the American state itself.

Bush's isolationist rhetoric in the 2000 election campaign, questioning the need for American troops to get involved in remote corners of the globe, was bound to be reformulated once Bush was actually burdened with (and appropriately socialized in) the office of a presidency that is now as inevitably imperial as it is domestic in nature. For this, the explicitly imperial statecraft that the geopolitical strategists close to the Republican Party had already fashioned was ready and waiting. September 11 alone did not determine their ascendancy in the state, but it certainly enhanced their status. Their response has revealed all the tensions in the American state's combination of its imperial function of general coordination with the use of its power to protect and advance its national interests. Defining the security interests of global capitalism in a way that also serves the needs of the American social formation and state becomes especially tricky once the security interests involved are so manifestly revealed as primarily American. This means that while threats to the United States are still seen by it as an attack on global capitalism in general, the American state is increasingly impatient with making any compromises that get in the way of its acting on its own specific definition of the global capitalist interest and the untrammeled use of its particular state power to cope with such threats.

Perhaps the most important change in the administrative structure of the American empire in the transition from the Clinton administration to the Bush II administration has been the displacement of the Treasury from its pinnacle at the top of the state apparatus. The branches of the American state that control and dispense the means of violence are now in the driver's seat; in an administration representing a Republican Party that has always been made up of a coalition of free marketeers, social conservatives, and military hawks, the balance has been tilted decisively by September 11 toward the latter.[15] But the unconcealed imperial face that the American state is now prepared to show to the world above all pertains to the increasing difficulties of managing a truly global informal empire—a problem that goes well beyond any change from administration to administration.

This could turn out to be a challenge as great as that faced earlier by formal empires with their colonial state apparatuses. The need to try to refashion all the states of the world so that they become at least minimally adequate for the administration of global order—and this is now also seen as a general condition of the reproduction and extension of global capitalism—is now the central problem for the American state. But the immense difficulty of constructing outside the core anything like the dense networks that the new American imperialism succeeded in forging with the other leading capitalist states is clear from the only halting progress that has been made in extending the G7 even to the G8, let alone the G20. For the geopolitical stratum of the American state, this shows the limits of any "effective states" approach outside the core based on economic linkages alone.

This explains not only the extension of U.S. bases and the closer integration of intelligence and police apparatuses of all the states in the empire in the wake of September 11, but the harking back to the founding moment of the post-1945 American empire in the military occupations of Japan and Germany as providing the model for restructuring Iraq within the framework of American empire. The logic of this posture points well beyond Iraq to all states "disconnected from globalization," as a U.S. Naval War College professor advising the secretary of defense so chillingly put it:

> Show me where globalization is thick with network connectivity, financial trans-actions, liberal media flows, and collective security, and I will show you regions featuring stable governments, rising standards of living, and more deaths by sui-cide than murder. These parts of the world I call the Functioning Core. . . . But show me where globalization is thinning or just plain absent, and I will show you regions plagued by politically repressive regimes, widespread poverty and dis-ease, routine mass murder, and—most important—the chronic conflicts that in-cubate the next generation of global terrorists. These parts of the world I call the non-integrating Gap. . . . The real reason I support a war like this is that the re-sulting long-term military commitment will finally force America to deal with the entire Gap as a strategic threat environment.[16]

In this "Gap" are listed Haiti, Colombia, Brazil and Argentina, former Yu-goslavia, Congo and Rwanda/Burundi, Angola, South Africa, Israel-Palestine, Saudi Arabia, Iraq, Somalia, Iran, Afghanistan, Pakistan, North Korea, and Indonesia—to which China, Russia, and India are added, for good measure, "as new/integrating members of the core [that] may be lost in coming years." The trouble for the American empire as it inclines in this strategic direction is that very few of the world's "noncore" states today, given their economic and political structures and the social forces, are going to be able to be recon-structed along the lines of postwar Japan and Germany, even if (indeed espe-cially if) they are occupied by the U.S. military, and even if they are penetrated rather than marginalized by globalization. What is more, an American imperialism that is so blatantly imperialistic risks losing the very appearance of not being imperialist—that appearance which historically made it plausible and attractive.

The open disagreements over the war on Iraq between the governments of France, Germany, and even Canada, on the one hand, and the Bush administration, on the other, need to be seen in this light. These tensions pertain very little to economic "rivalries." The tensions pertain rather more to a preference on the part of these states themselves (in good part reflective of their relative lack of autonomous military capacity) for the use of international financial institutions, the WTO, and the UN to try to fashion the "effective states" around the world that global capitalism needs. But the bourgeoisies of the other capitalist states are even less inclined to challenge American hegemony than they were in the 1970s. Indeed, many capitalists in the other states inside the empire were visibly troubled by—and increasingly complained about— their states' not singing from the same page as the Americans. In any case, the capitalist classes of each country—including the United States, where many of the leading lights of financial capital, such as Rubin and Volcker, were openly disturbed by the posture of the Bush administration on the war as well as economic policy—were incapable of expressing a unified position either for or against the war. Once again we can see that what is at play in the current conjuncture is not contradictions between national bourgeoisies but the contradictions of "the whole of imperialism," implicating all the bourgeoisies that function under the American imperial umbrella.

These contradictions pertain most of all to the danger posed to the broader legitimacy of the other capitalist states now that they are located in a framework of American imperialism that is so unconcealed. The American empire has certainly been hegemonic vis-à-vis these states, their capitalist classes, and their various elite establishments, but it has never entailed, for all of the American economic and cultural penetration of their societies, a transfer of direct popular loyalty to the American state itself. Indeed, the American form of rule—founded on the constitutional principle of "extensive empire and self-government"—has never demanded this. The economic and cultural emulation of the American way of life by so many ordinary people abroad may perhaps properly be spoken of as hegemony in Gramsci's terms. But however close the relationship between the American state and capitalist classes and their counterparts in the informal empire, this did not extend to anything like a sense of patriotic attachment to the American state among the citizenry of the other states. Nor did the American state ever take responsibility for the incorporation, in the Gramscian sense of hegemony, of the needs of the subordinate classes of other states within its own construction of informal imperial rule. Their active consent to its informal imperial rule was always mediated by the legitimacy that each state could retain for itself and muster on behalf of any particular American state project—and this has often been difficult to achieve in the case of American coercive interventions around the globe over the past fifty years. A good many of these states thus distanced themselves from the repeated U.S. interventions in Latin America and the Caribbean since 1945, and indeed since 1975, not to mention the American subversion of governments elsewhere, or the Vietnam War.

In this sense the unpopularity of American military intervention—and even its lack of endorsement by other advanced capitalist states—is not new. But this dimension of the imperial order is proving to have particularly important consequences in the current conjuncture. The American state's war of aggression in Iraq—so flagrantly imperial and so openly connected to a doctrine that expresses the broader aim of securing a neoliberal capitalist order on a global scale—has evoked an unprecedented opposition, including within the capitalist core states. Yet even in France and Germany where the opposition is highest, many more people today attribute "the problem with the US" as due to "mostly Bush" rather than to the "US in general." This suggests that the possibility of a "benign imperium" still exists even in the other advanced capitalist countries.[17] But insofar as the conditions making for American military intervention clearly transcend a given administration, and insofar as a benign imperium can hardly prove to be more than an illusion in today's world, this is a currency that could be less stable than the American dollar. This is especially significant: since the American empire can only rule through other states, the greatest danger to it is that the states within its orbit will be rendered illegitimate by virtue of their articulation to the imperium. To be sure, only a fundamental change in the domestic balance of social forces and the transformation of the nature and role of those states can bring about their disarticulation from the empire, but the ideological space may now be opening up for the kind of mobilization from below, combining the domestic concerns of subordinate classes and other oppressed social forces with the antiglobalization and antiwar movements, that can eventually lead to this.

It is the fear of this that fuels, on the one hand, the pleas of those who entreat the imperium to be more benign and to present itself in a more multilateralist fashion, at least symbolically; and, on the other hand, the actions of those who are using the fear of terrorism to close the space for public dissent within each state. This is especially so within the United States itself. The old question posed by those who, at the founding of the American state, questioned whether an extended empire could be consistent with republican liberty—posed again and again over the subsequent two centuries by those at home who stood up against American imperialism—is back on the agenda again. The need to sustain intervention abroad by mobilizing support and limiting opposition through instilling fear and repression at home raises the prospect that the American state may become more authoritarian internally as part of it becoming more blatantly aggressive externally. But the unattractiveness of an empire that is no longer concealed in its coercive nature at home as well as abroad suggests that anti-imperialist struggles—even in the rich capitalist states at the heart of the empire as well as in the poor ones at its extremities—will have growing mass appeal and force.

NOTES

This is an abridged and slightly revised version of "Global Capitalism and American Empire," in *The New Imperial Challenge: The Socialist Register 2004*, ed. L. Panitch and C. Leys (London: Merlin, 2003).

The source for the first epigraph is Harold Innis, "Great Britain, the United States and Canada," Twenty-first Cust Foundation Lecture, University of Nottingham, May 21, 1948, in *Essays in Canadian Economic History* (Toronto: University of Toronto Press, 1956), p. 407.

The source for the second epigraph is Michael Ignatieff, "The Burden," *New York Times Magazine*, January 5, 2003.

1. Compare W. Ruigrok and R. van Tulder, *The Logic of International Restructuring* (London: Routledge, 1995), especially chapters 6 and 7, against W. I. Robinson, "Beyond Nation-State Paradigms," *Sociological Forum* 13, no. 4 (1998); and see the debate on Robinson's "Towards a Global Ruling Class?" *Science and Society* 64, no. 1 (2000), in the "Symposium" in vol. 65, no. 4 (2001–2002) of that journal.

2. The argument here is much further elaborated in L. Panitch and S. Gindin, "Euro-Capitalism and American Empire," *Studies in Political Economy* (Fall–Winter 2003–2004).

3. John Grahl, "Globalized Finance: The Challenge to the Euro," *New Left Review* 8 (2001): 44. See also his outstanding paper, "Notes on Financial Integration and European Society," presented to the conference "The Emergence of a New Euro-Capitalism," Marburg, October 2002. On the increasing adoption of American management practices in Europe, see M. Carpenter and S. Jefferys, *Management, Work and Welfare in Western Europe* (London: Edward Elgar, 2000).

4. See Peter Gowan, "Making Sense of NATO's War on Yugoslavia," in *Socialist Register 2000* (London: Merlin, 2000).

5. W. A. Hay and H. Sicherman, "Europe's Rapid Reaction Force: What, Why, and How?" *Foreign Policy Research Institute*, February 2001.

6. *Economist*, May 27, 2003.

7. See Dan Bousfield, "Export-Led Development and Imperialism: A Response to Burkett and Hart-Landsberg," *Historical Materialism* 11, no. 1 (2003): 147–60. The counterargument, in terms of Japan's "leadership from behind," was best set out in G. Arrighi and B. Silver, ed., *Chaos and Governance in the World System* (Minneapolis: University of Minnesota Press, 1999).

8. See L. Panitch, "The New Imperial State," *New Left Review* 2 (March–April 2000).

9. Donald Sassoon, *One Hundred Years of Socialism* (London: I. B. Taurus, 1996), p. 207.

10. *Financial Times*, March 26, 2003.

11. Our interviews at the Bundesbank and the UK Treasury in October 2002 confirm this. Indeed, there often appears to be more contact across the Atlantic between these bureaucrats and their counterparts in the United States than there is among the various departments within these institutions.

12. Perry Anderson, "Force and Consent," *New Left Review* 17 (2002): 24.

13. See Peter Gowan, "The American Campaign for Global Sovereignty," in *Fighting Identities: The Socialist Register 2003*, ed. L. Panitch and C. Leys (London: Merlin, 2002), pp. 8–10.

14. Stephen Lewis interviewed by Jim Wurst, "The United Nations after the Gulf War: A Promise Betrayed," *World Policy Journal* (Summer 1991): 539–49.

15. The increased influence gained by the military, coercive, and security apparatuses in the wake of September 11 could be seen in that the first victory of the new war was scored at home, against the U.S. Treasury. It involved breaking the latter's long-standing resistance (lest it would demonstrate the continuing viability of capital controls) to freezing bank accounts allegedly connected to terrorist organizations (which mechanisms the U.S. state has always known about since it was involved in establishing these to facilitate money transfers to many of its favored terrorists in the past).

16. Thomas P. M. Barnett, "The Pentagon's New Map: It Explains Why We're Going to War and Why We'll Keep Going to War," *Esquire*, March 2003 (available at the U.S. Naval War College website at http://www.nwc.navy.mil/newrules/ThePentagonsNewMap.htm).

17. See the report on the Pew Global Attitudes Survey in the *Financial Times*, June 4, 2003, which shows that in France and Germany, where only 43 percent and 45 percent respectively have "a favourable image of the US" today, 74 percent of respondents in each country attribute the problem with the United States to "mostly Bush" as opposed to only 25 percent to the "US in general" or to "both." Interestingly, in those advanced capitalist countries where the U.S.

image is more positive (Canada, 63 percent; the UK, 70 percent) there is nevertheless a higher percentage than in France or Germany who see "the problem with the US" as due to the "US in general" or "both" (32 percent) rather than "mostly Bush" (60 percent). As for countries like Indonesia and Turkey, where "a favourable image of the US" has fallen from 75 percent and 53 percent respectively to only 15 percent today in both countries, it may be worth noting that whereas 45 percent of Turks attribute the problem to the "US in general" or "both," only 27 percent of Indonesians do so, in contrast with the 69 percent who see the problem as "mostly Bush."

PLANETARY FOREIGN POLICY

8

Anatomy of a Disaster: Class War, Iraq, and the Contours of American Foreign Policy

Stephen Eric Bronner

LEST WE FORGET

There was a new game in town when this article first appeared: the political establishment had decided it was time to forget the lies and blunders associated with the Iraq war. Europe was ready to reaffirm its bonds with the United States, the United Nations was trying to placate the superpower, and smaller nations were desperately trying to make a deal. The angry demonstrations of time past, the loss of "the street," no longer seemed relevant. It was indeed time to "get on with the job" of securing the peace. June 30, 2004, was to mark the departure of American troops. But now it is mid-April: more than three American soldiers are being killed per day, hateful mutilations of bodies have taken place, and uprisings initiated by private militias in both the Shiite and Sunni regions have shaken Iraq. Major cities like Adamiya, Kufa, Najaf, Shula, and Falluja—with its 300,000 inhabitants—are being bombed by missiles and invaded by tanks while a pattern of prisoner abuse has further undermined the already plummeting image of the United States.

President George W. Bush proclaimed victory months ago, but the war is not over. Precisely for that reason it is important to recall how the American public has been manipulated, the world bullied, and the fragile nature of the democratic discourse endangered since this war was declared by an administration inspired by imperialist ambitions and guided by the interests of the wealthy. New crises of planetary importance will present themselves in the future and it seems that the same strategy of mixing deceit with belligerence will be employed. An imperialist foreign policy, fueled by militarism and a hyper-nationalism, is also cloaking a new domestic form of class war. Battling the lat-ter calls for understanding the former. This indeed turns the need to remember into a political issue.

WINNING THE HEARTS AND MINDS

There are countless dictators in the world, and Saddam, though bad enough, was probably not the most gruesome. The United States cannot intervene everywhere. The question is why an intervention took place in Iraq. It has now been revealed that Saddam actually made various last-minute overtures to avoid war: his concessions apparently included unrestricted investigations for nuclear weapons by American inspectors and even, which admittedly pro-vokes suspicion, free elections. The possibility of peace, in any event, was ig-nored. But that's not all: reports by the State Department forecast the difficulties associated with rebuilding the Iraqi infrastructure, the looting that would follow opening the prisons, and the resentment that would greet Amer-ican troops. These reports were also ignored.

Another study commissioned by the current administration, by David Kay, the American expert leading the search for "weapons of mass destruction," states that Saddam Hussein was not building nuclear arms or in possession of large quantities of chemical weapons. Secretary of State Colin Powell has, meanwhile, admitted that no proof existed of an Iraq–al Qaeda link. The Iraq war, in short, was also not a logical outcome of the assault on Afghanistan in which a genuine international coalition supported an attack upon a Taliban regime complicit in the events of 9/11. Richard Haas, president of the Coun-cil on Foreign Relations, put the matter well: "Iraq was a war of choice, not a war that had to be fought."

The American public would never have supported a war against Iraq had it known then what we know now. Human rights became a fashionable justifi-cation only once the other justifications increasingly began losing their valid-ity. The pro-war clique of "realists" in the Department of Defense made their reputation attacking "idealists" who favored human rights. Current secretary of defense Donald Rumsfeld in 1984 offered support to Saddam during the Iran–Iraq War as a special envoy of the Reagan administration, while fully aware of the chemical weapons used against the Kurds, and Deputy Secretary of Defense Paul Wolfowitz actually stated in *Vanity Fair* in June 2003 that, while freedom from the tyranny of Saddam Hussein was an important aim of

American policy in Iraq, this alone was "not a reason to put the lives of American kids at risk." The mixture of arrogance and cynicism that marks the current administration indeed oozes from the words of Richard Perle, perhaps the most notorious of right-wing hawks, who—according to the *Guardian* (November 20, 2003)—told an audience in London that with regard to Iraq, "I think in this case international law stood in the way of doing the right thing."

All the claims have been shot down: Ahmed Chalabi, the favorite Iraqi exile of the White House and a prime source for claims concerning the existence of "weapons of mass destruction," now claims "we are heroes in error." The best that the administration can do now is state that Iraq's continuing search for arms justified the war and launch an investigation into the sources of the "false information" fed to the president. Debate over the illusory claims and the quality of information has produced a loss of memory concerning the real reasons for war: geopolitical dreams of controlling vast oil resources and four rivers—the upper and lower Zab as well as the Tigris and Euphrates—in one of the most arid regions of the world; intimidating Tehran, Damascus, and the Palestinians; a belief that American interests in the Middle East could no longer be safely left in the hands of Israel; the perceived need for an alternative to the bases situated in the increasingly archaic and potentially explosive nation of Saudi Arabia. Thus, the United States felt its presence in the region was required: larger interests than those of Iraq were at stake.

President Bush insisted after 9/11 that the war on terror would last a long time: years, decades, perhaps even generations. There was no single identifiable enemy: only an amorphous transnational terrorist movement and a shifting collection of rogue states harboring fanatics and preparing for nuclear war. The enemy could be anywhere, its hatred could only be irrational, and thus—with a paranoia fanned by the dreadful events of 9/11 no less than the flames of the administration's own propaganda—the Bush administration began to think anew about the calls to reconfigure the Middle East. Paul O'Neill, the former secretary of the treasury under President Bush, stated openly that President Bush and his top aides had begun talking of eliminating Saddam in the earliest days of the administration. Leading architects of the war such as Wolfowitz and Perle had, in fact, been calling for the ouster of Saddam as early as 1991, and it made sense for administrations to consider the contingency plans formulated in September of 2000 by neoconservative think tanks such as Project for the New American Century. These reports insisted on the strategic importance of dominating the

Gulf as well as creating a "worldwide command and control system" to deal with nations such as North Korea, Iran, and Syria that President Bush would later lump together and condemn as "the axis of evil."

FIGHTING THE GOOD FIGHT

The "war on terror," if that phrase any longer has any meaning, is not going away. Right-wing politicians in Washington continue to joke, "Sissies stay in Baghdad, real men want Tehran and Damascus." Every now and then a trial balloon goes up expressing new fears about Iran or Syria. Both are lambasted for aiding the attacks on American troops, harboring or selling nuclear weapons, and imperiling Israel and the stability of the Middle East. But public skepticism for yet another military adventure has grown. The military and economic miscalculations made in Iraq have thrown the Bush administration on the defensive. Its foreign policy is in shambles.

Relations between Europe and the United States will undoubtedly improve: it makes no sense for them to engage in an ongoing confrontation with the other. Both are too politically important, too economically powerful, and—also—too alike. The rifts remaining within the European Union require mending, which is only possible through a rapprochement with the United States, while the need for reliable allies has become obvious on the part of the hegemon. The United Nations for its part has now passed a resolution supporting American policy in Iraq. That, too, only makes sense. The United Nations cannot remain at loggerheads with its most powerful member: such a course would spell financial disaster and instability for the organization. Some degree of international cooperation over the future of Iraq, moreover, was probably inevitable. But tensions still remain: symbolic is different than military support and, while it is becoming ever more apparent that the United States cannot bear the costs of peace by itself, the billions in aid sought by the Bush administration are still not forthcoming. The European Union has offered $230 million and the administration will be lucky to raise an extra few billion dollars from its other allies.

But it is not simply a matter of money. This administration has also lost the moral high ground accorded the United States following the tragedy of 9/11. America is now seen by the publics of most nations as the primary threat to world peace and as a hypocrite willing to make war on weak states and then leave the mess to be cleaned by others. Even in Latin America, due primarily to the Iraq war, Zogby International found in a poll taken during the first week of January 2004 that 87 percent of "opinion makers" in the region disapproved of Bush's foreign policy, and another poll found that nearly a third of all Latin Americans, a twofold increase since 2000, had a negative image of the United States. The world senses that this administration no longer takes the constructive criticism of democratic allies seriously, while its own panel of experts has advised the Bush administration that "hostility toward America has reached shocking levels" among Muslims and that the "image" of the United States must change. The source of a new public relations campaign, however, will surely not be Afghanistan.

That nation is now witnessing a revival of the Taliban amid the armed conflicts between tribal chieftains, which recall the battles between American gangsters during Prohibition, and there is precious little sense of a deep commitment to reconstruction. The stable, secular, and democratic regime promised by the Bush administration has not come into existence. Admittedly, in Afghanistan, some financial and humanitarian aid has been given by the allies of the United States in what was an internationally supported military response to a regime harboring the criminals of 9/11. But further aid is assuredly imperiled by demands for support in Iraq. This is not a good sign. Any potential ally must think that American foreign policy is at cross-purposes in that part of the world. It is.

And the situation is not so different elsewhere. The original refusal of the Bush administration to consider providing material incentives for North Korea to liquidate its nuclear arsenal, the rejection of the policy followed by President Clinton, and the attack on those who would succumb to "blackmail" or appeasement have given way to negotiations with Pyongyang punctuated by bellicose blustering. The "road map" to peace between Israelis and Palestinians, which was originally predicated on overestimating the pliancy of Ariel Sharon and underestimating the popular support of Yasir Arafat, has also led nowhere. Israel has assassinated the leader of Hamas, Sheikh Yassin, and it has lifted any "insurance policy" on the life of Yasir Arafat. A unilateral withdrawal from Gaza and perhaps part of the West Bank is being prepared in order to avoid bilateral negotiations and further undermine any governing authority in Palestine.

President Bush clearly did not "ride herd" on both parties to the conflict, and, for all the talk about statehood, Palestinian independence was not guaranteed as a prerequisite for curtailing the violence. Annexation of land is awaiting the completion of the "fence" separating Israel from Palestine; settlements are still being built, terrorism inside Israel remains a threat, and the prospect of peace is further removed than it was before the Iraq war. Clearly the connection between security and settlements trumpeted by the bosses of Israel is an illusion, and, with the support given to the preemptive strike of Israel against supposed "terror bases" in Syria, the possibility of a general war in the region has increased. The belief that the fall of Saddam has created more stability in the Middle East is simply absurd, and, the way things are going, even the prospect of securing American military bases on Iraqi territory is in jeopardy.

There is nothing worse than a fearful bully: feint and retreat have supplanted any sustained foreign policy. Suspended between bellicose rhetoric and uncertain aims, the foreign policy of the Bush administration is adrift. Some half-cracked officials and advisors of this administration think that the cure, the best way to soften the impact of a failed policy in Iraq, is to gamble on a spectacular victory elsewhere. A bombing of North Korea or an invasion of, say, Iran will probably not take place while the United States is stuck in an Iraqi quagmire that is solely of its own making. But you never know. The influence of the lunatic right should not be underestimated and—as Machiavelli and Sun Tzu understood—it is always better to prepare for the worst.

THE PRICE OF VICTORY

The cost of the Iraq war has been far higher than anyone expected, and it will not be paid for a long time. More is involved than dollars and cents. American democracy has incurred dramatic wounds. The left laughs at those who would substitute the term "liberty fries" for "french fries." But it is no laughing matter. A wave of nationalism and xenophobia has been unleashed in a country that clearly retains what the great American historian Richard Hofstadter called a "paranoid streak." Coupled with the introduction of legislation like the Patriot Act, there have been calls for an "academic bill of rights," and threats to lift funding from institutes too critical of Israel and American foreign policy. Neoconservatives are expanding federal death penalty statutes and issuing subpoenas without the approval of judges or grand juries, insisting on maximum penalties while limiting plea bargaining, and constricting the right to counsel, bail, habeas corpus, and freedom from surveillance. A "watch list" of more than 100,000 suspects associated with terrorism is currently being designed. Justification for such measures is supplied by a seemingly endless number of "national security alerts" for which neither criteria nor evidence is ever supplied.

Billions of dollars—four to five billion dollars per month—have already been spent on the Iraqi conflict and far more than the eighty-seven billion dollars originally appropriated by Congress is on the way. Even before adding on well over $250 billion in war costs, the huge surplus inherited from the Clinton administration has turned into the largest deficit in the history of the United States. Tax cuts benefiting the rich exacerbate the situation, profits are not reinvested, and low-paying jobs without benefits are being substituted for high-paying jobs with benefits. While the richest 1 percent of Americans acquired more after-tax money than the bottom 40 percent combined, the state teeters on the edge of bankruptcy, thereby, of course (!), rendering new social programs unfeasible. Where wars have traditionally been associated with an expansion of domestic programs—consider the GI Bill in the aftermath of World War II or the complex of social programs associated with the Great Society during the conflict in Vietnam—that has not been the case this time.

Soldiers will have a much tougher time when they come back. Work requirements have been increased for welfare recipients, overtime has been eliminated for more than two million workers, child-care subsidies have been reduced throughout the country, and there is barely a single welfare program that has not felt the knife: a particularly mean-spirited example is in the virtual elimination of a tiny program costing $150 million to tutor the children of convicts. Union rights of workers engaged in the many agencies connected with the Office of Homeland Security have also been rolled back. Then there are the lives wasted and, especially for the Iraqis, the "collateral damage." The price of this conflict was purposely underestimated, later miscalculated, and is now understated by the current administration. If ever there was a president who deserved to be impeached, then it is George Bush Jr.

Congress, admittedly, set up two "bipartisan" committees to "investigate" the administration. In concert with a cowed and simpering media, however, they have tended to sweep under the carpet the sheer incompetence and blatant misuse of power by the Bush administration. Every now and then a little gem is dropped: the public will then learn about new developments such as the formation of a company known as "New Bridge Strategies," composed of businessmen close to the family and administration of President Bush, which is consulting other companies seeking slices of taxpayer-financed reconstruction projects. Most probably the mainstream media lost its bearings amid the outburst of euphoric nationalism that accompanied the outbreak of hostilities. But whether its ongoing laxity is due to intellectual laziness, a "club" mentality, or misplaced pragmatism is irrelevant. Independently minded people now look to other sources of information like the Internet. There they can find writings by a host of critics who insisted from the beginning that Iraq had no serious links to al Qaeda and that it constituted no threat, and certainly no nuclear threat, to the security of the United States. There they can find commentators who anticipated that the people of Iraq would not embrace the United States as a liberator and that any number of serious—if not intractable—problems would plague the postwar reconstruction.

Grassroots organizations like United for Peace and Justice, no less than Internet groups like MoveOn.org and Truth Out, have been doing a valiant job of speaking truth to power and demanding that the president and his cronies be held responsible for the debacle. The president's popularity has sunk dramatically from what it was in the aftermath of 9/11, due to the depressed state of the economy and growing cynicism about the failed policy in Iraq. But the forces arrayed against the opposition are mighty indeed: there is the timidity of the media, the cowardice of so many in the "mainstream" of the Democratic Party, and—of course—the $270 million that President Bush now wishes to raise for a reelection campaign whose advertisements are already condemning candidates who are "attacking the president for attacking terrorists."

FALSE HOPES

Propaganda in America won't change the "facts on the ground" in Iraq. Capturing Saddam Hussein won't either: it might even make things worse since, arguably, the only reason even more of the populace is not engaged in open resistance is the fear that the dictator will return to power. The original assumptions underpinning the policy of the Bush administration, in any event, were optimistic and naive. There will be no quick transition to democracy, Iraqis are not welcoming their liberators, terror is rampant, and the obstacles to reconstruction are clearly enormous. We now have the prospect of a protracted war and a long occupation. How long? Some in the administration believe that America should cut its losses, while others, like the director of the National Security Council, Condoleezza Rice, believe that Americans might have to remain in Iraq for a "generation." In order to justify his policy, the president has claimed that Iraq is now the "central front" in the international war against terror: why that is the case given what is occurring in Indonesia, Pakistan, Saudi Arabia, and elsewhere remains an open question. Ironically, in

Iraq, it hardly makes sense to speak of "terror" any longer—better to think of a traditional guerilla war against an imperialist military occupation.

Knee-jerk responses won't help matters: the situation is complex. Though most Baghdadis look forward to the creation of a democratic order, and probably believe that life will improve for them in five years, different groups within Iraqi society have very different notions of what "democracy" means and what institutions should govern the new polity. The constitutional efforts by the provisional government clearly lack broader legitimacy: profound disagreements exist over whether this new regime should take the form of a Western parliamentary democracy or an Islamic republic. Rifts also run deep not only between Sunni and Shiite Muslims, between moderates and fundamentalists within the Shiite community itself, but also between various minorities on the borders of Iraq. There is little doubt that not merely the degree of nationalism in Iraq but also the depth of competing ethnoreligious identification has become more intense than anticipated. Neither a civil war that might destabilize the region even more nor a partition, which would generate a permanent irredentism among Iraqis, is a far-fetched possibility.

Simply pulling out American troops—without transferring responsibility to a NATO or UN force under multilateral command—might hasten these developments. It will surely plunge Iraq into deeper chaos and ultimately empower a new set of antidemocratic forces. This would occur as security was handed over to Iraqi militias and police. Creating an Iraqi military and police force is a possibility: but leaders of the 50,000 Iraqis already recruited are coming from the old regime. Six hundred and fifty thousand tons of ammunition at numerous unsecured sites must serve as a temptation for tribal chieftains, gangsters, and the new leaders of paramilitary organizations. In contrast to the initial claims of the Bush administration that opposition to its policy is strong only among "dead-enders" like foreign religious fanatics and criminal gangs, according to most assessments, everyday Iraqis are becoming increasingly disgusted with the military occupation by the United States, and, among much of the population, collaborators are being treated like traitors. Introducing substitute forces from the United Nations or Europe might provide a solution: but that will not happen so long as command remains a prerogative of the United States. Senator Edward Kennedy has already stated publicly that Iraq is turning into "President Bush's Vietnam." There is a way out, but, so far, it has been *politically* unacceptable to the Bush administration.

No quid pro quo has been put on the table by the president. The ideological reason is most likely the general strategic decision to reject the multilateral foreign policy of the past—with its reliance on NATO, the UN, and various regional associations of states—in favor of a unilateral approach. But there are also practical reasons: domestic politics cannot simply be divorced from foreign policy. The domestic base of political support for the Bush administration has never had any use for the United Nations and it always understood NATO as an arm for implementing American foreign policy goals. As for the beliefs and interests of Bush supporters: conservative elites are adamant that American corporations closely tied to the administration retain their lucrative contracts for reconstructing Iraq and its oil industry, while the Christian Coalition and other groups imbued with nationalistic ideology would be furious should an "apology" for the invasion be made or the "victory," no less than the symbols of American military power, be compromised.

When the Iraq war broke out, without any sense of the different power constellations, references were constantly made to the dangers incurred by appeasing Hitler in the 1930s. Next the postwar era was invoked: Iran and Syria and other Middle Eastern states have been challenged by the United States to embrace democratic "regime change" just as Europe did following the defeat of Nazism. That is a laudable goal. But it becomes little more than posturing for domestic consumption, or veiled threats against the recalcitrant abroad, since no plans exist regarding how to introduce democracy or just what democratic forces in these nations should be supported. The Middle East lacks the indigenous traditions of liberalism and social democracy that marked European history. The context is radically different and the analogy is false. An analogy of a different sort, however, might prove useful in making sense of postwar Iraq and the intensification of anti-Americanism.

In the aftermath to World War I, a defeated Germany was forced to admit sole responsibility for the conflict, compensate the victorious allies, and surrender part of its territory, while its new democratic leaders were castigated as "November criminals" and "traitors" for supposedly collaborating with the enemy and signing the Treaty of Versailles. Nationalist fervor arose among the masses and also among soldiers who, unemployed following the peace, formed any number of right-wing paramilitary organizations. Chaos followed the war, left-wing revolutions were attempted, the economy collapsed, unemployment raged, and liberal politicians were assassinated at a rapid rate. The new republic never gained the legitimacy its framers expected and dreams of revenge festered.

Iraq in 2003 is obviously not Germany in 1918. But, while there are no left-wing revolutionary uprisings taking place in postwar Iraq, unemployment is now at about 70 percent, and other similarities are striking. A defeated nation—billions in debt to a variety of countries—must take responsibility for a war, which this time was obviously the work of its enemy, while this same enemy has instituted economic policies privatizing two hundred Iraqi firms, allowing 100 percent ownership of Iraqi industries and banks by foreign investors, and making it legal for all profits to be sent abroad. The new leaders of Iraq, Chalabi and his friends on the provisional council nominally ruling Iraq, fear for their lives. They inspire little enthusiasm and less trust: most of them are viewed as corrupt stooges of the United States, and it seems clear that any new Western-styled regime will suffer from a deficit of legitimacy. The country has been humiliated, territory might be lost, and the fabric of the nation has been frayed.

Historical no less than political miscalculations have produced terrible consequences. It was believed by officials of the Bush administration that the United States would be welcomed as a liberator and that democracy would be brought to Iraq: a full-scale guerrilla war is instead under way and only baby steps have been taken on the road to democracy.

No less than in Germany following World War I, intense nationalism provides the only locus of unity: this translates into hatred of the invader. Resistance to the United States is rapidly becoming a symbol for the anti-Western and antidemocratic fundamentalists in the region: linkage between Iraqi insurgents and "terrorist" forces, precisely what the Bush administration most feared, might actually come to pass. Responding to this situation has taken the form of employing police and military officers of the old regime while making deals with tribal chieftains and religious leaders. These are not reliable allies—neither by tradition nor by inclination are they disposed to democracy—and it is becoming ever more easy to imagine the emergence of a new authoritarian state lacking in gratitude to its creators and politically incapable of guaranteeing the United States a presence in the region. Perhaps things will turn out differently. But the future does not look bright for the forces of liberty.

A CLASS WAR

When the twentieth century began, among the Left in the socialist labor movement, it was generally believed that imperialism, militarism, and nationalism were the natural fruits of an inevitably more exploitative capitalism. That perspective is no longer fashionable. Imperialism is a word rarely used any longer in polite company; talking about a "system" is considered old-fashioned; while history is interpreted by many on the Left as an agglomeration of ruptures and contingencies. To be sure: speaking about inevitability is misleading and there is little left of orthodox Marxism. But still—today—imperialism, militarism, and heightened nationalism are functioning together amid an intense economic assault on working people and the poor. Not to see the interconnection between these phenomena undermines the ability to make sense of world affairs and respond to what more than one Nobel Prize winner has called the most reactionary administration in American history.

Imperialism need neither benefit the nation as a whole nor prove purely economic in character. It can serve only certain small powerful interests and it can project primarily geopolitical aims. Naomi Klein was correct when she noted in *The Nation* that, whether troops were withdrawn or power was ceded to international organizations, Iraq would still remain "occupied." There is nothing strange in suggesting that the reconstruction contracts awarded certain American firms and the economic arrangements introduced into Iraq, coupled with new geopolitical control of regional resources, are part of a new imperialist strategy undertaken by the United States, the *hegemon*, in a period marked by globalization. It cannot simply be a coincidence, after all, that rogue states almost always seem to be traditional in orientation, outside the orbit of global society, and with a citizenry that is brown or black. The United States is now already harshly criticizing Iran and Syria for failing to close borders, for building nuclear arms, and for posing a threat to planetary security. The propaganda machine is employing the same tactics that it used in Iraq: whether they will lead to the same result, of course, is another matter. Nevertheless, it makes sense that the Bush administration should believe that the United States must back up the worldwide revulsion against its words with worldwide fear of its might.

With its new strategy of the "preemptive strike" buttressed by its defense budget of more than $400 billion, bigger than that of the rest of the world put together, the Bush administration has explicitly linked its imperialist vision with a new militarism. Little wonder then that the United States should also once again lead the world in international arms sales: its profits of about $13 billion, with $8.6 billion going to developing nations, are substantially more than the $5 billion accrued by Russia and the $1 billion by France. Israel has already claimed for itself the right to engage in preemptive strikes, which it did in Syria, and the increasing sales of arms worldwide will make it likely that violence will increase worldwide as well. Such developments can *only* benefit the most dominant military power, the United States, since new interventions will most likely be required for purposes of "security" and new subservient regimes for the purposes of securing stability.

A belief in the need for unilateral action is the logical consequence of such policies rather than simply an irrational form of machismo. It also only follows that the political mind-set of those envisioning new imperial adventures and intensely preparing for war will tend to privilege the mixture of deceit and brutality in foreign affairs. But that is not something the American people can accept without undermining its sense of democratic identity. The rational justifications for imperialism and militarism therefore lose their importance. Americans become more sensitive to criticism. Old allies like France and Germany therefore are not simply evidencing disagreement but expressing their latent resentment, jealously, and ingratitude toward the United States. Everything becomes reduced to a conflict between "us and them."

Nationalism will thus take the form of identifying American interests with those of the planet. If others disagree they are then—by definition—either fools unaware of their real interests or enemies not just of the United States, but humanity. Internal critics of a misguided foreign policy, by the same token, suffer the same fate as old allies with different views. Their goodwill is denied from the start. They become "traitors," nothing more, and the need for vigilance against them and their kind must prove as unending as the war on terror itself: the Patriot Act and other attempts to curtail civil liberties in the name of national security and a national enterprise thus, once again, become logical extensions of a general imperial strategy rather than simply irrational expressions of paranoia. That all this actually serves the Bush administration by identifying it with the national interest, and the national interest of the United States with that of the world, is still not emphasized enough. The similarity between the current form of thinking and that of our old Communist enemies—who believed that what was good for the "party" was good for the nation and what was good for the Soviet Union was good for the world proletariat—is indeed striking.

Again: it is not a matter of this or that policy but of a new reactionary agenda and the assumptions behind it. The magnitude of the current crisis is still underestimated: what was called the "military-industrial complex" is working to the detriment of the nation, and the welfare state is being stripped to the bone. More than three million jobs have been lost since the new millennium began, which would require the creation of about 150,000 jobs per month not to recover the jobs already lost but simply to keep pace with the current decline. Little is being said about what it would take to counteract these trends in a meaningful way or, to put it differently, how to reclaim the heritage of the antitrust spirit, the New Deal, and the Poor People's Movement.

Intoxicated by "the end of ideology," content as usual to offer a perspective just a little less loathsome than their opponents, even most critics of the present administration are unwilling to engage American gunrunning, the economic exploitation of Iraq, and the reality of this new class war. More radical elements stand in the wings, and, arguably, even many within the mainstream are being forced to reevaluate. But the pressure must come from outside the ranks of the party. Sources for such pressure exist: huge demonstrations now forgotten bear witness to the depth of dissatisfaction with this current regime, and there exists a colorful mosaic of community organizations, interest groups, and progressive social movements.

Coordination and a common perspective on fighting this new class war are the problems, not simply "apathy." Now, more than ever, it is necessary to begin furthering a *class ideal*—a set of values and programs—that speaks to the general interests of working people within each of the existing organizations even as it privileges none. Propagating common values of resistance and articulating new programs of empowerment can only occur by working with the reformist organizations that we have: it cannot come from the top down, through sectarian action, or through vague calls for abolishing the system. No longer is it a matter of choosing between reform and revolution. The choice is instead between radical reform and resignation. But that choice is no less dramatic: the quality of our future depends upon making the right decision.

9

The "Islam Industry" and U.S. Foreign Policy

Irene Gendzier

In the days that followed 9/11, the Middle East and the question of Islam and politics were high on the public agenda. The shift in popular mood, a direct product of the terrorist attacks, made the search for explanations of what had led up to 9/11 urgent. But the long-taboo subjects of U.S. Middle East policy and Middle East politics were not subjected to widespread critical inquiry. Instead, the justification of policy was extended to include Islam in an agenda that was committed to maintaining business as usual.

In retrospect, far from promoting an examination of the conditions that had led to the attacks against Washington and New York on September 11, 2001, the events of 9/11 inaugurated another stage in the brisk business of deception. Instant experts on terrorism promised security without understanding. Confronting the dirty business of knowing why and how and who and the history thereof was sidelined. Instead, relying on "embedded journalists" in the field, the news unfit to print was safely unfurled, leaving 9/11 as a forbidding memory of evil with a foreign name.

In the frenzied atmosphere of manipulated fear that followed, a dizzying array of correct thinkers divided the world between those "for and against us," while bemedaled generals promised victory and no-think tanks contributed to miseducating the public, the better to prepare it for the permanent "war on terror."

To assist in this project were full-time opportunists prepared to take aim at intellectual institutions to ensure their regression. The case of the bill that awaits Senate approval, but was passed by the U.S. House of Representatives in 2003, calling for the monitoring of recipients of federal funding to ensure their conformity with a vision of the Middle East espoused by neoconservative pro-Israeli advocates provides one example.[1]

The singular preoccupation with Islam provides another, of a different kind. The increasing focus on Islam was not motivated by the commitment to launch a major educational campaign to instruct Americans about the religion, culture, or civilization of Islam. Rather, it represented the ideological manifestation of policy bent on exploiting the Islamic wave in the Middle East, hardly a new phenomenon in American practice. As the former counterterrorism expert Richard A. Clarke conceded, "We have been here before."[2] And as the same former official argued, it is necessary for Washington to formulate "a subtle and successful message about religion," in order to win the "war on terrorism" and to undermine the appeal of radical groups such as al Qaeda. In search of analogous situations, Clarke offered both the Cold War and the colonial war of France against Algeria, arguing that both offered Washington lessons in dealing with Islamic radicals, as he referred to al Qaeda. The first showed how the United States had learned "to sell . . . America, democracy, and capitalism" by launching culture wars and backing parties and movements, from Italy's Christian Democrats to, "ironically, Islamic movements in places like Afghanistan." The second revealed the failure of the French in not "addressing the ideological underpinnings," as in *The Battle of Algiers*, which Clarke recommended to his colleagues for viewing.

According to this scenario, the United States faced the equivalent of the Cold War in North Africa and the Middle East as well as central Asia, among other places, which required the ideological conversion of the natives to avoid the proliferation of guerrilla wars. How this might be done was proposed by some of those who contributed to the "Islam industry." Daniel Pipes in reviewing past practice recalled that "to get Pakistani permission to arm the Afghan mujahidin against Soviet forces in the 1980s, the CIA had disproportionately to supply the Islamists."[3] But the situation had changed "now that militant Islam is the greater evil—or, at least, the more dynamic one," hence the need to readjust U.S. policies.

The "Islam industry" can be situated in this context, as an example of the culture war seeking to legitimize U.S. policy. The prime contribution of the "industry" was the production of conformist works of "misrecognition," supported "as much by advocates of Islamism as by western opinion, expert and

inexpert, purporting to find, over and above the complex and multiple histories and present conditions of Muslim peoples, a homogeneous and timeless
Islam, construed as a culture beyond society and history, a repository of
'meaning.'"[4]

The approach appealed to true believers who argued that the revival of Islam represented a return to an essential, authentic Islam, devoid of the corruption of foreign influence. It was taken up by apologists who regarded the
notion of such a revival as a sign of immutable cultural difference beyond critical inquiry. It was also taken up by those who approached it as evidence of the
nature of the enemy faced by the United States in the "war on terror." In so doing, the self-appointed "experts" whose voices dominated discussion of the
subject and its reflection in the media diverted attention from the domestic
roots of Islamist opposition as well as the role of foreign interests to the debate on authenticity and historical intra-Muslim divisions, the better to
demonstrate the urgency of supporting U.S. policy. The talk of Islam, the
good, bad, and indifferent, was thus predicated on defining the new enemy, on
identifying the insurgents according to a confessional map of their religious
and political identity. But it was the latter category that mattered.

The litmus test was compatibility with U.S. interests, not religious affilia-
tion, hence the variations and opposing tactics whereby U.S. support was extended to religious as well as antireligious movements. That such calculations
had the capacity to backfire and produce unintended consequences was another matter. But to outward appearances, U.S. policy appeared nondiscrimi-
natory, and it was, insofar as religious identification was irrelevant. In the case
of Latin America in the early 1980s, in policies involving some of the very figures active in the George W. Bush administration, the designated enemy was
the Catholic Church, thanks to its opposition to U.S.-supported dictators and
its vow to help the poor.[5]

In the case of U.S. policy in the Middle East, the exploitation of religion in
no way suggested a different criteria for secular parties or movements. In
Lebanon's civil wars, Washington favored the maintenance of a confessional
system whose political results conformed to its interests. It demonstrated no
appreciation of the secular underpinnings of democracy. In Iraq, the long
years of U.S. support for Saddam Hussein, on the other hand, were hardly
premised on an appreciation for the secular character of the Baathist party.
Nor was the 1991 U.S. move to abandon the Shiite resistance in southern Iraq
to the Iraqi tyrant's murderous response a sign of anti-Shiite politics, any

more than the pro-Shiite politics pursued by Washington in its 2003 invasion and occupation of Iraq were a sign of a turnabout on this score.

The comments—albeit confused—of Reuel Marc Gerecht, former CIA agent, in the neoconservative publication the *Weekly Standard* underscore the point. Writing in the midst of the crisis over Falluja, Gerecht called for "classic counterinsurgency tactics," for "Marines to storm the place."[6] But he called for more, albeit in contradictory terms, and his concluding passage was nonetheless clear. As Gerecht argued:

> We should state loudly and often that we will oppose any UN plan that diminishes the democratic throw-weight of the Shiite majority in Iraq. We believe that all Iraqis ought to have constitutional protections guaranteeing their individual rights, but the United States is not in favor of Lebanonizing Iraq into religious and ethnic cantons. This means that on most matters—except those specifically enumerated in a new constitution—the Shiites, if they vote as a bloc, will legislatively carry the day.

The thrust of Gerecht's message was that the Shiite grand ayatollah Sistani "is America's most essential ally in Iraq, regardless of whether Americans and the Iraqis like to publicly admit it." This, then, was the epitome of the good Muslim and his, the good Islam, while the rebel actively resisting the U.S. occupation, Muqtada al-Sadr, represented the opposite.

As journalists, commentators, and various experts pursued the nondebate on Islam and politics in the Middle East, the voices that went unheard were generally those of Arab and non-Arab critics. The omission made sense. It guaranteed the exclusion of unpalatable considerations that undermined the justifications of policy and war and made a mockery of the "Islam industry."

While hewing to different interpretations, critics of Islamist movements in and outside of the Arab world were in agreement on basic propositions concerning the Arab world. Among them was that the diverse manifestations of Islamic fundamentalism "have different underlying political content and functions, determined by their different *immediate* objectives."[7] And as the author of "Eleven Theses on the Resurgence of Islamic Fundamentalism" wrote in 1981, two years after the Iranian revolution, "Muslim movements remain essentially political movements. They are thus the expression of specific sociopolitical interests that are very much of this world."[8] The delineation of the social origins of such movements and those to whom they appeal sheds light on a phenomenon that transcended national boundaries.

The conditions that stunted the development of the lower middle class and impoverished workers were recognizable signposts across North Africa and the Middle East and elsewhere. They were direct products of the neoliberal victory whose implementation rested on authoritarian regimes whose leaders were regularly upbraided for failing to promote democracy. Under the circumstances, the emergence of militant opposition movements, including those assuming a religious form, offered no surprise. But the nature of such movements and their evident rejection of radical alternatives forced a confrontation with the conditions of the latter's failures.

Those who examined earlier periods of Arab history and politics, such as Aziz al-Azmeh, not only sought to dispel the obscurantism in vogue in dealing with "the Muslim question," but they also urged readers to examine the circumstances in which past Islamic movements had arisen. Azmeh pointed to the "marginal pietistic and proto-fascist youth militias and sporting club movements in the 1920s and 1930s; some in brown shirts, others in grey shirts, mainly active in Egypt, but also in Syria broadly conceived."[9] He noted that they had been "nurtured" as well as generously supported primarily by "petro-Islamic agencies and their obscurantist systems of public education."[10] Arab regimes were complicit in these combinations, as well, compromised in their relations with Islamist forces on one hand and with the petro-princes on the other. These were the very same regimes protected by foreign leaders, including those of the United States, whose calculations of power and interest long superseded their much-publicized commitment to democracy.

The question of the relationship between the policies and the politics of the giant oil exporters was not new, nor was the protection of such regimes afforded by foreign interests. Increased security allocations and increasingly swollen defense budgets that characterized the main oil producers of the Arab East were widely understood to be essential features of such regimes. Such connections were not widely advertised as crucial to an understanding of U.S. policies or Arab politics.

These were not the kinds of issues raised for public discussion before or after 9/11. It was warnings about the culture wars that took over, magnifying fear and confusion about "them," the terrorist cave dwellers and their flying agents who swore in the name of Islam. After 9/11 the "Islam industry" thrived. There was no debate on its offerings, or indeed on whether a fast-food serving of Islam was the key to understanding what happened on September 11. An editorial in the *New York Times* on October 14, 2001, referred to "America's deeply cynical relationship with Riyadh." But it was not the nature of that relationship or the broader context of U.S. interests in the Middle East, of which it was a central part, that embedded commentators and like-minded "experts" recommended as the urgent fare for public inquiry. It was another kind of investigation, one in which the agenda was to document the inherent extremism of Islam and in so doing to demonstrate the irrelevance of conventional methods of diplomacy and warfare, and therefore the necessity and legitimacy of the "war on terror."

In works such as *What Went Wrong?*[11] well-known specialists provided accounts of Islam and the West in the Middle East, pointing to their failures in the face of modernization, while suggesting the importance of grasping the broad contours of "the crisis of Islam."[12] The complicitous role of Western governments and allied intellectuals in condoning abuses of power by secular as well as religious leaders in the Middle East was underlined, with proper selectivity. Political calculations of self-interest, identified in cases that were sketched in, applied to those who in the past had backed Islamist movements to protect themselves against a "revolutionary wave. Such are the movements encouraged at various times by the Egyptians, the Pakistanis, and notably the Saudis."[13]

Works such as these stopped short of exposing such alliances or the full network of those involved. Attention was shifted instead to the notoriety of Islamic movements, and not to the notoriety of conditions—political and economic—involving Arab regimes and those of its allies, including the United States, in which such movements found an increasing appeal. Under the circumstances, grasping the outlines of the "crisis of Islam" became urgent, since "a significant number of Muslims—notably but not exclusively those whom we call fundamentalists—are hostile and dangerous, not because we need an enemy but because they do."[14] For those who "still see the West in general and its present leader the United States in particular as the ancient and irreconcilable enemy of Islam, the one serious obstacle to the restoration of God's faith and law at home and their ultimate universal triumph," there was no way out "but war to the death, in fulfillment of what they see as the commandments of their faith." In the end, then, it remained for Western leaders, notably, those of the United States, to recognize that they faced a religious war, one in which "the war against terror and the quest for freedom are inextricably linked, and neither can succeed without the other."[15]

Other works trod a similar path, insisting that "the notion of good and bad Islamists has no basis in fact. Yes, militant Islamic groups, ideologies and tactics differ from each other in many ways—Sunni and Shi'i, working through the system and not, using violence and not—but every one of them is inherently extremist."[16] To policy makers looking for answers, the recommendation was practical. Distinguish "between Islam and militant Islam,"[17] as Daniel Pipes suggested. As to those "seeking the causes of militant Islam, it is probably more fruitful to look less to economics and more to other factors. Although material reasons deeply appeal to a Western sensibility," Pipes observed, "they offer little guidance in this case."[18] Proper guidance was to be found elsewhere; by "appreciating the religious, cultural, and political dimensions, we may actually begin to understand what causes militant Islam."[19]

Pipes aside, the context in which Islamist movements emerged in the immensely varied landscape that stretches from North Africa to the Mediterranean and central Asia was one marked by regimes with low levels of political tolerance and a distinctly uneven allocation of wealth and services and, in many instances, by a record of opportunistic alliances with Islamist forces designed to undermine left-wing parties, strategies to which foreign governments sometimes lent clandestine support. The overt position of movements loosely classified under an Islamist umbrella corresponded to a variety of positions, nationalist in some instances, transnationalist in others. Common to all was the claimed centrality of an Islamist identity that demanded the creation of an Islamic state. In the interval, it was their response to daily humiliations and grievances that generated support, a support whose elasticity made precise measurement difficult but one that forced a confrontation with the limits of existing regimes and opposition parties.

What were the circumstances that contributed to the emergence of such movements? Was it a response to the 1967 defeat of Arab states by Israel? Was it the result of economic stagnation, the adoption of structural adjustment programs and privatization menus that punished all but the few? Was it the result of falling oil prices that affected not only the oil-producing states but the rest who depended on their subsidies?

In the late 1970s, the Egyptian government faced the wrath of those opposed to the regime's domestic politics, the toll of its structural adjustment policies, the consequences of its political repression, and the significance of its recognition of Israel in 1978. The same year witnessed the Israeli invasion of southern Lebanon, a move inseparable from Israel's continuing efforts to subvert the PLO in the West Bank and Gaza. That move was to foment changes in Lebanon's Shiite political community leading to the emergence of Hizbullah.

It is useful to recall the impact of domestic changes in Israeli politics in this context. The 1977 electoral success of the right-wing Likud Party enhanced the power of the Israeli fundamentalist movement, the Gush Emunim, whose religious justifications of claims to Judea and Samaria, the West Bank, were legitimized by the secular party that replaced the Labor Party.

Twenty-seven years later, with another Likud prime minister, and a vastly expanded Israeli presence on the West Bank, U.S. journalist James Bennet, writing in the *New York Times*, confirmed that such settlers were "vehemently opposed to any withdrawal. Many view the territory that Israel conquered in the 1967 war as part of Jews' birthright, delivered to them by God through what they consider Israel's miraculous victory."[20]

The archnationalist Zionists who were members of the Gush Emunim were not Israel's disinherited; that classification in the 1970s had belonged to the Israelis of Sephardic origin. Their radical members joined organizations such as the Black Panthers. Thirty years later, the composition of Israeli society had undergone major change as a result of foreign immigration, including that of Russian Jews.

Those on the margins of Israeli society, as Nitzan and Bichler argue, were "ravaged by neoliberalism and disillusioned with the doublespeak of both Labour and Likud, [and] shifted their allegiances to religious and ethnic political parties, such as SHAS and Yisrael Ba-aliyah." And as the same authors add, "the emphasis of such parties on ethnicity, racism and religion has been welcomed by the elites as a cheap way of diverting attention from class divisions."[21]

By general agreement among students and observers of the Middle East, the landmark event that transformed the region in this period was the 1979 revolution in Iran. For the United States and its regional allies accustomed to relying on the shah, the shock of 1979 provoked a reassessment that led to the realignment of the United States with Saddam Hussein and to support for his regime in the ensuing war with Iran. Religion was not the key to the U.S. response to Tehran, whatever the reaction of U.S. officials to a revolution that defined itself in religious terms. Nor were religious considerations uppermost as U.S. allies, with Washington's backing, it appeared, supported anti-Soviet mujahideen in Afghanistan, in an effort to undermine Soviet influence in that country, and to hasten Moscow's collapse.

In 1980, the major U.S. ally in the Middle East, Israel, covertly extended its support to Hamas, the Islamist movement that later emerged on the Israeli and U.S. list of terrorist organizations. Israel's support of Hamas was no more indicative of Tel Aviv's support for Islamist organizations than were Washington's comparable moves in other locations. In Israel's case, the objective was to undercut the authority of the secular Palestine Liberation Organization.

Two years later, Israel launched a full-scale invasion of Lebanon that resulted in its occupation of the Lebanese South and its wooing of Lebanese Shiites. But among the consequences of the Israeli invasion was the intensification of the strife within the Shiite community alluded to above, which resulted in the breakaway from 'Amal and the emergence of the more openly defiant Hizbullah.

According to Ilil Shahar, writing on "the Israel connection" in the Israeli daily *Ma'ariv* (March 30, 2004), in the late 1970s Israeli policies looked favorably on Islamic movements: "Israel aided and abetted it, in the hope of counterbalancing the PLO." The former defense minister of the Labor government, Fuad Ben Eliezer, described this period as one of "blindness and wishful thinking." At the time, however, according to the same source, the Israeli government did not consider "Islamic movements through the sights of Apache helicopters." On the contrary, it favored such organizations in an effort to undermine the PLO. "Under the auspices of the Israeli Administration in the territories they were allowed to build mosques, to receive Saudi funding which was pouring into the territories and consequently to earn the support of thousands of Palestinians."

Some twenty years later, the earlier policies were all but forgotten, if indeed they had ever been known to the general public.

On February 24, 2004, the Israeli mainstream newspaper *Ha'aretz* published the views of the Israeli deputy defense minister, Ze'ev Boim, who wanted to know "why much of local, regional and world terrorism is directed by extremist Muslims." No reference appeared here to Israel's earlier policies toward Hamas, let alone to extremist Israelis. Boim wanted to know "what is it about Islam as a whole and the Palestinians in particular? Is it some form of cultural deprivation? Is it some genetic defect?" One month later, the Sharon regime approved the assassination of Sheikh Ahmed Yassin, founder of Hamas. Six days later, his successor as head of Hamas, Abd al-Aziz Rantisi, became the next official target.

Among secular Palestinians, Yasser Arafat, now reviled by the Israeli leadership, had long been bitterly condemned for his suppression of independent critics, including those who exposed his corrupt rule and his compromised policies. Those who supported the Palestinian Initiative, a statement of principle endorsed by Palestinian professionals and political independents, envisioned a democratic political alternative that would serve the needs of the people, including "its need for liberation, for democratic freedoms, and for public debate and accountability," as Edward Said wrote in the December 19–25, 2002, issue of the Egyptian weekly *Al Ahram*.

It was not a secular democracy but the prospect of a more representative government that some believed to be in the making in Algeria ten years earlier, when the military intervened in the oil-rich, security-conscious, and highly militarized state. An estimated 150,000 Algerians died in the ensuing civil war. The Algerian case riveted the attention of those persuaded that the rich, oil-producing North African state was on the verge of a historic transformation. Instead, blocked elections following the strong showing of the FIS, the Islamic Salvation Front, were followed by years of civil war, a war whose history remains obscure. Who was responsible? Islamist movements? The military? Outside forces?

According to Lord Eric Avebury, vice chairman of the Parliamentary Human Rights Committee, United Kingdom, in his preface to *An Inquiry into the Algerian Massacres* (1999), "explanations attributing all these dreadful crimes to one political organisation do not hold water."[22] The vice chairman maintained that "the whole phenomenon has been seen through the distorting lens of a prejudice, which casts political Islam as the enemy of democracy, and those who aborted a democratic process as the defenders of democracy."

As A. Zerouali observed in his analysis of the "responses of the Arab-Muslim world," while many believed in the necessity of an independent investigation to determine what had transpired in the Algerian tragedy, there was little likelihood of such an inquiry under Arab regime auspices. The reason offered was that such regimes "will only help each other muzzle their political opponents and critics. They can work closely together only when it comes to crushing dissent, stifling free speech and censoring the media."[23] The point was not that an all-Arab investigation was useless, but that its formation would necessarily involve interference by "undemocratic and repressive regimes."

Those who called attention to the long-term roots of the Algerian crisis of the 1990s pointed to secular trends. They looked at the effects of structural adjustment policies begun a decade earlier, which, combined with the fall of oil prices in 1985, had contributed to undermining the very sectors of the economy they were designed to enhance. It was not the Algerian middle class that benefited from such programs, which neither promoted industrialization nor significant manufacturing. The deterioration of the situation of the middle class accelerated in the intervening years, while Algeria's poor increased in numbers and desperation. The major beneficiaries of this transition appeared to be those in charge, in a process that led to increased allocation for security and the military. It was under such circumstances that Islamist and other movements proliferated, albeit without challenging the existing economic policies of the regime, and without touching the oil-rich zone where foreign investment, including that of U.S. companies, was involved.

More than a decade later, Moroccan economic conditions attracted international attention in the wake of the Madrid train bombings of March 2004, as some of the accused were traced to Morocco. Observers hastened to make connections between deteriorating economic conditions, the failings of a "stunted democratic system," and the emergence of the Justice and Development Party, "one of the strongest in the country."[24] But the same journalist noted that it was not only the poor who turned to Islamic parties, pointing to the experience of Moroccans who had lived in Europe and returned to join such parties and movements. Then there was the experience of Maghrebi workers in Europe, a matter of more general concern to governments with increasing immigrant populations. Why the expanding numbers? In late April 2004, the Spanish prime minister was reported to have informed his aides that he would "lobby for greater European political and economic support for Morocco to help contain that nation's rising fundamentalism. That support would include more development aid to a nation of 30 million people with high unemployment and more than half the population under the age of 25."[25]

Across the Maghreb, as in other parts of the Arab world and central Asia, the deterioration of material and political conditions led journalists such as Ahmed Rashid to charge "local governments and the international community alike" with failing the peoples of this region, "offering them little but massive repression, unemployment, poverty, disease, and war."[26]

The case of Imam Abdulkarim Abdullayev is worth considering. In the spring of 2004, Imam Abdullayev was busy contemplating attacks attributed to "Islamic militants, probably with ties to international terror groups," in his hometown of Tashkent, in Uzbekistan.[27] At the time, Abdullayev reminded observers that it was urgent not to ignore "that there are a lot of economic problems here, not enough work." He recommended the advisability of "a more democratic system" in an environment where political repression obliged silence. The absence of democracy was not contested by U.S. journalists, who recognized that 80 percent of the population lived in poverty in a society "without a free press or legal political opposition," which led many to "underground Islamic groups, some of which preach violence."

Other accounts of Uzbek difficulties identified "Uzbek law-enforcement" as a factor contributing to the suppression of opposition to President Islam Karimov's economic policies as well as to those described as "brutally repressive policies" directed against dissident groups of Islamic origin.[28]

Reflecting on the situation in the country in April of 2004, Daniel Pipes appeared less concerned with his earlier claim that "the factors that cause militant Islam to decline or flourish appear to have more to do with issues of identity than with economics."[29] Facing the situation in Uzbekistan, Pipes's analysis moved to realpolitik. Support the leader. The situation resembled that of the Cold War, he argued. "It's a highly complex situation. There's no universal rule."[30]

With a population of twenty-five million, Uzbekistan was not only the largest state of central Asia in a region of immense oil reserves. Uzbekistan and its neighbors were described by Dan Gardner in the same article as being "overwhelmingly Muslim and poor, making them potential targets for destabilization by Islamist terrorists, while Mr. Karimov's regime is fiercely secular and has ruthlessly suppressed Islamist organizations."

There was another dimension to Uzbekistan's appeal. As U.S. Deputy Defense Secretary Paul Wolfowitz reminded Congress several years ago, "No one could have anticipated in the summer of 2001 that the United States would be basing forces at Karshi Khanabad, Uzbekistan, or conducting a major military operation in Afghanistan."[31] It was not difficult to predict, however, that the presence of U.S. military installations across this and neighboring regions might elicit opposition.[32] On the other hand, in "stable" regimes free of democratic habits, such opposition could be handled. In the late 1990s, for example, the Clinton administration had undertaken the wooing of the Algerian government to obtain its cooperation in the "war on terror," and, at about the same time, U.S. oil companies obtained approval for their advance into the Algerian oil sector, a move welcomed in Algiers, which correctly assumed its appropriate upgrade as a result.

There was no talk of Islam or Islamist opposition movements in such a context; the business of negotiating contracts would not be interrupted by such considerations, provided the proper "stability" was ensured.

The tacit understanding in these and comparable circumstances was that ensuring such stability involved control over dissidents, Muslim or other. Such was to be the recommendation to U.S. policy makers by those who argued that "the overriding goal of U.S. policy must be to keep Islamists from seizing power."[33] In the process, as Pipes noted, Washington would have to support some distasteful allies, "even when that means accepting, within limits, strong-arm tactics (Pakistan, Egypt, the PLO), the aborting of elections (in Algeria), and deportations (Israel)."[34]

Given the nature of such proposals and the dutiful blindness toward the conditions fueling political despair, there was little question that the problems the "Islam industry" claimed to be addressing would intensify.

NOTES

1. Zachary Lockman, "Behind the Battles over US Middle East Studies," *Middle East Report Online*, January 2003, http://www.merip.org/mero/interventions/lockman_interv.html.

2. Richard A. Clarke, *Against all Enemies* (New York: Free Press, 2004), p. 263.

3. Daniel Pipes, *Militant Islam Reaches America* (New York, W. W. Norton and Co., 2003), p. 50.

4. Aziz al-Azmeh, "Postmodern Obscurantism and 'the Muslim Question'" *Journal for the Study of Religions and Ideologies*, no. 5 (Summer 2003): p. 23, http://hiphi.ubbcluj.ro/JRSI/html%20version/index/no._5/aziaalazmeh-articol.htm.

5. Noam Chomsky, *Hegemony and Survival* (New York: Metropolitan Books, 2003), p. 91.

6. *Weekly Standard*, May 3, 2004, online edition.

7. Gilbert Achcar, *Eastern Cauldron* (New York: Monthly Review Press, 2004), p. 48.

8. Achcar, *Eastern Cauldron*, p. 49.

9. al-Azmeh, "Postmodern Obscurantism," p. 27.

10. al-Azmeh, "Postmodern Obscurantism," p. 27.

11. Bernard Lewis, *What Went Wrong?* (New York: Oxford University Press, 2002).

12. Bernard Lewis, *The Crisis of Islam* (New York: Random House, 2003).

13. Lewis, *Crisis of Islam*, p. 23.

14. Lewis, *Crisis of Islam*, p. 28.

15. Lewis, *Crisis of Islam*, p. 169.

16. Pipes, *Militant Islam Reaches America*, p. 46.

17. Pipes, *Militant Islam Reaches America*, p. 47.

18. Pipes, *Militant Islam Reaches America*, p. 62.

19. Pipes, *Militant Islam Reaches America*, p. 63.

20. James Bennet, "Sharon Coup: U.S. Go-Ahead," *New York Times*, April 15, 2004, p. A6.

21. Jonathan Nitzan and Shimshon Bichler, *The Global Political Economy of Israel* (London: Pluto Press, 2002), p. 356.

22. Youcef Bedjaoui, Abbas Aroua, and Meziane Ait-Larbi, eds., *An Inquiry into the Algerian Massacres* (Geneva: Hoggar, 1999), p. xvii.

23. A. Zerouali, "Responses of the Arab-Muslim World," in Bedjaoui, Aroua, and Ait-Larbi, *Inquiry into the Algerian Massacres*, p. 845.

24. Craig Smith, "A Long Fuse Links Tangier to Bombings in Madrid," *New York Times*, March 28, 2004, p. 12.

25. Marlise Simons, "Spain's New Premier Pays Visit to Morocco," *New York Times*, April 25, 2004, p. 8.

26. Ahmed Rashid, *Jihad: The Rise of Militant Islam in Central Asia* (New Haven, CT: Yale University Press, 2002), p. x.

27. Seth Mydans, "Uzbeks' Anger at Rulers Boils Over," *New York Times*, April 8, 2004, p. A6.

28. Alex Rodriguez, "Uzbek Unrest Blamed on Policies," *Chicago Tribune*, April 4, 2004, p. 4.

29. Pipes, *Militant Islam Reaches America*, p. 53.

30. Dan Gardner, "Shaking Hands with the Devil," *Ottawa Citizen*, April 10, 2004, p. B1.

31. Michael Kilian, "US Expanding Military Sites in Mideast, Asia," *Chicago Tribune*, April 23, 2004, p. 4.

32. Kilian, "US Expanding Military Sites."

33. Pipes, *Militant Islam Reaches America*, p. 49.

34. Pipes, *Militant Islam Reaches America*, p. 50.

10

Multilateralism: For a New Political Enlightenment

DRUCILLA CORNELL AND PHILIP GREEN

"Even if the realization of this goal of abolishing war were always to remain just a pious wish, we still would not be deceiving ourselves by adopting the maxim of working for it with unrelenting perseverance."

—Immanuel Kant, *Metaphysical Principles of Justice*

I.

The war in Iraq has descended from an officially celebrated "victory" of our new foreign policy and its commitment to preemptive strikes against anyone who gets in the way of the United States to a political and human disaster of epic proportions. None of the bloodshed that still eats at the heart of Iraq, and at the fraying fabric of American civil society, bothers anyone in charge, or their apologists in the media; nor does the continued, and escalating, international revulsion at what the United States has wrought. As for the future, the fall of Saddam Hussein may well have come as a liberation for most Iraqis, but still the Iraqi prospect is one about which the administration seems utterly indifferent: tens of thousands of casualties that will never be counted, endless civil strife, starvation, the collapse of public health and the economic infrastructure. None of this counts when placed in the scales with the reelection prospects of the occupier-in-chief. Even now, the United States continues to make it clear that the world community, in the form of the United Nations, will not be allowed to help with the occupation and restructuring of the desert we will have created, except on terms supervised and dictated by us. As with everything else, the United States continues to act unilaterally; not even the faithful ally Britain has been able to bring its prime minister's moral concerns to a table at which corporate greed has become the main principle of constitution making and distribution. How did such a political, moral, and human disaster come about? For us, the answer is simple: the unilateral desertion by the United States of all established principles of international law, together with its administration's contempt for democratic standards of justice and fairness at home. Liberation, though welcome if it ever truly does come to pass, will not be welcomed by anyone for long if it has been brought about only by extending the rule of lawlessness and caprice across the globe.

Before the invasion, the vice president remarked that he is proud rather than insulted when he is called a gunslinging cowboy; proud both because he is a Westerner and because such gunslinging is what the world needs. The real truth in his remark is that the gunslinging cowboys of the administration don't have any other ethic than might makes right; as has been said of various tyrants of the past, they understand only force. Thus, even though the invasion and conquest of Iraq continues in this vein—with the sight of its attendant destruction at last escaping from the new system of embedded reporting and being visible to Americans as well as the rest of the world—we now more than ever need to fight against the adoption of this ethic. Although alternative ethical and political ideals have been made to seem impossibly distant, we must not surrender to the administration's political "realism." On the contrary, we must salvage such ideals, for they are crucial to building movements and institutions for abolishing lawless violence—what the United States unleashed on Iraq in the horrifying name of shock and awe.

But we also need to develop a political analysis that transcends the rhetoric of the good, democratic United States and its few unquestioning allies versus a world of evildoers and their witting or unwitting collaborators, the world of "with us or against us" that characterizes the propaganda of the Bush administration. Crucial to the complexity of this analysis is the recognition of two salient points. First, the legitimacy of U.S. unilateral mobilization of force anywhere abroad at any time is shored up domestically by the systematic undermining of our most basic constitutional liberties; and by the growing militarization of our culture and economy, to say nothing of the attendant demolition of civil society, public education, health care, social services, public safety, and the basic needs of anyone other than billionaires. Second, the only foreign policy compatible with the recovery of our precarious democracy is a true multilateralism, rather than American imperial dominance, as the governing principle of international politics.

II.

By multilateralism, we mean that each nation-state as a matter of right should be accorded the dignity of its sovereignty by other nation-states, and thereby deserves the same respect that the United States demands for itself and for its laws. Of course, in an age of nuclear weapons, international terrorism, genocide, and state torture, the principle of multilateralism must be subject to reasonable objections. A state that engages in "ethnic cleansing," invades its neighbors, sponsors terrorism, or refuses to accept internationally sanctioned limits on weapons of mass destruction becomes an outlaw state. However, except on the most extreme occasions, a state's moral wrongdoing enters the international political arena by masquerading as self-defense, deterrence, cultural preservation. Over and against such a state, some other political entity must assert the rule of law, pronounce the sentence of outlawry, and, if necessary, legitimize the use of counterforce. But who can legitimately do this?

By itself, no single nation-state has the moral authority to play that role. Therefore, true multilateralism is inseparable from recognizing the centrality of the United Nations, an organization that since its inception has had as its major long-term goal collective security, defined not only as the full termination of particular wars, but also as the end of war as a means of resolving conflicts between sovereign nations. This ideal presumes a form of federalism that secures the freedom of each state in accordance with international law and right, and affords each state an equal voice in the federation. To be sure, the UN's actual practice over the last few decades has lagged far behind its stated ideals; it is, after all, a bureaucracy often no better than any other. On the other hand, its record in food aid, refugee relief, the provision of children's health needs, and even in its peacekeeping efforts is impressive compared to that of most nations—especially the United States. And we must remember that, to a large degree, the UN's well-publicized shortcomings in its peacekeeping role are due to the United States' refusal to commit its economic power and military might to peacekeeping efforts in the way it has unilaterally used that might toward destructive and violent political ends. Truly supporting the UN would require helping it to obtain the resources necessary to enforce its charter, not making it beg for its yearly dues.

What does multilateralism look like, then, under the current UN Charter? First of all, "humanitarian" invasions must always proceed under the authority of the UN Security Council, and they must be based on cooperative efforts among nations, since by definition they deal with collective causes—human rights violations, genocide, civil wars, and so on. To say that, it must be emphasized, is not to say that we ought to give a blanket endorsement to the practice of invasion for allegedly humanitarian purposes, even were it to take place under the auspices of the UN. That a regime treats its inhabitants horribly cannot be made the occasion for aggression, or perpetual war would be the principle of human affairs. The world is and always has been full of tyrants and torturers, and the list of nations, past or present, whose inhabitants, all other things being equal, would probably be or have been better off under a different regime is potentially endless, depending only on one's point of view: Syria, Cuba, China, Nigeria (the regime of woman-killers), Algeria, Iran, North Korea, Saudi Arabia, the Union of South Africa before the end of apartheid, the Sudan, Myanmar, Argentina under the generals, Chile under the colonels; and there are those who, as we know, would add, say, Venezuela today to the list, or Israel. The point is not that any item on this list is defensible, but that none is. All other things are never equal. On rare occasions, as was almost certainly the case in Rwanda/Burundi, and may have been the case in ex-Yugoslavia, the utilitarian calculus of lives likely to be saved by armed intervention, versus the unknowable future costs of a supposedly beneficent but humanly destructive intervention, may be overwhelmingly clear and unarguable. Iraq was no such occasion. Though we in the United States must in some sense rejoice at Saddam's absence from the lives of the Iraqi people, we should not in any way rejoice at his overthrow; for there is no possible way in which that calculus, applied to Iraq, could justify having our contemptuous subversion and perhaps perversion of the fundamental principles of international law, that national sovereignty is to be respected, and that aggressive warfare for any reason must always be an option of last resort.

In any event, we know that prior to the fateful night of March 19, George W. Bush did not proclaim that the war in Iraq was primarily to be a humanitarian intervention seeking a regime change in the name of freedom and democracy, no matter whose auspices were going to justify it. Rather, throughout the fall and winter, after the passage of UN Security Council Resolution 1441, the administration's rhetoric focused chiefly on whether Saddam Hussein and his regime had refused to comply with the UN demand that they completely disarm themselves of weapons of mass destruction. Only after March 14, when Hans Blix argued with full documentation that slowly but surely Saddam Hussein was being disarmed and that his government posed no serious threat to the United States, did the administration return to its earlier, occasional rationale for a unilateral invasion. This should not be an occasion for surprise; the historical record is full of interventions undertaken for "humanitarian" reasons (e.g., the U.S. invasion of Grenada, or of Panama) that disappeared from sight the day after victory.

In the same way, the political discourse of security and self-defense has also been cynically deployed by the Bush administration ever since September 11. Shortly after September 11, in Security Council Resolution 1373, the Council recognized that the kind of terrorism perpetrated against the United States by al Qaeda presented a difficult problem of enforcement to the UN: how could it proceed to defend not just the United States but the countries of the world from what Richard Falk has called megaterrorism, and at the same time allow the United States to defend itself, given that terrorism of this magnitude could not be addressed by means of traditional political negotiation? An earlier Security Council resolution, 1368, was used by the Bush administration to justify its attacks on Afghanistan in the name of U.S. self-defense, even though self-defense had already been expanded beyond its traditional definition, since the war was declared against the Taliban regime for harboring and funding al Qaeda. This definitional expansion was widened to include George W. Bush's bellicose condemnation of what he called the axis of evil—an axis in which any nation that defied U.S. military or economic operations could be condemned as a threat to U.S. security, thereby justifying a retaliatory attack precisely as a matter of self-defense.

This paradoxical expansion of self-defense can only be offered in the language of just war theory because nothing in the language of the UN Charter could accommodate or justify it. Just war theory, however, turns on two basic moral principles: proportionality and discrimination between combatants and noncombatants, both of which purportedly limit human suffering by making war, as we have said, an absolute last resort. Resolution 1368, conceived as it was to deal with more traditional threats of one nation to another, thus had to be stretched even to extend to the U.S. pursuit of al Qaeda cells in Afghanistan. It was certainly not meant to justify the aggressive foreign policy of the United States, because it has to be read against the basic presumption of the UN that war, as the *last* resort, is justifiable only when all other efforts at collective or national security have failed. Nothing, then, in the implicit UN endorsement of the U.S. bombing and invasion of Afghanistan undermined the fundamental fact that only the Security Council should have decided if and when military action against Iraq was necessary. Indeed, the General Assembly held an emergency meeting in the first week after the war began—a meeting not televised or reported widely by the U.S. press and media. Resolutions decrying the war as illegal and shock and awe as a crime against humanity were brought to the floor of the Security Council, though they were not passed. But the very fact that the meeting occurred illustrates that, by its actions, the United States has significantly undermined the UN as an international institution designed to promote the ideal of peace and collective security.

In any case, let's pretend that a material breach of the UN's post–Gulf War resolution on disarming Iraq's weapons of mass destruction had been brought to light by the UN's weapons inspectors. Of course, no such "breach" has ever seen the real light of day, despite feverish investigations accompanied by "revelations" that disappeared by the next day's headlines. This fact aside, though, what should have been done in accordance with the ideal of multilateralism during the past few months amid increasing U.S. warmongering and boorish threats of U.S. unilateralism? Very simply, the governing resolution ought to have been followed, and the ultimate decision as to what means of enforcement should be used against Iraq ought to have been made by the United Nations and not by the United States. But this did not happen precisely because the United States counted votes and realized that it could not win, despite its unsuccessful (though clearly cynical) attempts to gather votes by arm-twisting, bullying, leveraging, and bugging the phones of Security Council delegates (as reported by the *London Observer* on March 2). Indeed, in retrospect it seems likely that the Bush administration (or elements within it) never intended to win UN sanction for an invasion, but rather preferred to both make war and discard the UN's pretensions to be a force for collective security at the same time. In this respect it is apparent that the supposed treaty that ended the Gulf War was not a genuine treaty but rather a mere temporary suspension of hostilities in the name of an imposed "truce." Because of the horribly punitive sanctions to which the people of Iraq were subjected, this "truce" was really a continuation of war by other means. Thus the ostensibly new war against Iraq actually began years ago, and that treaty itself should have been impugned, because the United States clearly intended to strike again at Saddam Hussein under its very terms, as soon as it could find an excuse (weapons of mass destruction) and muster enough international support—or at least establish a pretense of having tried to do so.

Arguments that national sovereignty is a thing of the past are thus beside the point. No one, after all, can pretend that U.S. sovereignty is dead and buried. This is all the more reason why the United States should be accorded full respect as any other state is—nothing less, but also nothing more. Certainly one doesn't need to be a cynic to know that weapons and money ultimately make the decisive decisions in world politics. Nevertheless, it is also true that naked power can abjure coercive rule precisely in order to gain moral authority for its actions. An enlightened superpower would be a state that sought to establish on the level of international relations the respect for the political dignity of all other states, dignity normally provided to individuals by modern democratic constitutions (though, admittedly, constitutions may take as many different forms as democratic regimes themselves). In the first instance, such a state would seek forms of conflict resolution consistent with international law through means other than war, rather than militarily defending its own naked economic and political interests. For the United States, this would mean, first and foremost, that it must join an international criminal court (something it has consistently refused to do) and thereby show its commitment to the political enlightenment represented by international law. Instead, the United States quite clearly pursues what Joseph Stalin would have recognized as a doctrine of "sovereignty in one country."

Of course, international laws and institutions are only as good as the nation-states that abide by and support them, since the particular mechanisms of enforcement within individual states are not powerful enough to enforce them worldwide. The nations of the world, then, are responsible for strengthening these laws and giving them political reality by respecting them. After September 11, some Americans on both the Left and the Right argued forcefully that the bombing of Afghanistan was unnecessary, devastating to an already devastated country. We are among those who would have supported, as an alternative, police action and a criminal investigation culminating in an international criminal trial. Both courses of action would have been in full accordance with international law. Moreover, they would have been the most effective means of actually bringing the perpetrators to justice. The bombing of Afghanistan caused severe harm to the people of that country, and yet for all the political bombast, cultural invective, and military zeal that accompanied it, Osama bin

Laden remains at large and, today, seemingly almost forgotten. Even pursuing a goal most of the world endorsed, the United States managed to subvert the only principles that could legitimize a long-run counterterrorist policy. That is not surprising—by now it is all too clear that even "counterterrorism" has only been a fig leaf to cover the administration's real goal, the pursuit of empire.

Of course the disarmament of states with nuclear power, whether or not they belong to an arbitrarily constituted "axis of evil," is also central to multilateralism—perhaps the most crucial goal of all. But if it is going to have legitimate status as one enlightened nation among others, the United States must be the first state to throw down the gauntlet and begin the disarmament process. For if the United States is to be just one nation-state in a federation committed to peace and collective security, then it should have no more need than any other nation for nuclear weapons—weapons of terror designed only to kill mass civilian populations. The United States does not need, under its own totally recalcitrant control, what is many times over the largest and most threatening military force in the world.

III.

This is yet one more reason why, at home, we must oppose an ever-expanding debt economy capable of financing an infinite war. "There is no cause for suspicion," Immanuel Kant wrote in his famous essay on perpetual peace,

> if help for the national economy is sought inside or outside the state. But a credit system, if used by the powers as an instrument of aggression against one another, shows the power of money in its most dangerous form. For while the debts thereby incurred are always secure against present demands (because not all the creditors will demand payment at the same time), these debts go on growing indefinitely.

Kant's point was not that all debts are bad, but that the running of an ever-growing military debt cannot but undermine the state's capacity to maintain basic institutions that meet the needs of its citizens and promote democracy.

Thus we are returned to the question of democracy at home. More and more it is becoming apparent that the administration's ultimate goal is the destruction of democracy as we have known it, and its replacement by a permanent regime of oligarchy. As we have said, our own civil society is steadily weakening, and some of its institutional necessities—equal economic opportunity, care of the poor and the helpless, equal justice in the courts, maintenance of cities and their infrastructural lifeblood—are threatening to disintegrate. Democracy must begin at home. The ultimate American political fantasy is that a regime that trashes equality at home has carte blanche to spread it abroad. So we must pay close attention to the fraying domestic fabric of democracy, while abroad we must replace the discourse of "democratic" liberation—in truth, a discourse of *novum imperium*—with a more properly political discourse of mutual support and reciprocity. As the strongest among equals but nonetheless still a moral and legal equal, the United States must involve itself in transnational agreements and accords that seek to solve problems clearly unsolvable by any one nation-state. It is both unrealistic and normatively undesirable for any state as powerful and wealthy as the United States to be isolationist. Historically, isolationism has always been supernationalist and opposed to collective security; today's imperialists, then, are but the old isolationists in a new context—new emperors, as it were, in the same old clothes.

An archetypal example of what a real attempt at mutual support might look like is the recent international support behind the Kyoto global warming treaty, a treaty the United States refused to sign, arguing that it was unfair because it used a point system that required the wealthier countries of the world (the wealthiest, of course, being the United States) to assume a greater responsibility for curtailing their burning of oil than other poorer countries in dire need of industrial development. This point system was eminently realistic, and unimpeachably fair, about how much burden some of the poorest countries in the world could shoulder in the name of a world problem—the gargantuan hole in the ozone layer. In the name of respect for a long-term goal of reaching a more egalitarian distribution of the world's resources, reciprocity must take into account different levels of responsibility. Another example of a world problem that can only be addressed by transnational accords and agreements is the AIDS epidemic currently ravishing whole areas of Africa and Asia. Millions of people around the globe are dying on a weekly basis from AIDS. We will need to seek a world solution to that problem because no nation or individual—even one as wealthy as Bill Gates—is up to the task. But even after verbally committing a relatively paltry sum to that end, the administration still allows economic blackmail and political scare tactics to keep sex education and the distribution of condoms from being implemented in nations that desperately need them. What kind of nation among nations marshals virtually infinite resources to fight a war against one hideously brutal tyrant but turns its back on much less expensive, less interventionist, and less destructive policies that might avoid hundreds of millions of hideously brutal deaths?

Criticizing U.S. policies in this way, it's necessary to keep in mind two things: first, that endless imperial expansion in the name of democracy is not taking place as the democratic will of the American electorate; second, that we are referring to the newest phase of U.S. imperialism, not to the political novelty of American imperialist dominance (for such dominance has been ongoing and, *pace* Michael Hardt and Antonio Negri, threatens to continue untrammeled). Because an out-of-control executive branch currently fuels the reckless use of unconstrained power, we remain committed to the claim—at once historical and political—that the U.S. Constitution is a document that reflects a deep and profound suspicion of unchecked executive power. For the Constitution not only establishes checks and balances between the major branches of the government; but it also contains a bill of rights that defends the freedom of individuals against abuse by the United States. It thus should protect U.S. soldiers from the abuse of fighting an illegal and unjust war. The best way to have supported our troops *and* supported democracy was to demand that Resolution HJ20 in the House of Representatives, which would have stripped Bush of his right to continue to wage the war, be removed from committee and brought to the House floor. Genuine American patriotism and multilateralism need not be at variance. After all, patriotism must begin with a defense of the Constitution—a political reclamation of the very political rights upon which the USA Patriot Act is trampling.

We have all heard the language of freedom and rights replaced by the language of security. No one would deny that a certain amount of security is necessary to live. This does not mean just security against terrorist attacks. It also means that we need the security of knowing that we will not be spied on in our own homes. We need the security of not being thrown in prison unless we have committed an actual crime. We need the security of dissent in all forms—the dissent necessary for individual citizens to defend what they understand to be the values of their country. We need economic security, in the form of jobs, health care, and decent school systems for our children.

As crucial as it is, then, the question concerning how we can be safe from terrorism can only be answered through a resolute commitment to law, right, and equal justice—in other words, through a commitment to multilateralism as the guiding principle of international politics. That is the only way that the United States can become a nation-state that respects international law, the UN, and the sovereignty of other nation-states—an enlightened nation-state.

11

Chances for a Left Foreign Policy

DICK HOWARD

A leftist (or "progressive") American intellectual is expected to criticize his government.[1] That seems to be the reason that many Europeans were astonished, for example, to find the name of a Socialist intellectual like Michael Walzer coexisting peacefully with people of rather different convictions on petitions supporting the Bush administration response to September 11. And when the progressive American speaks foreign tongues, it is expected that he will go on to deplore American isolationism—or unilateralism, or both, as sins of equal evil. He will be expected, in short, to be more European than the Europeans. Hence, let me say at the outset, in French, that "tout comprendre n'est pas tout pardonner." And let me explain myself by adding, in German, a sort of Feuerbachian *Umkehrung* of Marx's famous Eleventh Thesis: "Die Politiker haben die Welt nur verändern wollen, es kommt aber darauf an, sie zu verstehen."

I will propose here some ideas toward elaborating a leftist approach (which is not simply an alternative) to current American foreign policy choices. But to do so, I must first criticize some interpretations of those policies because they use categories that describe foreign policy choices as they existed during the Cold War but are only apparently relevant today. I will then sketch a historical framework for understanding some constants in American foreign policy choices as part of a *democratic* political dynamic. In this context, the task of the intellectual changes; criticism no longer suffices. The difference between the Left and the Right is replaced by an opposition between democratic and antidemocratic politics. The progressive intellectual—and the Europeans who worry about the American hegemon—have to imagine forms of political intervention that encourage the openness of democratic debate while avoiding the antipolitical temptations that are particularly strong in the sphere of foreign policy.

ARE THE OLD CATEGORIES STILL ISEFUL?

The first reactions to September 11 were that nothing would remain the same, that the old political clichés had lost their meaning, and that leftist intellectuals could not simply repeat their hardy stance of opposition and the pacifist opposition to power.[2] Yet that cannot be true; change does not occur overnight. Geopolitical relations remain over the long term; political cultures do not change in the blink of an eye nor do national habits. And recent surveys of public attitudes toward government or toward basic liberties show a remarkable constancy. (Indeed, one finds similar reactions to the Pearl Harbor emergency, save that Americans now are more tolerant of Muslims than they were then of Japanese.)[3] Perhaps, as many Europeans told us, America was finally entering the real world, forced out of her narcissism and compelled to recognize that if she is a *primus*, she is nonetheless a primus inter pares, among equals. But that expectation has yet to manifest itself concretely.

The political response of the Bush administration seemed to reflect the weight of habit. This was the unilateralist government that had refused to sign the Kyoto accords, had denounced the ABM treaty that interfered with its dream of a missile defense, and was determined to eliminate Saddam Hussein regardless of the opinion of its allies. Those allies' invocation of Article 5 of the NATO treaty as an expression of solidarity was briefly noted and quickly forgotten as the Bush team took its own initiatives in Afghanistan, accepting token offerings from the allies while giving them no voice in return. Its attitude was summed up in Secretary of Defense Rumsfeld's pithy remark that this time (as opposed to the haggling that almost crippled the intervention in Kosovo) the mission would determine the coalition rather than the coalition determining the mission. The fact that Rumsfeld referred to a coalition, not an alliance, is significant: an alliance implies a shared global vision elaborated by consultation and deliberation among equals; a coalition is heteroclite—it uses its members as expendable "spare parts" to fill temporary needs. Similar disdain for multilateral cooperation was starkly evident in the recent decision by Washington to "unsign" (rather than simply not send to the Senate for ratification) the Rome treaty creating an international court; at a time when the "war" on terrorism would seem to call for such a transnational institution, the Bush administration defiantly insisted that it would go its own way.

It may be that this picture of unilateral immobility is overdrawn; foreign policy is always a work in process that is subject to many different influences. Some of those influences are personal—and so the optimists remind us that Colin Powell remains secretary of state;[4] and after many long months of silent cooperation motivated by fear of electoral backlash, the Congress and the Democratic Party seem to be asserting its critical autonomy. There are other, external, influences, the grist of "realism" in foreign policy mills—which is why the intention of eliminating Saddam Hussein has been put on hold, and the United States has finally found it necessary to play a role in the Israeli-Palestinian conflict (even though it seems unsure what that role is to be, and how it is to be played, and whether it can influence either the Israelis or the Saudis). Still other influences are domestic and electoral—as when a free-trading president imposes steel tariffs to win votes in Pennsylvania and Ohio, supports agricultural subsidies for the same purpose in Iowa and Nebraska, or pursues an antiquated Cuban embargo in deference to votes in Florida (also needed to reelect his brother as governor). It is hard to measure the weight of these incremental shifts, or the backlash that they could bring, for example, among supporters of a new round of global trade expansion.

Those who want to see an incremental learning process rather than immobility suggest that a president who had barely traveled outside the country and a Congress whose majority leadership takes pride in its provincialism[5] have abandoned the historical American politics of *isolationism.* Insofar as foreign policy played a role in the 2000 campaign, it was epitomized in Bush's denunciation of so-called "nation building" and multilateral interventions into the affairs of others.[6] Thus, on taking office, the not-quite-legitimate president broke with tradition by ostentatiously reserving his first visit for Canada, and his next for Mexico (neglecting England, and Europe). In this regard, a major victim of September 11 has been the agenda of intracontinental free trade: an expanded NAFTA, regularization of immigration with the new, democratically elected Mexican president, and regained fast-track trade liberalization authority (now euphemistically called "trade enhancement"). Commerce cannot replace politics, nor can it hide political imperatives. The tariff on steel products has harmed relations with Brazil; Chile has received no rewards for its liberal economic policies, while Argentina confronts the results of a dollarized economy out of control. The war on terrorism has added complications to the early and simple agenda. To take a recent example, how can one decrease tariffs on tuna fishing for the drug-infested, unstable regime in Colombia when this will create unemployment among the Muslim fishermen in the terrorist-harboring regions of the Philippines?[7]

In this context, it appears that the Bush administration has moved from isolationism toward a recognition of a multifaceted world whose complexity it could not master. As a result, it has now sought to reduce this complexity by exerting unilateral control. Not for nothing does the United States spend more on national defense than the next fifteen nations *together*; not for nothing do the Americans tell their European allies, *Modernize or be marginalized.* And whereas the Europeans protest and demand to be treated as equals, the recent signature of a new (475-word, ignoring, among other things, tactical weapons) missile treaty as well as acceptance of American withdrawal from the ABM treaty suggests that the Russia of Mr. Putin has understood the hard realities of a new American century. Europe, on the other hand, seems to be fulfilling the (low) expectations of Defense Secretary Rumsfeld, who recalls bitterly his period as U.S. ambassador to NATO a quarter century ago, in 1973–1974.

But are these categories—isolationism, multilateralism, and unilateralism—still useful for a characterization of American foreign policy? Isolationism has a long tradition; but it stands opposed to *both* multilateralism and unilateralism, which are themselves opposites. This duality leads to confusion; it conceals differences that, particularly in the new post–Cold War era, are politically important. Think of some recent examples. Unilateralism need not be the action of an imperial power snuffing out freedom as it works its will; it may be necessary when the wrangling of coalition partners prevents action at times when human rights (or lives) are in peril, as in Bosnia, Kosovo, or recent cases in Africa. Multilateralism can be functional for the creation of a world of mutual interdependence whose members will reciprocally civilize each other's behavior; but it can also be a formula for pious words that make impossible practical deeds—as in the cases just mentioned. Even isolationism can have different meanings. It need not be the stance that wishes to hear or see no evil and is condemned to pay the price of its good-natured naïveté; nonaction denounced as isolationism may be the recognition that not every problem can be solved immediately and that simple solutions cannot be imposed upon people unwilling or unable to admit them—indeed, there are problems that can only be solved after they fester for a time until the times are ripe.[8]

CATEGORIZING DEMOCRATIC DYNAMICS

There are good reasons, both geographical and historical, to repeat the usual description of U.S. foreign policy as congenitally isolationist. One of the founding moments of American democracy, George Washington's "Farewell Address," marks not only a recognition of the limits of political power in a pluralist society but contains also the warning to his countrymen to avoid "entangling alliances." This phrase, learned by every American schoolchild, has become what Walter Russell Mead calls "the foreign policy equivalent of the Bill of Rights."[9] One of the goals of Mead's remarkable new book, *Special Providence: American Foreign Policy and How It Changed the World,* is to show that, even before the creation of the new nation—indeed, as a political condition of its creation, which depended on French, Dutch, and Spanish alliances—Americans knew, and practiced skillfully, the art of foreign policy. More than that, Mead's claim is that—as opposed to the contemporary stereotype—foreign policy has been one of the chief issues dividing the contesting political parties, at least until the achievement of a certain "mythical" modus vivendi with the outbreak of the Cold War.[10]

Mead analyzes historically and illustrates pragmatically four currents—as opposed to the now-ambivalent categories inherited from the Cold War—associated with historical figures of the American past. The result goes beyond the dichotomy with which Henry Kissinger introduced his *Diplomacy,* when he distinguished the naive idealism of Wilson from the hardened balance-of-power realism of Theodore Roosevelt.[11] Mead's first category reflects the primacy of business and commerce throughout American foreign relations: *Hamiltonians* stress the alliance of government and business to ensure stability at home and integration into the world economy. *Wilsonians* then introduce a moral dimension that wants to spread American values in order to create a peaceful world under the rule of law. *Jeffersonians* strive above all to protect democracy at home, and therefore avoid unsavory alliances by Hamiltonians and risks of war run by Wilsonians. Finally, populist *Jacksonians* insist that domestic and foreign policy must ensure the security and well-being of the people; while they don't seek foreign quarrels, when war becomes necessary, these Jacksonians demand that it be fought to the finish.

Because of their historical specificity, Mead's categories are able to take into account the dynamics of political competition because, in order to remain the same, each of them must mutate as political conditions change. This flexibility is double: it takes into account changed socioeconomic conditions as well as the contending political parties. For example, the original Hamiltonian vision of the way to achieve the primacy of trade and commerce was formulated in Hamilton's "Report on Industries," which defended the protection of "infant industries" by means of a high tariff. Such protectionist policies could only be maintained at the end of the nineteenth century because protected industries still paid good wages and guaranteed secure jobs. By the middle of the twentieth century, however, American economic power meant that lower tariffs (i.e., free trade) would benefit the economy—but now wages and jobs came under pressure. If a new Hamiltonian policy was to be enacted, it would have to find new allies, perhaps among the (nationalist) Jacksonians, since its former supporters had gone either to the Wilsonians (the NGOs opposing exploitation) or to the Jeffersonians (attacking business power as a threat to democracy). Hamiltonian politics would, in other words, have to change in order to remain the same.

Mead's categories also permit the tracing of a multitude of potential cross-alliances in changing historical conditions. His account of the Wilsonians' "missionary spirit"—which antedated Woodrow Wilson—clarifies the status of his categories. This spirit was present at the foundation, when the colonists left the Old World to seek not only religious freedom but the blessings that accompanied it. Their heirs expanded this mission, taking their creed across the continents, and bringing in their wake government interventions that to the nonhistorian's eye could look like a new colonialism. But the Wilsonians had no monopoly on virtue; the Jeffersonian democratic creed not only competed with their moralism but warned against its excesses, fearing that such interventions could become a threat to the foundations of democracy.[12] Where the Wilsonian might fight "a war to end all wars," the Jeffersonian would seek to negotiate, try to put off the moment of decision, or stand on the sidelines while cheering for the virtuous. But at this point, the temporary alliance of Jeffersonians with those Jacksonians who supported a democracy because it left them alone would come under pressure, since these populist Westerners were slow to anger but fierce in self-defense once aroused. At this point, the Jacksonians' populism could turn into a patriotism that would allow them to rejoin the Hamiltonians in defense of a national cause that holds together as long as neither side looks too closely at its own premises.

Leaving aside the historian's question of the accuracy of these classifications, they do seem to offer a recognizable picture of America. What is significant is that they do not coincide with actual party lines; they point rather to the ingredients of shifting coalitions, and they can reflect different policy goals—or lead participants to change their policies (or to compromise) in order to maintain their original intentions. Mead attributes the success of American foreign policy to the competition among these basic categories; and he recognizes that the domination of one or the other would be harmful (which is why he dismisses at the outset the "myth" of the Cold War and a unified America for which only one policy is possible or just). His critics deplore this flexibility because it lacks predictive power; his thesis seems nonfalsifiable because he can always explain *post festum* new combinations or splits and realignments.[13] For example, Hamiltonians among the Clinton administration appealed to the civilizing effects of Montesquieu's "doux commerce" while Hamiltonians in the Bush camp are more crudely pro-business. Wilsonians might well ally themselves with the former, who are making the world safe for their own (modern forms of) missionary work; but other Wilsonians would insist that globalization destroys the dignity of indigenous cultures. This second group could in turn find allies among those Jeffersonians whose fear for the fragility of democracy leads them toward isolationism. But the historical fact that Jeffersonian fear of big government led many of them to oppose U.S. entry into World War I, to reject the League of Nations, and above all to appease the new totalitarians in the 1930s discredited this orientation. What remained of their influence depended on an alliance with the Jacksonians, which disintegrated with the Vietnam War. Both tendencies were appalled by the effects of the war at home and by the corrupt Vietnamese government it defended; but the Jeffersonians wanted to cut and run, which, to the Jacksonian, was a violation of a code of honor that cut more deeply than the fear for the safety of domestic democracy.

Mead draws two conclusions from his analysis. The first is that the interplay of these four political tendencies accounts for the unquestionable successes of American foreign policy, including the victory in the Cold War. He wants his readers to learn from this history, and to recognize that foreign policy has been fundamental to the history of American democracy. The second conclusion is more contemporary and pragmatic. He suggests that the Hamiltonian and Wilsonian came together after 1989 to provide the basis of the New World Order, whose "rise and retreat" he chronicles. Free trade plus globalization joined with increasingly powerful NGOs to pursue the creation of rule of law and the spread of democracy while protecting human rights. But this coalition was short lived; the other two tendencies affirmed themselves, and history did not come to an end, after all. What then of "the future of American foreign policy"? "I believe," says Mead, "I owe it to readers to declare my preference among the schools." His carefully hedged adhesion is to Jeffersonianism, whose "caution," and "conservation of . . . liberty and lives, and . . . passion for limits" is said, finally, to be the ideal that motivated John Quincy Adams and James Monroe in 1823.[14]

I want to propose a different conclusion from Mead's stimulating account. The constant interplay among the four categories that he describes means that none of them can uphold the claim that it has a monopoly on wisdom, that it expresses *the* unique national interest, or even that it expresses the vox populi. Mead's analysis suggests that foreign policy success, particularly in the post–Cold War world, is not predicated on such (real or imagined) national unity; indeed, the totalitarian disasters of the twentieth century in the Soviet and German (and Japanese) cases resulted from just such unitary presuppositions. The task of the democratic intellectual is not to propose another vision of unity that claims to be superior to those failed attempts. That was the project of the progressive intellectuals who rallied to Jack Kennedy, only to find themselves unable to escape from their Vietnam nightmare because their politics was defined by the moral imperatives of Cold War anti-Communism. But their equally moralist left-wing critics could only adopt an "anti-anti-Communist" stance that had nothing political to offer, especially in the domain of foreign policy. Mead's account suggests the direction in which to search for a new politics; although he doesn't say it in so many words, democracy for him is not simply a means; it can also be an end to be sought in the post–Cold War world.

POLITICAL DYNAMICS IN THE POST–COLD WAR WORLD

The end of the Cold War appeared to leave the United States alone on a world stage that had no overarching structure. Omnipotence was coupled uneasily with impotence, in the Balkans, in Rwanda, in the pious words and absent deeds of the Clinton years. In 1994, Henry Kissinger argued in *Diplomacy* that the ethical basis of the unity of American Cold War politics was useless in the emerging political-strategic world; American power was in fact limited and could be exercised only if it rediscovered the principles of diplomatic realism of which Kissinger claimed to be a master. Seven years later, in his first chapter of *Does America Need a Foreign Policy?* Kissinger posed the question: "America at the Apex: Empire or Leader?" Empire, he argued, is not a policy;

it confuses strategy with economics, while ignoring the political, cultural, and spiritual impact of the new technological world. Leadership is exercised through alliances, such as NATO. An alliance differs from a guarantee of collective security, which is merely a juridical promise that, like a UN resolution, will not be carried out if major participants fail to act.[15] Europe, argues Kissinger, could become merely such a zone of collective security if America does not revitalize and repoliticize the NATO alliance. This is the more important since a unified Europe (either in the German Fischer proposal, or in the French multispeed mode, or in Blair's confederal version) would face the United States only once decisions had been made, at which point it would not be possible to revise them as a result of discussion with the Americans. Kissinger's worry is clear, but his formula for leadership leaves no role for a European partner (only for European partners: divide et impera is an earlier form of Kissinger's favored realpolitik).

Kissinger's rejection of the old political concept of empire may be too facile (and self-interested); after all, the power and reach of twenty-first-century America has no historical parallels. Recall the time when optimism about a Soviet revival under Gorbachev's perestroika was widespread; historian Paul Kennedy's best-seller, *The Rise and Fall of the Great Powers: Economic Change and Military Conflict from 1500 to 2000* (1987), convinced many that the result of America's "imperial overreach" would be an inevitable decline. Today, Paul Kennedy has to admit that while Rome was limited by the Persian and Chinese empires, and the size of the British navy was equal only to the next two navies, the United States stands alone. More aggressively, the *Wall Street Journal* editorialist Max Boot, writing in the conservative *Weekly Standard*, suggests that September 11 resulted not from foreign resentment at America's action in the world but from the insufficient involvement of the United States in its true mission. In the same vein, Robert D. Kaplan, whose *Balkan Ghosts* (1993) was said to have dissuaded Clinton from his aggressive "lift and strike" option for Bosnia, drew a similarly amoral lesson in *Warrior Politics: Why Leadership Demands a Pagan Ethos* (2001). If order is to be imposed in an anarchic world, the American cop will have to do the job—and he will be applauded for his work by willing masses already seduced by the pleasures promised by America's vaunted "soft power."[16]

What theorists of empire forget is that America acquired its hegemony without any specific political project other than its moral righteousness—the end of the Cold War was more a Soviet defeat than an American victory (an arms race to the death, what the Germans call *tot-rüsten*, rather than a duel of utopias). Indeed, Bush's national security adviser Condoleezza Rice wrote in *Foreign Affairs* in 2000 that since the end of the Cold War American foreign policy seemed to have lost its direction.[17] She was not alone in that analysis. But she is not alone either, today, in her revision of that analysis, whose new premise is that the post–September 11 period is "analogous to 1945–47," when the doctrine of containment was elaborated and made operational. But the author of the remarkable article that contains Rice's recent claim, Nicholas Lemann, puts her analysis into a broader and more worrisome imperial context, one that began under the direction of Bush *père*, aided by then defense minister Cheney, who proposed his own hard-nosed vision of a post–Cold War world, only to watch with frustration as Bill Clinton—in the words of Condoleezza Rice's *Foreign Affairs* article—was guilty of "an extraordinary neglect of the fiduciary responsibilities of the commander in chief."[18]

The proposed post–Cold War imperial policy is often associated with the names of Deputy Defense Secretary Paul Wolfowitz and Vice President Cheney. Its academic label was provided by Zalmay Khalizad (now American proconsul in Afghanistan): it is the passage from "containment to global leadership." This project, or vision, seems to have only become truly possible with the shedding of American blood on September 11. However America acquired its hegemonic position, its rulers now intend to keep it, by all means necessary. And those means include preemptive strikes (possibly even nuclear),[19] the redrawing of regional maps, and the intervention needed to create what is called euphemistically a "democratic zone of peace." Another, less euphemistic label for this project is proposed by Colin Powell's chief intellectual adviser, Richard Haass, who occupies the office first held by George Kennan, the father of containment theory. In an interview with Lemann, the State Department's Richard Haass suggests that there are "limits of sovereignty" that prevent governments from abusing the rights of their citizens; and there are legitimate interventions that prevent them from doing so. More important, such limits also prevent governments from supporting terrorism or from producing weapons of mass destruction—whose possession legitimates "preventive, or peremptory, self-defense." Obviously, such a policy would have its first application in Iraq, permitting the son to fulfill the task left for him by his father.

But are the proponents of such a policy right in thinking that September 11 will permit them to gain public support? The cynic might reply that the manner in which this administration has used the metaphor of the war on terror to prevent not just dissent but even the questioning of its policies by members of the opposition (or by Republicans like Richard Shelby or Dan Burton) will ensure public support by its manipulations. What can the progressive intellectual do in the face of this onslaught? What can Europe do?

Turning first to the intellectual, from whose position I began this discussion, he is assumed to be a critic of the American policy. The stance of the intellectual as critic is an old one. During the Cold War, the progressive intellectual could only be a critic of one of the competing world systems, without reflecting on the manner in which his critique implied at least tacit support of the other system. In the American context, this meant that the Left was "*anti*-anti-Communist," with the result that it had nothing positive to defend, no ideals to realize, no project for the future. Typical of this attitude was the oldest existing weekly journal of the Left, the *Nation*.[20] To put the matter differently, the leftist intellectual acquired the habit of finding all glasses to be half empty; there was never any question of finding one to be half full—and in need of further positive measures. As a result, at the end of the Cold War (if not before, which is another debate), the Left had no contributions to ongoing political debates, and was blind to its Eastern *compagnons*.

But "the" Left was and is (and should not be) so unified as these last remarks imply. There was an antitotalitarian Left too, one that contributed to the overcoming of the Soviet order. It was not so strong in the United States as, for example, in France. Learning from Eastern European dissidents who recognized the need to ensure the rights and freedoms, this new Left recognized the radical political implications of democracy—which is not simply another justification of capitalist economic exploitation. Although it was a minority among the Left, this new direction (and its Eastern friends) seized upon Basket III of the 1975 Helsinki Accords, which conservatives denounced as a sell-out in which the West recognized the legitimacy of the Soviet imperium. Despite Henry Kissinger's attempt to reclaim this achievement for himself,[21] there is no reason for a progressive Left to allow him to take the credit and play the Democrat. Why should the Left not claim that the glass is half full? There is no reason, for example, for a critical Left not to agree with the State Department's Richard Haass about the limits of sovereignty (although it might dissent from the possible preemptive nuclear strikes suggested by Paul Wolfowitz). The Left should favor interventions to encourage democracy.

In this same context, one sees how the categorical framework of Walter Russell Mead offers a possible guideline for European political action as well.

Two points in particular seem promising. If it is true that the democratic nature of American foreign policy depends on the constant interaction—call it checks and balances—of the four political tendencies, then Europeans should be on guard to ensure that their words and actions do not favor the domination of one or the other tendency. Democracy in U.S. foreign policy is good for Europe as well. Second, the lability of the flexible categories, which can enter into various alliances at different historical conjunctures, suggests that European reaction to American actions needs to bear in mind that these policies are not the result of a single unified will expressing itself in the one and only form it can possibly take. American actions result from multiple interactions; the imposition of a tariff on steel, or the decision to intervene in Iraq, is not preordained; such actions result from political coalition building, and there is no reason only to criticize when the fact that coalitions are built by partners means that the temporary alliances can also be drawn apart and reconfigured by sufficiently subtle approaches. In a word, as with the intellectual, Europe has to remember that, despite appearances, America remains a republican democracy, plural in its values and open to the future. It is a glass that only appears half empty; if we understand that it is also half full, we are on our way to realizing what Marx should have intended when he wrote the Eleventh Feuerbach Thesis, with which I proposed to begin this discussion of intellectuals and foreign policy.

NOTES

1. The exception that proves the rule is the scandal that arose fifty years ago when *Partisan Review* published its famous issue "Our Country and Our Culture," in its May–June 1952 issue.

2. This is of course not true for all leftist intellectuals—or intellectuals who think of themselves as leftists, as is the case most clearly for Noam Chomsky, whose blame-America-first politics have not changed since September 11. In German, c.f. the pre-September article by Jörg Lau, "Onkel Noam aus dem Netz," in *Die Zeit*, no. 31, July 26, 2001, p. 29. More generally, c.f. the biting criticism of similar positions by Ian Buruma and Avishai Margalit, published under the ironic title alluding to Edward Said's famous polemic, "Occidentalism," in *New York Review of Books*, January 17, 2002, pp. 4–7.

3. C.f. Adam Clymer, "US Attitudes Altered Little by Sept. 11, Pollsters Say," *New York Times*, May 20, 2002, p. A12, reporting on the fifty-seventh annual meeting of the American Association for Public Opinion Research. Attitudes toward gun control and capital punishment did not change; nor, despite the perception that religion had become more important for people, did patterns of church attendance. While the public did support some more restrictions of civil liberties, this was typical of past crises, and was expected to recede, as

in the past. Nor was there greater support for an increased role of government more generally, despite predictions by commentators, including this one!

4. And Colin Powell too seems to think that he has been able to change the attitudes of the president, as he notes in a recent interview, pointing to Bush's having learned from the "bad handling" of Kyoto, and the lesson of patience in dealing with the Chinese after the downing of a U.S. spy plane. The latter case taught Mr. Bush to let his subordinates, including the State Department, "shape the situation for the president for a little while." C.f. David E. Sanger, "On the Job, Bush Has Mastered Diplomacy 101, His Aides Say," *New York Times*, May 22, 2002, pp. 1, 10.

5. Texas Republican Dick Armey, the House majority leader, takes pride in never having traveled to Europe. Tom DeLay, the House whip soon to replace Armey as leader, has recently been voicing his misgivings about the Enlightenment. C.f. Harold Meyerson, "Axis of Incompetence," *American Prospect*, May 20, 2002, pp. 18–19.

6. There is a long and honorable precedent for this attitude, which is perhaps best articulated by John Quincy Adams, the theoretical force behind the creation of the Monroe Doctrine, which long guided American foreign policy after 1821. Sounding perhaps like the "compassionate conservative" that Bush wanted to represent, Adams wrote that

> wherever the standard of freedom and independence has been or shall be unfurled, there will be America's heart, her benedictions and her prayers. But she goes not abroad in search of monsters to destroy. She is the well-wisher to the freedom and independence of all. She is the champion and vindicator only of her own. . . . She well knows that by once enlisting under other banners than her own . . . she would involve herself beyond the power of extrication. . . . She might become the dictatress of the world. She would no longer be the ruler of her own spirit.

It is worth noting that I am citing this passage from Henry Kissinger's *Does America Need a Foreign Policy?* (New York: Simon & Schuster, 2001), p. 238.

7. C.f. the news analysis by Keith Bradsher, "Quandary on Trade," in the *New York Times*, May 21, 2002, p. W1.

8. Isolationism can also take an aggressive form, as in the previously mentioned case of Chomsky, for whom whatever the United States does is harmful; or it can be adopted by his right-wing political opposite, Patrick Buchanan, whose recent book is called *America: A Republic Not an Empire*.

9. Walter Russell Mead, *Special Providence: American Foreign Policy and How It Changed the World* (New York: Knopf, 2001), p. 59. I will make use of Mead's categories, but do so in a different context. Mead's concern, as his subtitle indicates, is to vindicate the success of a democratic foreign policy; mine is to look at the dynamic underlying that politics. Mead is a diplomatic historian who uses his framework to retell a coherent story, but his categories are too general to deal adequately with contemporary politics, as is clear in former assistant secretary of state for public affairs James P. Rubin's review in the *New Republic* (March 18, 2002, pp. 29–33).

10. That this diplomatic involvement was not simply verbal or commercial is argued also in a recent book by *Wall Street Journal* editor Max Boot, *The Savage Wars of Peace* (New York: Basic

Books, 2002). Boot discusses what he calls "small wars" which led America in the 114 years before 1900 to undertake 184 landings on foreign soil. Mead's first chapter is a lengthy factual refutation of claims that America has always been isolationist and indifferent to foreign policy.

11. Henry Kissinger, *Diplomacy* (New York: Simon & Schuster, 1994). In fact, Kissinger begins with a chapter on the post–Cold War "New World Order" that argues for the relevance of rereading the history of diplomacy. He then presents Roosevelt and Wilson under the title "The Hinge," before returning directly to Richelieu, William of Orange, and Pitt. Without overemphasis, Mead's book is clearly directed against Kissinger's European "realist" orientation. He suggests that once America became a dominant economic power, and particularly with the "myths" of the Cold War, the economic dimension of American foreign policy was forgotten and the image of an immature "isolationist" America that had now grown up could become dominant. C.f. chapter 3, "Changing the Paradigms."

12. Mead assimilates John Quincy Adams to the Jeffersonian creed—despite the political differences that had separated Adams's father and Jefferson. Mead cites as one proof of his claim the same passage from Adams cited by Kissinger in note 7, above. This would seem to imply that the "compassionate conservative" Bush was also a Jeffersonian—despite his clearly Hamiltonian trade policies. But as was seen in the text, the modern Hamiltonians needed new allies—why not seek them out here, among Jeffersonians, who, like everyone else, had to change their politics in order to remain consistent with themselves?

13. This is the argument of James P. Rubin's review (note 10, above). Rubin is unfair, however, in that he uses a series of newspaper columns published by Mead over the past decade in the *Los Angeles Times* to show the inconsistency of Mead's own political analysis. This confuses the task of the editorialist and that of the political historian.

14. Mead, *Special Providence*, pp. 331, 334.

15. Kissinger was writing before Donald Rumsfeld had invented the above-mentioned distinction between an alliance that determines a mission and a mission that determines the alliance. One has to admit that Kissinger is, like it or not, a historically schooled thinker—which is not the case for the present regime. For a critique of Kissinger, c.f. Stanley Hoffmann's review-essay, "Yesterday's Realism," in the *American Prospect*, July 20, 2002, pp. 33–37. Hoffmann argues that Kissinger "dodges the problem that has plagued realists ever since Morgenthau. . . . Is there a clearly defined and delimited national interest?" His answer is that "while Wilson's hyperbolic statements rejecting 'a standard of national selfishness' are easy to dismiss, his belief that this age requires us also to think about 'the interest of mankind' is not so easily ignored" (p. 36). As I have suggested following Mead, Hoffmann too concludes that "on the whole, Wilsonians understand better than realists do: that what happens within a country is often more decisive than calculations of power balance" (p. 37).

16. For a summary of these arguments, c.f. Emily Eakin, "All Roads Lead to D.C.," *New York Times*, March 31, 2002.

17. Condoleezza Rice, "Promoting the National Interest," *Foreign Affairs*, January–February 2000, pp. 45–62.

18. C.f. Nicolas Lemann, "The Next World Order," *New Yorker*, April 1, 2002, pp. 42–48. The citation from Condoleezza Rice is on p. 51 of the article in *Foreign Affairs*.

19. By a curious detour through primitive Afghan conditions: How to get to caves? How to dig deep? This is an example of a (coherent) logic run wild, a precautionary example.

20. It is worth noting that, in the wake of September 11, the *Nation* did open to more serious debate, for example between the still consistently anti-American Alexander Cockburn and his more critical colleague, Christopher Hitchens, both Britons who have long written mainly in the U.S. leftist press.

21. C.f. *Diplomacy*, pp. 759–61. But Kissinger has to admit that without the dissidents there would not have been a breakthrough. It is worth noting that in this context, Kissinger brings up once again (p. 756) the above-cited passage from John Quincy Adams to explain his position—viz., to cheer on the dissidents while remaining on the sidelines.

IV

COSMOPOLITAN HOPE

12

The Two Faces of Globalization

MICHAEL J. THOMPSON

"The time for petty politics is over: the very next century will bring with it the struggle for mastery over the whole earth—a compulsion to politics on a grand scale."

—Friedrich Nietzsche, *Beyond Good and Evil*

We think of globalization as a monolithic and inexorable process, gripping provincial and cosmopolitan alike, transforming the globe—slowly, but assuredly—into a cohesive network of markets, political institutions, cultural sensibilities, and norms. It is as if the world were moving toward what the Christian philosophers of the medieval age knew as the *Cosmopolis*: a world political community united by Christianity and the Church. But the reality of globalization is considerably more complex. The optimistic assessments of globalization are couched in the rhetoric of economic and technological diffusion. Both critics and defenders of globalization overwhelmingly focus on its economic dimension: on its ability either to impoverish or enrich countries traditionally banished to the periphery of global economic growth and development. But the problem of globalization is not ultimately economic but political in nature. The impulse that streams outward from the West and gives impetus to globalization, such as Western science and capitalism, has not been matched by an acceptance of Western moral and political ideas—and it is this crucial disconnect that needs to be addressed.

When, in 1904, Max Weber penned his seminal study of the origins of Western modernity, *The Protestant Ethic and the Spirit of Capitalism,* the central concern that inspired his analysis was not the origins of Western capitalism and the roots of modernity in and of itself. Rather, Weber begins his enquiry with a much broader and, for contemporary readers, much more profound concern: Why is it that the West has become more developed in its economic, political, and social organization than other cultures? How and why is it, in other words, that the West is "modern" and the rest are not? What is the reason for the apparent uniqueness of the West in developmental terms? Today, the mere statement of such a question sparks controversy and a flurry of accusations ranging from orientalism to "occidentalism." But Weber's broader question—especially within the context of globalization—is more relevant now than when he first articulated it at the dawn of the twentieth century.

For Marx, what we now call globalization is nothing more than the result of the very logic of capitalist expansion, which would carry with it a modernizing process as it knocked down feudal arrangements of property and labor. The spread of capitalism meant the transition from feudal relations to bourgeois property relations. Many readers of the *Manifesto* still recall the lines of praise that Marx heaped on the transformative powers of capital in the global context:

> The bourgeoisie, by the rapid improvement of all instruments of production, by the immensely facilitated means of communication, draws all, even the most barbarian, nations into civilization. The cheap prices of its commodities are the heavy artillery with which it batters down all Chinese walls, with which it forces the barbarians' intensely obstinate hatred of foreigners to capitulate. It compels all nations, on pain of extinction, to adopt the bourgeois mode of production; it compels them to introduce what it calls civilization into their midst, i.e., to become bourgeois themselves. In one word, it creates a world after its own image.[1]

Although the quote drips with nineteenth-century language, it shows that Marx and Engels comprehended the mechanics of capitalism and the cultural process of modernization that accompanied it. The concern was not simply with how capital worked, but it was also a concern with how capitalism effected fundamental changes in culture and politics. Globalization is therefore a twofold process: on the one hand, there is the emergence of certain *institutional forms*—whether it be in terms of the economy or the polity—and, on the other hand, there is also a globalization of *ideas,* and by ideas I mean the moral and political ideas that have their roots in the Western Enlightenment. And these ideas can progressively transform the political and cultural landscape of developing countries. Modernity can no longer be equated merely with the adoption of certain technologies, with certain forms of financial institutions, and with merely formal kinds of political "democracy."

Globalization has shown itself to be a largely differentiated or, even better, an *uneven* process of social development and change. Whereas the neoliberal "end of history" thesis was heralded with decidedly pseudo-Hegelian optimism just after the fall of Communism, the reality of globalization plainly shows that liberal democracy has not become the paradigm for political institutions and political culture throughout the world, especially in the former Soviet states, which were seen, as of only ten years ago, to be the fallen victims of liberal capitalism's superiority over Communism and socialism. Much of the current mainstream discourse about globalization heralds it as a process of transformation that will culminate in global economic prosperity and political freedom. But what if this is not the case? If there are two faces of globalization, then this would mean that the transformations throughout the globe are not the result of some new globalized invisible hand, but the more complex result of the ways that different political traditions and interests utilize it. It would mean that both the messianistic neoliberal doctrine—which weds capitalism with democracy and prosperity—as well as the Marxian one, linking the spread of global capitalism with modernization, would be suspect, and that a more nuanced understanding of the globalization process is needed. Dealing with this problem and its various implications will be one of the great political tasks of this century and, undoubtedly, beyond.

GLOBALIZATION'S TWO FACES

Seeing globalization as a dual process of development between technological and scientific change on the one hand and moral and political change on the other points toward an inevitable conflict. The essence of this conflict is between the diffusion of capital, technology, scientific forms of thought, and the institutions needed for multinational trade and the diffusion of moral and political ideas that can erode both older forms of political and social hierarchy and authority inherent in many political and cultural institutions as well as guard against the modern effects of new forms of economic organization, market liberalization, and new forms of state oppression. Whereas neoliberal thinkers can argue for the liberating effects of economic globalization, the exclusion of the political—and more specifically here, political theory—is not only harmful, but seriously misguided as well.

In the West, it is no accident that the scientific revolution and the age of political revolution coincided with one another. "Tout a changé dans l'ordre physique; et tout doit changer dans l'ordre moral et politique," said Robespierre at the peak of the French Revolution, but globalization has not brought such revolutionary transformations in morality and politics on a global scale even as technological and economic change have spread. This is the essence of the uneven process of globalization, by which I mean not simply an unevenness of economic development, but, perhaps more importantly, that the rapid industrialization and economic modernization of much of the world is not being accompanied by what in the West was the expansion of political rights and the moral and political consciousness of human freedom and ethical autonomy. In this sense, understanding globalization means discussing the ways that both of these forces—the technological and scientific on the one hand and the moral and political on the other—are being shaped, understood, and incorporated by other cultures.

The first face of globalization therefore relies heavily on two different impulses: first, the need to expand markets and the need for those markets to be supported by certain kinds of political and legal institutions. The second impulse is the drive toward social modernization via the use of Western science and technology. This first face of globalization—which I will call here the *technical-rational*—has had the deepest and most pervasive impact in transforming global society because it is the most obvious of the two. It is obvious in the sense that technological innovation is easily copied and always desperately needed, whether it be in the form of enhancing industrial production or new forms of communication or agricultural techniques. The technical-rational dimension of globalization is the result of the spread of technological knowledge and Western science; it is the culmination of centuries of progress in abstract scientific thinking—in the natural sciences and mathematics—and the enhancement of practical knowledge, culminating in the efficient manipulation of nature. The worldview that inevitably accompanies it is one that objectifies nature for instrumental ends.

But this is not confined to the natural sciences. The social sciences, too, are part of this face of globalization. New forms of economic structure must accompany many of these new forms of technology. Patterns of investment, finance, banking, and the like need to be learned and such institutions need to take root if the success of integrating into the global economy in any effective and beneficial way is to come to pass. Economics therefore becomes one of the primary social sciences for development and modernization; its "laws" taking on a truth status that only a Newton or a Huygens could bestow upon them. Similarly with political science: certain rational bureaucracies and procedures need to be implemented so that some degree of a rule of law is instituted. What was once considered a hypothesis about the relationship between the development of capitalism and the evolution of democracy has become a full-blown ideology that guides the institution building and policy making of political development in the context of globalization.

This discussion of political ideas leads me to the second face of globalization, which I will call the *moral-political*. It consists of the outgrowth of certain concepts of social relationships and forms of political organization. I call it moral-political precisely because it is, in fact, a set of political and moral traditions that have the capacity to shape the narrow, instrumental mind-set that follows once the rationality of technology and economic development sets in. The moral-political face of globalization can serve as a progressive force that rails against preliberal and sometimes feudal forms of social arrangements from castelike systems to traditions that impose hierarchies in terms of race, gender, or class. A product of Enlightenment rationalism, it remains one of the most efficient and radical ways that globalization can effect the social and political transformation of other cultures and put them on a path toward realizing some sense of political freedom. Indeed, if the first face of globalization emerges out of the scientific revolution of the eighteenth century and the theories of economic management and social organization that have emerged since that time, then the moral-political face of globalization emerges from a similar root—from the Western Enlightenment's revolution in political and moral consciousness: the need for social and political equality, religious tolerance, ethnic pluralism, secular democratic institutions, and the construction and maintenance of a rational public sphere. And it is for precisely this reason that it is considered dangerous.

Democracy requires—as Enlightenment thinkers from Spinoza through Locke and Kant knew far too well—a *cultural* component that would serve as a ground for new political institutions grounded in a moral conception of freedom and equality. One of the interesting problems with the notion of "globalizing democracy" is not that the institutions cannot be exported, but that there is little attempt made to transform the moral dimensions of different political cultures so as to effect such a transformation. The problem arises when the two faces of globalization come into conflict with one another, and this is precisely what we see happening in much of the world. One can look at China as an example: a country that selectively adopts Western science and technology but makes every effort to limit Western moral and political ideas—from liberal democracy to conceptions of human rights—from taking root. What develops in such instances is a one-sided form of capitalism where markets that are hooked up to the global economic network are fused to a form of bureaucratic authoritarianism grounded in traditional forms of political authority. This is the direct result of an uneven globalization process where the imperatives of economic and technological modernization supersede the moral and political transformations that globalization can also disseminate.

It is not difficult to see that of the two faces, one has increasingly become more hegemonic: the technical-rational paradigm (which itself encompasses modern economic techniques of finance and planning) is becoming increasingly predominant without the counteracting force of the moral-political. There is a growing sense that, speaking globally, we are encountering on a much larger scale something akin to what C. P. Snow saw happening within Western culture in the postwar period: that the "two cultures" of science and humanism were growing ever more apart and the result of this cleavage would be an overspecialization and dehumanization of science and a corresponding intellectual erosion of the humanities. This would produce a split culture where each pole was unable to inform the other. The result would be fatal for Western civilization, Snow believed, and he was convinced that bridging the gap between the two cultures was getting increasingly difficult since "once anything like a cultural divide gets established, all the social forces operate to make it not less rigid, but more so."[2] The two faces of globalization therefore pose an inherently political problem: the presence of a divide between the movement toward modernization in technological and economic terms on the one hand and, on the other, political concerns for democracy and human welfare and political rights, to which the technical-rational dimension is becoming increasingly immune. We are not witnessing a new imperial age by any single nation but, rather, by a social system: of capitalism stripped of democratic accountability; of industrialization without crucial environmental protections; and of other economic transformations that are driving social and political inequalities ever deeper and disenfranchising large portions of the world's population as they unfold.

And this is precisely where the conflict between the two faces of globalization can be glimpsed. Capitalism neither sets the stage for nor does it encourage the development of democracy. Similarly, globalization should not be associated with the diffusion of capital and democracy as an inherent aspect of its evolution and growth. The conflict between the two faces of globalization therefore brings us into a new phase of global systemic coordination that privileges the technical-rational aspects of modernity at the expense of the moral-political dimension. In the end, it would seem that Weber's pessimism about the spread of instrumental reason has won out over Marx's optimism about the progressive impetus of modernization, but only if the political reflection on human development, rights, and welfare is privileged at the expense of the narrow economic view of globalization that currently dominates the intellectual discourse on the subject.

Political action is grounded in moral conviction; without the evolution of basic humanistic traditions of thought and their development it is unlikely that effective forms of social and political contestation can develop against the effects of global change brought about by the natural effects of the expansion of markets on the one hand and those indigenous forms of social oppression and political power that remain stubbornly intact. Belief in the innate human face of economic globalization is standard ideology today, having its roots in the market fundamentalism that characterizes naive apologists for a globalization that is evolving in terms of the market. And it is for this reason more than any other that the moral-political face of globalization ought, therefore, to be seen as crucial and, indeed, as the necessary correlate to the planetary sweep of technical, scientific, and economic change.

ARE THERE MULTIPLE MODERNITIES?

If the two faces of globalization have a different impact on different societies transforming them as they infiltrate, is it possible that they will produce different modernities? This idea has become prevalent in recent years since it seems the only way to deal with what many observers see as the different cultural responses to globalization. But this is, I think, a mistake. What we see emerging as the world becomes more "global" is the resurrection of old nationalisms and provincial struggles. We may see the penetration of Sony and McDonald's throughout the countries of South Asia, the Far East, and Africa, but we are seeing at the same time political divisions around ethnic and nationalist lines. There is no mélange of different modernities, no wellspring of cultural variety, but a global fragmentation that threatens all forms of perpetual peace. The first face of globalization is indifferent to this reality. It can squeeze into any ethnic crevice to spread its goods and its technological rationalism. But this does not change the political dimension of things. Political change comes from the emergence of new moral and political ideas—ideas that are incorporated by a culture, transforming it by shedding light on its own indigenous and regional political problems and by initiating new ways of thinking and new values that can offer new solutions to such problems.

It is therefore wrong to critique the globalization of economic institutions as being inherently against the interests of the developing world. The spread of capital in and of itself may be the only way to destroy many forms of global poverty and stagnation—Marx's insight about the power of capital, in this regard, is worth retaining. What does need to be emphasized are the democratic preconditions for such economic institutions and policies. It has become a fruitless strategy to identify economic globalization with a global laissez-faire capitalism; the expansion of markets, industries, trade, and investment must be premised on certain democratic goals and be accountable to democratic coordination. Without this crucial emphasis on the political, globalization will continue its uneven effects and create a world more stratified than before and more unresponsive to change. Politics must be premised above economics—by making markets accountable to human ends rather than the means for realizing human interests, economic globalization can be used to improve the standard of living of billions.

It was Weber's belief that the twentieth century would continue down the path laid out by the last decades of the nineteenth. States would strengthen and centralize their bureaucracies, different forms of capitalism would converge, and the process of rationalization and secularization brought about by the progress of scientific thought would continue along its path of disenchanting the world. But what we have seen is a remarkable resilience in the abilities of cultures to hold on to their ways of life and react against the cultural ideas of the West. At times this is the result of legitimate political struggles against capital or other forms of unwanted change. However, there are also movements—from al Qaeda to nationalist parties from the Balkans to the Far East—that desire nothing more than opposition to the ideas of civil and human rights as well as, in many cases, of democracy itself. There has also been, as Meera Nanda has insightfully shown, a resistance to Western science itself, and the rejection of Western ideas is couched in the political project of ethnic particularism.[3] Such an antimodernism emerging in the very shadow of the expansion of modernity is nothing new, but its implications in an era of intense globalism have meant a political reaction to the West and many of the notions of secularism and democracy that are seen as being exported as moral and political models for a new global order. Of course, global terrorism is one strain of this antimodernism, but what is perhaps more dangerous in the long run is technological and economic modernization fused to reactionary political ideas and culture, what Jeffrey Herf termed "reactionary modernism."[4] Whereas Herf was describing the political economy of the Third Reich, it is still a useful way of looking at where much of the developing world—China is once again an excellent illustration—is headed: not toward fascism but a turn toward nationalism and an emphasis on national identity that often leads to a rejection of political ideas commonly seen as "Western," from liberal democracy to tolerance and principles of universal human and civil rights. Globalization may integrate markets and expand cultural horizons, but it causes its own brand of fragmentation as well, on a global scale.

The discourse of human rights is an interesting example of this. Whereas it was once seen as an inevitability that certain forms of human and civil rights would be adopted over time by more and more nations, we have seen remarkable resistance to such a tendency. Ethnic cleansing, the repression of minorities, the suppression of civil rights, and the increasingly bleak conditions of the global working class are all testaments to the limits of human rights in practice. This is not to say that there have not been successes and improvements to social welfare; but what we are seeing is a growing tendency toward a general reactionism and political breakdown along ethnic lines in spite of— or perhaps it is better to say as a result of—an increased globalism. In addition, we are witnessing the emergence of new forms of capitalism—such as in China, but in other places as well—where a liberalization of markets and the development of higher-level industrial production is accompanied not by an increase in democratic sensibilities and a flowering of civil society and democracy but by authoritarian state policies that show no sign of weakening and even less sign of resistance from within. In the Middle East, stubborn forms of dictatorships and monarchies show little sign of withering away. In Africa, few states have been able to withstand decline into ethnic strife. Globalization in economics and technological modernity has had little effect on politics since there has been too little globalization in moral-political ideas and values. There is little debate about this reality; there is increasingly less openness to such ideas; there is no dialogue of civilizations. Only by providing a political path—grounded in moral values of equality, justice, and tolerance—can the oppressed find any kind of voice that can then articulate itself institutionally.

And this is the essence of what globalization can offer: it is not that Western political ideas and institutions should be adopted uncritically by non-Western cultures; what it does mean is that the fundamental moral and political ideas of the Western Enlightenment can find affinities with rationalist traditions in almost every culture and its philosophical and religious traditions; it is simply a matter of finding affinities between the rationalist and humanistic ideas of these traditions and pushing them to their concrete political conclusions. Only in this way can we speak of cosmopolitanism and not hegemony, and of a more flexible, culturally nuanced conception of political and social freedom and political universalism grounded in the precepts of reason and not in superstition and blind tradition.

The roots of a political conception of cosmopolitanism derive from Immanuel Kant. Kant's essential idea was that the modern world would pose a problem in the ways that a global community of nations would deal with one another. He saw a distinction between a legal order that would regulate the ways that nations engaged with one another (*ius gentium*) and another order that went a step further, dealing with the sphere of universal humankind and the rights associated with that universality (*ius cosmopoliticum*).[5] A concern with internationalism therefore turns into a concern for the cosmopolitan: a universal moral groundwork lying beneath the particularities of cultural difference. What Kant called the cosmopolitan (*Weltbürgerrecht*) level of justice was predicated on the universal principles of equality, freedom, and communication. He saw it as a new ethical and political category that consisted not of an arbitrarily assigned right that could be attributed to humankind, but a universal attribute of all human beings. In this sense, Kant advocated a groundwork for the universal basis for morality and politics that could serve as the foundation for a world federation of nation-states two centuries before the onset of what we today call globalization. But there is a need to rethink some of these core ideas in the light of the political and philosophical dilemmas that globalization has put forth to political theory.

The discussion of the two faces of globalization should lead us to the conclusion that the political rather than the economic and technological dimensions of globalization should be emphasized and be the focus of current debates about global change. The reason is simple: it is only through politics that the seemingly inexorable and "natural" process of global change can be directed, steered, and made to serve universal human ends rather than those of a minority of the community—whether that community is local or global. This can be accomplished by pursuing economic policies that are accountable to public goals, which itself can only be achieved by means of democratic state intervention in economic affairs. The politics of globalization therefore needs to take on a more cosmopolitan perspective, and this begins not with politics itself, but a new sense of moral awareness that will overcome inherited forms of inequality and those traditions that impede the development and expansion of rational and secular political life.

It is in the realm of politics that we must see the real transformative potential of globalization since it is there that the real stuff of history can be changed: the evolution of new political forms of life can only come about once the moral foundations of political actors have begun to transform, and democratic institutions—in order to have any kind of efficacy and sustainability—will require enlightened societies as well. But the extent to which the moral-political impulses of Western Enlightenment political thought are prevented from developing and taking root in the social orders of the present is precisely the extent to which progressive political and social change will be muted and its potential effects nullified.

In the final analysis, it may be that new economic forms of organizing the economies of developing nations are the primary way to solve the problems of poverty even as they create problems that are more difficult to manage, such as those associated with mass urbanization and vast economic inequality. But what so many commentators on globalization seem afraid to say is that the moral foundations of cultures need to transform before workable, robust, and sustainable forms of democracy can be founded and developed. Only cosmopolitan political ideas that are grounded in a rational universalism, rather than one of a panoply of ethnic particularisms, will be capable of revealing the rational foundations for a universal set of political rights that also have roots in the indigenous philosophical, political, and moral traditions of peoples in different cultures. Only in this way can a set of global rights that are universal in nature even as they appeal to the particular cultural semantics of diverse peoples emerge. And, in the end, this may be the only way to ensure some sense of what Kant understood as a cosmopolitan politics, one "necessary for the sake of any public rights of human beings and so for perpetual peace."

NOTES

1. *The Communist Manifesto*, in *Marx and Engels: Basic Writings on Politics and Philosophy*, ed. Lewis Feuer (New York: Anchor Books, 1959).

2. C. P. Snow, *The Two Cultures and the Scientific Revolution* (New York: Cambridge University Press, 1961), p. 18.

3. See Meera Nanda, *Prophets Facing Backward: Postmodern Critiques of Science and Hindu Nationalism in India* (New Brunswick, NJ: Rutgers University Press, 2004).

4. Jeffery Herf, *Reactionary Modernism: Technology, Culture, and Politics in Weimar and the Third Reich* (New York: Cambridge University Press, 1984).

5. For an interesting discussion of Kant's ideas on global order and cosmopolitanism, see Sankar Muthu, *Enlightenment against Empire* (Princeton: Princeton University Press, 2003), pp. 186–200.

13

Is a Global Ethic Possible?

KARSTEN J. STRUHL

In September 1993, representatives of one hundred and twenty of the world's religions assembled in Chicago to convene a Parliament of the World's Religions. This marked the one hundredth anniversary of the 1893 World Parliament of Religions, which had initiated a worldwide religious dialogue. The task in the 1993 parliament was to discuss a draft of a global ethic written by Hans Küng, a well-respected ecumenical German theologian. Six thousand participants discussed this draft and amended it. The final draft, entitled "Declaration toward a Global Ethic,"[1] begins with two assumptions. The first is that in order to confront the major problems of our age (war, the assault on the Earth's ecosystems, global economic disparities and poverty, religious hatred and intolerance) a new global order is necessary. The second is that such a new global order requires a global ethic and that the basis for a global ethic already exists, because there is within the religions of the world a "common core set of values." However, such a global ethic, the declaration insists, would not be limited to the world's religions as, once properly formulated, it "can be affirmed by all persons of ethical convictions, whether religiously grounded or not." In short, the task was to formulate a consensus on a core set of values that could be agreed upon by all religions and, indeed, by all persons of reasonable ethical sensibilities. The declaration then begins to describe this consensus as the principle that "every human being must be treated humanely." This principle, in turn, can be derived from a fundamental ethical norm that can be found in all the world's religions and ethical systems, an ethical norm known as the Golden Rule—"What you do not wish to be done to yourself, do not do to others. . . . What you wish done to yourself, do to others." The declaration then highlights four specific ethical guidelines that, it claims, follow from this basic principle. These are: (1) a "commitment to a culture of nonviolence and respect for life," which includes a concern not just for humans but also nonhuman animals and plants; (2) a "commitment to a culture of solidarity and a just economic order"; (3) a "commitment to a culture of tolerance and a life of truthfulness"; and (4) a "commitment to a culture of equal rights and partnership between men and women" that would oppose any form of sexual discrimination and exploitation.

In the same year that the Parliament of the World's Religions discussed Küng's draft, Leonard Swidler, a colleague of Küng who is at the Department of Religion at Temple University in Philadelphia, wrote his own draft of a global ethic, which was subsequently presented to a number of international conferences and then posted on the Internet in the hope of reaching a wider audience and of generating responses. His draft on the Internet has undergone a number of revisions, the last of which was in September 1998. Swidler's draft, entitled "A Universal Declaration of a Global Ethic,"[2] also takes the Golden Rule as the ultimate basis of a global ethical consensus. He then proceeds to list eight basic principles of a global ethic and ten "middle ethical principles." Both these sets of principles and especially the middle principles are much more specific than the principles of the parliament's declaration. They also seem more a Western articulation of a general ethic—for example, that every person should be "free to exercise and develop every capacity, so long as it does not infringe on the rights of other persons."

Since these two drafts were written, there have been various attempts to move the project for a global ethic beyond religious circles. In 1995, the World Commission on Culture and Development issued a UNESCO report that called for a global ethic that would provide the basis for a change in attitudes, social priorities, and patterns of consumption necessary to secure "a decent and meaningful life" for all human beings throughout the world.[3] In 1996, the Interaction Council, composed of thirty former heads of state, urged that a global ethics be developed to meet the problems of the twenty-first century. In 1997, UNESCO initiated a "Universal Ethics Project," which brought together philosophers and theologians representing a variety of ethical traditions. Such a universal ethic, the UNESCO document declares, would have a different ontological status than the UN Declaration of Human Rights in that it would provide the philosophical principles from which those rights could be derived.[4]

I think we can expect that there will be many more such attempts to discuss and to formulate a global ethic. The question I wish to raise is whether a meaningful global ethic, an ethic that is substantive enough to speak to the global problems that confront us in the twenty-first century, is possible. Can such an ethic become a social reality? I want to suggest some philosophical and practical problems posed by the global ethic project, whether it takes shape in a Parliament of the World's Religions or within the orbit of the United Nations. I will suggest that we are not likely to achieve a meaningful global ethic through the forums within which it is now discussed and that, therefore, we need to reconceptualize the project.

THE PROBLEM OF A MINIMAL CONSENSUS

The hope of the various drafts of a global ethic is that it is possible to come to a minimal consensus on ethical norms. It is important to mention at the outset that such a minimal consensus must be more than a very general statement of agreement, for it must be capable of generating norms that can address the kinds of world problems for which the global ethic is conceived. The various drafts of a global ethic attempt to do this insofar as they attempt to derive certain substantive guidelines or middle-range principles from their most general principles. What I want to do in this section is discuss the problem of attempting to develop such a substantive minimal consensus.

There are several aspects to this problem. The first is how to decide who participates in the dialogue that attempts to reach such a minimal consensus and how the dialogue is to be conducted. Let us examine this problem first in terms of a consensus among the world's religions. There are, as mentioned above, two major religious drafts. At the Parliament of the World's Religions in 1993, Küng's draft underwent only one revision, a change in title. So it is reasonable to say that both drafts represent predominantly the viewpoint of their respective authors and that at the parliament the "consensus" generated was the result of a managerial process. The philosopher John Hick, who was one of the respondents to Swidler's "Universal Declaration of a Global Ethic," has suggested that Swidler's draft is essentially a reflection of post-Enlightenment Western Christianity and that there need to be other initial drafts from other cultures and other religions.[5] While I take Hick's suggestion to be a reasonable one, two problems yet remain—who will be the initiators of the plurality of drafts and who will discuss them in order to reach a minimal consensus. The parliament's version of the global ethic represents at best a consensus among the liberal progressive wing of the world's religions. What about the fundamentalists? Should they also be party to the dialogue? Khalid Duran, who offers a Muslim perspective in response to Swidler's draft,[6] argues that fundamentalism, which he believes represents a minority position within Islam, will insist that *shari'a* (Islamic law) be the basis of a global ethic and will "seek to impose their exclusivist vision on others." Duran suggests, therefore, that the fundamentalists within all the world's religions be excluded from the dialogue. But if we do this, then we do not have a real consensus among the world's religions, only at best a consensus among their progressive liberal wings. Zoltán Turgonyi has posed the problem sharply. Within each religious tradition, we have to ask "who has the right (or duty) to represent the worldview in question. . . . And should we exclude from dialogue heretics? But if we wanted to treat all possible interpretations of a certain religion as equals, in the end we should invite every believer."[7] And it is highly unlikely that if we did so, we would get a meaningful minimal consensus that could even begin to serve the goals for which the parliament's declaration was drafted. Furthermore, even if we could somehow get a substantive consensus among all sectors within the world's religions, we are still left with the problem of how we get a consensus that goes beyond the world's religions. Who shall represent these people? It is hardly likely that there is even a consensus among the people within a given culture that can give us anything like the principles suggested by the declaration. Should we, then, suggest that we use the majority of the culture as a standard or only "progressive" people within the culture?

There is a second aspect of the problem of developing a minimal consensus. However we delimit the scope of the participants, we can still anticipate that there will be some significant disagreements, and it is by no means clear how these disagreements can be reconciled. Sallie King, in discussing the differences between the parliament's draft of a global ethic and Swidler's draft, observes that it is

> scandalous that two versions exist and in a sense are vying against each other, especially when one considers that they both were drafted by white, prosperous, Catholic men who are from the dominant world culture (one German, one American). If these two scholars from closely related backgrounds cannot reconcile their differences and produce a single draft, then how can anyone expect

people from other religious, national, and ethnic backgrounds to agree to either proposal.[8]

If, following Hick's proposal, we allow a plurality of drafts from various representatives of the world's religions, we can assume that they will be significantly different. On what basis would we decide which elements of these drafts to use as the basis for a minimal consensus? Suppose we appeal to the scriptures of each religion and try to find, within these texts, certain ethical ideas in common, for example, the Golden Rule. What would follow from this? Even among liberal progressives within a given religion, there is room for different interpretations of the implications of certain ethical norms, and we can certainly expect that the interpretations would vary even more widely between representatives of different religions. The underlying problem is that any interpretation of the ethical norms derived from the religious texts will depend on an ethical judgment. So we are back to square one. How do we come to a consensus when ethical judgments differ? Since different people within the same religion have different ethical evaluations of the implications of any moral norm, it is not even clear that we can come to a consensus within a single religion, let alone a consensus among the world's religions.

This leads to a third aspect of the problem of developing a minimal consensus. It is somewhat doubtful that we can find a genuine moral consensus among the world's religions if we look at them as a totality. For example, there is a very different understanding of the meaning of violence within Islam and Buddhism. Of course, one can draw from certain passages in Islam a preference for nonviolence over violence, but, given Islam's affirmation of jihad as an obligation of Muslims (granted, there are different interpretations of what this means), it is hard to see how this is compatible with Buddhism's fundamental commitment to ahimsa (nonharm) as a general principle of nonviolence. I shall return to this problem in the next section of this paper.

THE BASIC PRINCIPLE: TREATING EVERY HUMAN BEING HUMANELY AND THE GOLDEN RULE

It is probably true, as both Küng and Swidler have argued, that every religion, and perhaps every ethical tradition, has some version of the Golden Rule in both its negative and positive form. This, as I noted earlier, is taken to be the underlying basis for the general principle formulated by the Parliament of the World's Religions—that every human being must be treated humanely—and for the basic principles and "middle principles" that Swidler articulates. However, there are two difficulties with the use of the Golden Rule as the basis for a global ethic. The first was alluded to by G. B. Shaw, who said, "Do not do unto others what you would have others do unto you. Others may have different tastes." The call here is for greater specificity. Some people may have different kinds of sexual desires, so that to allow them freedom to engage in the sexuality that is to one's taste but not to allow them a form of sexual activity that one abhors is a lack of respect for the sexual freedom of other individuals. The rule could be amended by allowing each individual the right to pursue his or her sexual tastes. But this formulation immediately needs more amending, since someone's sexual taste may include rape, sex with children, and other forms of activity that most of us believe are oppressive to others. So the injunction might become, "allow each individual the right to pursue his or her sexual desires so long as they do not harm others." This, however, is a specific liberal formulation of the rule. Many cultures would insist that forms of sexuality that individuals might want and that do not directly harm another are nonetheless a violation of God's commandments, intrinsically unhealthy, or harmful to the community as a whole. Another problem, often acknowledged as a general problem of the principle of liberty, is that the idea of what is harmful has no clear consensus even among intellectuals in the West. Why, for example, is indirect harm to be excluded from the calculation of moral harm?

A further problem arises if we amend G. B. Shaw's statement as follows: "Do not do unto others as you would have others do unto you. Others may have different roles and obligations." Thus, within certain African countries, it is customary for all women of a certain age to be circumcised (which has very different implications for women than it does for men, since it removes at least part of the clitoris). Western feminists and perhaps most people in Western countries would consider this oppressive and a violation of fundamental human rights, but the practice is often defended by women within those cultures. Islam prescribes the wearing of a veil for women, and, in some Islamic cultures, wearing the veil has implications that Western feminists find extremely oppressive. The point I am making is that what is often seen in Western cultures as a fundamental violation of the idea of treating everyone humanely and of the Golden Rule is not at all a contradiction to large numbers of people in the cultures within which those practices occur. For those cultures, there is no contradiction between the Golden Rule and female circumcision or the mandatory wearing of the veil and all that it implies, since these demands are put on all women and women are understood as having intrinsically different social obligations.

A second problem arises with respect to the scope of the concern. "Do not do unto others." But which others? The conquistadores like Columbus, Balboa, and Cortes and members of the clergy who took slavery to be morally legitimate did not see their actions as contradicting the Golden Rule.[9] They simply assumed that the indigenous population in the Americas and slaves from Africa were not fully human and, therefore, did not deserve the same respect as those who were. Or they assumed, with Aristotle, that some humans were less equipped intellectually and morally than others and were, therefore, fit only to be the servants and slaves of their superiors. While most of the world's people now hold slavery to be immoral, racist and colonial/imperialist assumptions still persist among large numbers of people in a variety of cultures, often in overt and aggressive forms. And even where there is an explicit rejection of racism and colonialism, these assumptions persist more subtly. The suffering of those in other nations and in other cultures and religions is accorded a lesser place than the suffering of those in one's own nation or who belong to one's own religion or culture. Often this is justified by the assumption that those who belong to other cultures have some trait or traits whose difference justifies us in not granting them equal concern: for example, "they don't put the same value on human life as we do." These assumptions are often part of certain religious beliefs. For example, many Christians believe that those who are not Christian are not saved. Furthermore, perhaps the majority of the human population in the West excludes nonhuman animals from the Golden Rule. For example, Swidler's "Universal Declaration," while insisting that nonhuman animals be treated with respect, nonetheless insists that "humans have greater intrinsic value than non-humans," a claim that would certainly be disputed by many adherents of Buddhism and Hinduism. In short, "do unto others" or "do not do unto others" does not tell us which others we should or should not include.

THE CHALLENGE OF ETHICAL RELATIVISM

There is a deeper problem with the attempt to formulate a global ethic. The declaration of the Chicago parliament states, "We affirm that there is an irrevocable, unconditional norm for all areas of life." In other words, the declaration assumes that a global ethic presupposes ethical absolutism? The assumption is that a minimal consensus concerning moral norms requires that there be absolute ethical norms, norms that are independent of historical time and place. Given this assumption, a global ethic must be able to avoid the challenge of ethical relativism.

Ethical relativism claims that different frameworks of moral discourse are fundamentally incommensurable. Gilbert Harmon offers an interesting analogy to make this plausible.[10] Consider Einstein's theory of relativity in which all motion is relative to some spatiotemporal framework; therefore, something that moves in relation to one spatiotemporal framework may be at rest in relation to another. In the same way, Harmon argues, moral norms are relative to general moral frameworks. Therefore, what may be right within one moral framework may be wrong within another. For example, those on opposite sides of the ethical divide on such issues as vegetarianism, abortion, and euthanasia may very well agree on all the facts. But they make very different assumptions about the value of nonhuman life and the sanctity of human life as such. Furthermore, even when there seems to be agreement on certain values, there may be important moral disagreement. Harmon gives as an example the general consensus that murder is wrong. But this doesn't take us very far, as murder is defined as "wrongful killing." That murder is wrong may be perfectly compatible with the idea in some societies that a master can kill his slaves, that a husband can kill his wife, and that infanticide and human sacrifice are morally acceptable.[11] To all this, the ethical absolutist might argue that the reason for such moral diversity is that some people are better placed than others and, therefore, that some ethical judgments are correct while others are incorrect. To this, the ethical relativist replies that just as in Einstein's relativity theory there is no privileged spatiotemporal framework, so there is no way to judge that one ethical framework is superior to another. From this it follows that there is no such thing as being better placed to know the moral truth. One's moral judgment is always relative to some ethical framework, and there is no way to privilege any ethical framework above another. The challenge of ethical relativism, then, is how to find such a privileged position.

The problem is not so easily overcome by attempting to extract some common ethical norm from the world's religions. Consider again how the same ethical norm can function within different religious frameworks. Within at least certain interpretations of Islam, the idea that women and men are equal in the eyes of God is not, as I have suggested in the previous section, incompatible with the idea that men and women need to have different spheres and that women have special obligations that men do not. Buddhism, Islam, and Christianity might agree in general that violence as such is bad. But their understanding of what violence is ethically permissible will differ. In other words, while people within different religious or cultural traditions might appear to come to a consensus on certain ethical claims, their interpretation of those claims might well be different, because the meaning of those ethical claims is imbedded within a larger ethical-religious framework. And we have no access to a transcendent "God's eye" position that can privilege one of these ethical frameworks above the other.

Is there a way out of this problem? Let us recall that the problem arises because it is assumed that a global ethic presupposes ethical absolutism, that it presupposes universal moral norms that have an unconditional validity. However, there is an alternative way of deriving universal norms, one that does not require ethical absolutism.[12] We can attempt to derive certain universal norms from human nature, specifically, from the needs that all human beings have in common. This view, sometimes referred to as "ethical naturalism," has a long philosophical lineage from Aristotle to thinkers like Spinoza, Marx, John Dewey, and Erich Fromm. On this view, moral values are tools that enable us to fulfill our common needs, and if the latter can be objectively ascertained, so too can the former. One problem with this point of view, however, is that while we have certain basic "survival needs" like the need for food, sex, social support, and recognition, even these needs are organized and manifested within a specific social and historical context. In other words, our needs are "socially patterned."[13] If our needs are socially patterned, then there is no core transhistorical human nature to which we can appeal. From this it follows that the attempt to derive moral values from human needs must be historically and socially situated. However, even if our needs are historically developed, it might still be possible to develop a global ethic. Perhaps it is possible to derive a global ethic from the historical development of our common human needs at this historical juncture. If so, there would be certain norms that, while not transhistorical, are nonetheless valid for our specific historical epoch. Universal norms, then, need not be absolute norms.

Is a moral universalism based on the assumption of universal human needs that have been historically developed able to survive the ethical relativist critique? There are three difficulties. The first is that different cultures and religions within the same historical epoch place different value on those needs, value that is derived from their respective ethical frameworks. Furthermore, the ethical framework may be different with respect to the question of universality itself. There are some cultures, or at least elements within certain cultures, that eschew the very value of universalism or, at the other extreme, that insist that only the moral norms derived from religious revelation, as they understand it, have universal validity. Second, there may be groups within a given culture or within the world at large whose needs are inherently antagonistic to one another. For example, in a Marxist analysis, the needs of the agents of capital and of the proletariat are necessarily antagonistic to one another. However, one hardly has to be a Marxist to recognize that the agendas of those who govern the international corporations and global agencies like the International Monetary Fund and the World Trade Organization are at odds with the needs of most people in the less developed world. Finally, even if there are certain indisputable common human needs that we can recognize at this historical juncture, we can derive certain universal norms from them only if we make the added assumption that our moral community is wider than our specific national or religious culture. In other words, unless we care about the needs of those beyond our culture we cannot deduce universal norms.

UNIVERSAL NORMS AND OUR MORAL COMMUNITY

This last problem can be illustrated by a talk that Richard Rorty presented at the Second UNESCO Philosophy Forum in 1996.[14] Rorty argues that universalism presupposes that all human beings should be part of a common moral community. One problem with that assumption is that the possibility of forming such a community rests on the assumption that there can be a vast redistribution of wealth. This is because if "you cannot render assistance to people in need, your claim that they form a part of your moral community is empty." But what if we cannot? What if we who live in the advanced industrial countries cannot reasonably assist those in the less developed countries without destroying the standard of living that we want for ourselves and our children? If this is so, and Rorty thinks that it might very well be so, then the "rich parts of the world may be in the position of somebody proposing to share her one loaf of bread with a hundred starving people." Rorty suggests that the problem may be analogous to the problem of triage. Just as doctors and nurses may have to decide which victims can be given aid and which cannot, so those of us in the advanced industrial countries may have to decide that we cannot afford to render significant assistance to impoverished people in the underdeveloped world. If this is the case, then they cannot be considered part of our moral community, just as those who doctors decide not to save can no longer be considered members of their moral community. And if they are not a part of our moral community, there can be no universal ethic. To restate Rorty's conclusion in the terms of ethical naturalism, if there is not a willingness to concern ourselves with the needs of all the people in the world, then we cannot derive a universal ethic from universal needs.

Whether the problem that Rorty poses is comparable to triage is highly problematic, as the argument for triage presupposes that the physical survival of some may require the sacrifice of others. However, Rorty does not claim that rendering assistance to those in the less developed world threatens our survival. All he claims is that our accustomed lifestyle may be threatened. Furthermore, Rorty's analysis makes no attempt to situate the problem historically. Why is it that we in the advanced industrial countries have so much bread while others have so little? There is much evidence that these global inequalities are the result of centuries of colonial exploitation, slavery, and imperialist aggression. In other words, it is precisely because they have so little that we have so much. Nonetheless, I think one of Rorty's assumptions is right—that if we cannot care about people throughout the world, then it is meaningless to say that they are part of our global community. To what extent, then, does our ability to genuinely care for and render assistance to those outside our country rest on our global political economy and its existing resources? I raise the question this way to suggest that there are three variables—political economy, resources, and caring—and will, in the next section, argue that their relation is far more complex than Rorty makes it seem.

COMPASSION AND THE POLITICAL ECONOMY OF A GLOBAL ETHIC

The problem of resources is partly a problem of what can be sustained by our planet, and it is not likely that our planet can sustain the extension of the standard of living of, say, the American upper middle class to the world in general. It has been suggested that it would require five earths to enable the world's population to consume the amount of energy per capita that is consumed in Los Angeles, California.[15] Paul Wachtel, an American psychotherapist and ecological theorist, puts it this way:

> To imagine a billion Chinese using resources and polluting the air and water at the rate we do, and in addition 700 million Indians, 400 million Latin Americans, and 500 million Africans, and numerous other people as well, is to recognize that

our present notions of what constitutes the good life absolutely *require* that most of the world be poor. Only by changing the way we use resources and define our needs is there even a chance for all the world's billions to prosper.[16]

This might seem to support Rorty's position. However, Wachtel's analysis points in another direction. The focus of his work is on the way in which American affluence has created psychological impoverishment. Industrial growth has not made Americans happier than they were previously. Americans have made a Faustian bargain. Their obsession with economic growth, he argues, has confused quantity of goods with the quality of life. To take one example, the automobile, which has become the symbol of American freedom and spontaneity, means that people spend hours on crowded highways going to work and breathing air that literally kills them and their children, not to mention that the number of automobile accidents in a year far exceeds the casualties in many wars. Overall, Wachtel notes that the American middle-class lifestyle leads people to treat themselves as machines who must work longer hours to get the things that advertising tells them they must want, causing a variety of stress-related diseases. It is a vicious cycle in which hyperindividualism and the obsession with material things erodes community ties, which, in turn, creates a need for even more material goods to fill the vacuum. The result is the ideology of economic growth and consumption. The point I want to draw from Wachtel's analysis is that the attempt by those in the advanced industrial countries to maintain their present lifestyle at the expense of much of the world may, in fact, be to the psychological (and physical) detriment of themselves and their children.

There is another problem as well, which has been elaborated at great length within Buddhism and is also beginning to be discussed in contemporary Western psychological literature. To shut off our capacity for compassion, our capacity to care about others, is to diminish our own capacity for feeling and joy. Even when triage in a medical setting is absolutely necessary, it must take a severe toll on the emotional life of the medical personnel who participate in it. And when those of us who come from the advanced industrial world shut our hearts to the suffering of others—to the poor and homeless in our own country as well as the billions of people of the world who do not have enough to feed their families or obtain even the minimum medical care—we impoverish our emotional selves. In other words, there is a point at which self-interest and altruism meet and that point is compassion.

Humanity is not facing anything like the situation of having one loaf of bread for one hundred starving people. We certainly have enough resources and productive ability to provide food, shelter, clothing, and decent medical care for every person on the planet. There is nothing about the resources of the planet alone that condemns so much of the world's population to poverty and a dehumanized life. What condemns so many people to disabling poverty is the way these resources are used, the choice of energy, and the distribution of wealth. In other words, the problem is not the lack of resources but our global political economy. To put this in terms of Rorty's analogy, we can grow enough grain to make the amount of bread sufficient to feed all of humanity. The problem is that we are putting too much of our productive energies and resources into the baking of luxurious cakes that are being consumed by only a small part of the planet; and the cakes have so much sugar and fat that they are unhealthy for those who consume them.

This leads to the discussion of the third variable—political economy. We live in what is often described as the age of globalization. On the surface, this means that we live in a world that is increasingly integrated on the economic, technological, and political levels. We take for granted what only two decades ago was barely imagined—the Internet. We live in a world where a highly integrated global communications system seems capable of reaching every corner of the planet almost simultaneously. However, at the deeper level, globalization is a conjunction of two processes. As Peter Marcuse puts it, what might be called "really existing globalization" combines "developments in technology and developments in the concentration of power," specifically economic power.[17] Globalization, then, is specifically corporate capitalist globalization. It is globalization from above. What is called globalization, then, is a particular organization of the world in which global corporations and other transnational economic agents—for example, the International Monetary Fund, the World Bank, and the World Trade Organization—organize production on an international scale, determine the forms of technology and energy, and control the division of labor and the distribution of goods. These same transnational agents have near monopoly control over the global communications industry and undermine the capacity of many nation-states to attend to the needs and interests of their own citizens. It should be no surprise that these transnational economic agents have as their priority not the welfare of the world's people but the maximization of corporate profit. The result is that the economic, social, and ecological problems that the proponents of a global ethic wish to confront have become worse, and the gap between wealth and poverty is increasing internationally as well as within nations. For example, eighty countries, according to a 1999 UN report, have per capita incomes that are lower than they were a decade ago. Some 1.2 billion people live below the absolute poverty line. More than two billion earn less than two dollars a day. Almost one billion people are unemployed. "Four hundred and forty seven billionaires have wealth greater than the income of the poorest half of humanity. . . . The assets of the three richest people were more than the combined GNP of the 48 least developed countries."[18]

It is often said that there is no alternative to globalization and, in one sense of the term, this might well be true, since, unless humanity destroys itself, we can expect an increasing integration of economic and technological organization as well as the growth of a global communications system. It might, however, be possible to break the link between the present economic organization and technological development. In other words, it might be possible to envision a form of globalization that is not globalization from above. In fact, globalization from above is already being challenged by a growing international movement that is sometimes misnamed the "antiglobalization" movement but that I think is more appropriate to call the movement of "globalization from below." Its goal is not to destroy the global integration of technological development and communications systems but to create a different global culture, one that is not run by an international corporate elite, one in which the global institutions that dominate economic and political life are democratically accountable.

At the moment, the movement comprises a diverse group of ecologically concerned citizens, feminists, consumer advocates, indigenous peoples who protest the exploitation of their tribal lands, landless peasants from the less developed world, rank-and-file workers protesting such international trade agreements as NAFTA, Third World groups who oppose the structural adjustment policies of the International Monetary Fund and the World Bank, anticorporate activists, groups in opposition to global sweatshops, advocates of small farmers, human rights groups, peace groups, civil society organizations, movements for global justice, and so forth. These groups are not only diverse in terms of specific issues but often are ideologically diverse. They are often more anarchist than Marxist. They include radical feminists and a variety of liberals. At the World Social Forum at Porto Alegre, Brazil, in February of 2002, which was attended by 70,000 participants from 150 countries, there was a sharp division between reformers whose main goal was to lobby and negotiate with international financial institutions and trade organizations and those who were interested in creating new organizations of popular power.[19] Nevertheless, while it is indeed a diverse movement, there is an emerging convergence between its members. However different they may be ideologically and in terms of their specific social priorities, they "share an opposition to transnational corporations and to the neoliberal government policies which enable them to flourish."[20] They support each other's specific agendas and have made themselves felt collectively at huge protests in Seattle, in Washington, D.C., in New York City, in Genoa, in Prague, and at the World Social Forums in Porto Alegre and, most recently, in Mumbai, India (where 100,000 people from 132 countries attended). This kind of political activism and networking may be the embryo of a new revolutionary movement, a revolutionary movement with a vision of how the world could be organized from below, a movement that could develop a consensus on common values for an alternative global order.[21]

CONCLUSION: GLOBAL ETHICS AND GLOBAL STRUGGLE

It is time now for me to make my own position on global ethics clear. For reasons that I have indicated above, I do not think that, at this point in time, it is possible to have a minimal consensus among the world's cultures that will have substantive implications. I do not think that it is possible to construct a meaningful global ethic through dialogue between representatives of the world's religions, through dialogue within philosophical and social scientific think tanks, or through dialogue at UN conferences. I do not by this mean to demean these attempts, for they may have useful political and international functions just as the UN Declaration of Human Rights has useful political and international functions. However, for the reasons I have indicated above, I do not think that we can construct a global ethic through dialogue alone. The possibility of a global ethic that could become a social reality requires not simply dialogue but political struggle. It requires a struggle for a new global order.

Ethics, then, is conditioned by politics. At this historical juncture, there is a plurality of global ethics competing against each other, each putting forward a vision of what the global order could be. Those in the positions of power within the existing global order offer various top-down managerial visions of a global order and put forward values that serve those visions. Fundamentalists within each of the world's religions offer values animated by their respective religious visions, values whose immediate function is to further their respective political agendas. Political activists who have demonstrated in the streets of the world's major cities and who attend the World Social Forums are beginning to put forward an ethical vision generated by their struggle for a new global order.

For this last group, their ethical vision may be considered a global ethic in the making. As their goals begin to converge through their networking and political struggle, they may develop a consensus on a core set of values that can ground a more comprehensive ethical vision of a new global order. And as the struggle continues, it may be joined by those who meet in the Parliaments of the World's Religions, by important elements of the philosophical and scientific community, and by those who attend UN-sponsored conferences. In this sense, insofar as they join the struggle for a new world order, they too may be part of this global ethic in the making.

What all this means is that a global ethic at this juncture in history is possible only as a heuristic. There can be no substantive consensus among the world's cultures and groups, because there is not yet a common global culture. The possibility of a global ethic that is more than a heuristic depends on a new world order, one in which there really is a commonality of needs among the world's citizens, one in which there is an authentic global culture that can generate a global ethical framework. It is only within such a global culture that a minimal consensus on ethical norms could be developed.[22] The possibility of a universal ethic would be based on the reality that all of humanity is part of a unified global community. Our community would be the world. And if such a global culture was ecologically oriented and open to deep compassion, I believe that our community would include more than just humanity. An ecologically based compassion would allow for the inclusion of nonhuman life as part of our global community.

NOTES

An earlier version of this article was presented at the First Moscow International Conference on Comparative Philosophy, "Moral Philosophy in a Pluralistic Cultural Context," sponsored by the Institute of Philosophy, Russian Academy of Sciences, in June 2002. I would like to thank Marietta Stepaniants, who organized that conference, for her encouragement and support. I would also like to thank Bat-Ami Bar On, Henry Rosemont Jr., Elizabeth Suzanne Kassab, John Pittman, Richard Olsen, John L. Hammond, John Lutz, and Ross Gandy for their insightful criticisms and comments.

1. The full text of the final draft can be found in Hans Küng, ed., *Yes to a Global Ethic* (New York: Continuum Publishing Co., 1996). This book also has comments on the parliament's declaration from a variety of internationally known persons—Lev Kopelev, Rigobertu Menchu, Patriarch Bartholomew I, Crown Prince Hassan Bin Talil, Yehudi Menuhin, Elie Wiesel, Desmond Tutu, Aung San Suu Kyi, etc.

2. This draft, along with a number of responses, can be found on the Internet at http://astro.temple.edu/~dialogue/Center/intro.htm.

3. This report, entitled "A New Global Ethics," can be found on the Internet at http://kvc.minbuza.nl/uk/archive/report/chapter1_3.html.

4. The discussion of "The Universal Ethics Project" can be found on the Internet at http://www.unesco.org/opi2/philosophyandethics/pronpro.htm.

5. John Hick, "Towards a Universal Declaration of a Global Ethic: A Christian Comment," http//astro.temple.edu/~dialogue/Center/hick.htm.

6. See http://astro.temple.edu/~dialogue/Center/duran.htm.

7. Zoltán Turgonyi, "Universalism, Relativism, and the Possibilities of a Global Ethic," paper delivered at the conference entitled "The Age of Global Dialogue," organized by the Institute of Philosophy of the Hungarian Academy of Sciences, Budapest, 1997, www.philinst.hu/intezet/tz01_p.htm.

8. Sallie King, "A Global Ethic in the Light of Comparative Religious Ethics," in *Explorations in Global Ethics*, ed. Sumner B. Twiss and Bruce Grelle (Boulder, CO: Westview Press, 2000), p. 123.

9. In 1610, a Catholic priest in America wrote to the Church in Europe to ask whether slavery was in accord with Catholic doctrine. He received the following reply from a Brother Luis Brandon.

> Your Reverence writes me that you would like to know whether the Negroes who are sent to your parts are legally captured. To this I reply that your Reverence should have no scruples on this point, because this is a matter which has been questioned by the Board of Conscience in Lisbon, and all its members are learned and conscientious men. Nor did the Bishops who were in Sao Thome, Cape Verde, and here in Lando—all learned and virtuous men—find fault in it. . . . Therefore we and the Fathers of Brazil buy these slaves for our service without any scruple.

Howard Zinn, *A People's History of the United States* (New York: Harper Collins, 2003), p. 29.

10. Gilbert Harmon and Judith Jarvis Thomson, *Moral Relativism and Moral Objectivity* (Oxford: Blackwell Publishers, 1996). This is a debate between these two philosophers in which part I on "Moral Relativism" was written by Gilbert Harmon and part II on "Moral Objectivity" by Judith Jarvis Thomson.

11. In the early days of ancient Rome a husband could legally kill his wife. In ancient Sparta, infanticide was widely practiced and accepted. As for religion, in 1487 the Aztecs sacrificed 20,000 members of other tribes in order to dedicate their Great Temple to their god Mexitl.

12. Given the constraints of space, I have omitted discussion of the classical alternative that attempts to account for ethical absolutes on pure philosophical grounds—Immanuel Kant's *Fundamental Principles of the Metaphysic of Morals*. While Kant's solution is ingenious, I think it can be shown to be circular. Its argument is a transcendental one that would demonstrate the conditions under which absolute moral norms are possible. Kant, however, does not prove that there are absolute moral norms. In any case, Kant's solution has been debated for more than a century without coming close to a philosophical consensus.

13. I am indebted for this term and for much of the analysis that follows to Milton Fisk, *Ethics and Society: A Marxist Interpretation of Value* (New York: New York University Press, 1980).

14. See www.unesco.org/phiweb/uk/2rpu/rort/rort.html.

15. C. Douglas Lummis, *Radical Democracy* (Ithaca: Cornell University Press, 1996), p. 69.

16. Paul L. Wachtel, *The Poverty of Affluence* (Philadelphia: New Society Publishers, 1989), p. 28.

17. Peter Marcuse, "The Language of Globalization," *Monthly Review* 52, no. 3 (July–August 2000): 24.

18. Jeremy Brecher, Tim Costello, and Brendan Smith, *Globalization from Below: The Power of Solidarity* (Cambridge, MA: South End Press, 2000), p. 7. The statistics mentioned are from this work.

19. The World Social Forum at Porto Alegre was conceived as an alternative to the World Economic Forum, which was meeting at the same time in New York City. For further discussion of this historic forum, see James Petras, "Porto Alegre 2002," *Monthly Review* 53, no. 11 (April 2002): 56–61.

20. Barbara Epstein, "Anarchism and Anti-globalization," *Monthly Review* 53, no. 4 (September 2001): 10. Epstein's article is an excellent overview of the ideological tendencies within the movement and especially of its anarchist tendencies.

21. For an excellent attempt to develop a specific vision of an alternative form of globalization, see "A Report of the International Forum on Globalization" (cochairs of the drafting committee, John Cavanagh and Jerry Mander), *Alternatives to Economic Globalization: A Better World Is Possible* (San Francisco: Berrett-Kohler Publishers, 2002).

22. There might still be a variety of ethical frameworks, but there would be an overarching common culture within which an ethical core with substantive implications could be extracted. With a genuine global culture, the problem of antagonistic needs of different groups and different peoples would be, if not entirely eliminated, at least minimized.

14

Playing the Angel's Advocate: Human Rights, Global Realism, and the Politics of Intervention

Kurt Jacobsen and Alba Alexander

States, not unlike people, are selective as to the targets of their moral outrage. At the start of the 1990s President George Herbert Walker Bush brandished his "vision thing" of a new world order where states benignly apply their resources to policing the planet.[1] The progressive spark in this project was that major powers should deploy their weaponry to nip incipient horrors in the bud. The tantalizing promise was that, in exchange for retaining expensive military assets and refurbishing outworn alliance systems, the major powers would prevent genocide, oust cruel regimes, and aid popular forces throughout the world. Yet Bush operated firmly within Francis Fukuyama's "end of history" universe, where, ordained by a pecuniary world spirit, democratic capitalist states call the shots according to their own interests, as any scrutiny of peacekeeping activities of the UN reveals.[2] The cynical view is that human rights provides camouflage for pure greed and power grabs. Is that really all there is?

Do human rights pose a challenge to "business as usual" in international relations? Thrasymachus in Plato's *Republic* beheld "justice or Right as what is in the interest of the stronger party" and imposed on all the hapless rest, with Glaucon chiming in that morality is "merely a matter of convenience" and, long before Machiavelli, that we should "want not to be but to seem just."[3] These pessimistic sages seem all too resoundingly revalidated in a post-9/11 era. "If force creates right, the effect changes with the cause; every force that is greater than the first succeeds to its right," Rousseau lamented. "As soon as it

is possible to disobey with impunity, disobedience is legitimate; and the
strongest always being in the right, the only thing that matters is to act so as
to become the strongest."[4] While bullies revel in the cruel joys of might makes
right, most analysts, but for rather major exceptions like Thucydides, omit its
perils.[5] If every citizen were cynical there would be no cause for hypocrisy or
deceit.

The worry for U.S. elites is that the American public may withdraw a blank
check, that they will become "isolationist," which is defined as anyone who
puts the welfare of local average citizens over the welfare of the affluent at
home and abroad. This is no idle concern. Regarding trade, some 80 percent
of the U.S. public supports liberalization while observing that business benefits the most affluent, and so, in equal numbers, the public wants strong labor
and environmental standards.[6] This stance is quite a sophisticated one that
surpasses that of many unnuanced experts one readily can name. Yet any
power elite seeks to evade democratic controls, and for good reason. As
Chalmers Johnson observed regarding the wider rough-and-tumble realm of
foreign policy, "If the US resists the establishment of a court that can prose-
cute individuals for war crimes, it is precisely because its global imperialist activities almost inevitably invite the commission of such crimes."[7] While there
is little question that some elements of the 1948 Universal Declaration of Human Rights are impracticable or are unwelcome in some societies on grounds
of sheer lack of resources, that objection surely can be construed as much as a
spur to material and social progress as an argument against it.[8] Such a political-
economic course evokes a "New Deal writ large" from the reformist heights of
the Roosevelt administration.[9] Or, as Ruggie recently suggested, it augurs an
"embedded liberalism," not only revived but gone global.[10]

POWER PLAYS AND WORD PLAY

State leaders resort to rhetorical ruses to cover hidden purposes, but also because moral invocations appeal to those citizens who genuinely want justice,
not just improvements in the bank balances of the top decile of the populace.[11] The vision of a transcontinental "reaction force" dispatched to avert,
say, the Rwandan massacres or the depredations of the Balkan wars is an en-
ticing one. (Instead, we behold the travesty of a brutal "Extreme Reaction
Force" that specializes in abusing unindicted prisoners at Camp Delta in
Guantánamo Bay.)[12] Realists, however, counsel that we look at deeper (if not
at all) levels of what is going on. And you don't have to be a Marxist to notice

that economic factors play a strong role in such decisions.[13] The best anyone can expect, according to world-weary realists, is for interventions to occur abroad when humanitarian crises overlap sufficiently with national prospects either for gain or foiling threats.

But words too exert an impact, they can form a commitment, and they pose bluffs that can be called, at least on occasion.[14] Risse-Kappen, for example, claims that "the processes of argumentation, deliberation and persuasion constitute a distinct mode of interaction" that is very different from material-based rational calculation. Accordingly, actors "engage in truth seeking with the aim of reaching mutual understanding." A huge literature has been spawned by scholars emphasizing the role of nonstate actors contriving through "boomerang effects" and such to induce reluctant states to act in accordance with higher values.[15] Keck and Sikkink, for example, reflect a wider opinion when they write approvingly about "transnational advocacy networks" striving "to uncover and investigate problems, and alert the press and policymakers" about neglected problems or plights.[16] They seem to see this phenomenon as a net plus for planetary politics, and as unsusceptible to manipulation, or not so much as to matter. Yet, just as many NGOs are corporate entities or government conduits, so too advocacy networks can be constructed to serve, or be turned to, the purposes of groups whose prime objective is heartily partisan.[17]

Even Risse-Kappen allows that "there are social circumstances in which acting instrumentally is appropriate and legitimate"—and that is the rub. Where are these lines drawn and by whom? By NGOs? By unspecified concerned citizens? By an impeccable array of dissembling diplomats? By party-appointed flacks? By public relations firms such as Hill & Knowlton or Ruder Finn or Burson-Marsteller? To Hill & Knowlton we owe the emotive tale of incubator babies tossed to the floor by Iraqi occupiers in Kuwait in 1990. Ruder Finn expertly demonized the Serbs in very short order on behalf of its Bosnian Muslim and Croatian clients.[18] Burson-Marsteller is who you call when you are a corporation that has wreaked undeniable mass havoc: for example, Three Mile Island, Bhopal, or the Torrey Canyon oil tanker spill.[19] The first thing that a minority in a "far away land that we know little of," to quote Neville Chamberlain about Czechoslovakia, does these days is hire a sophisticated public relations firm to plead its case. Advocacy and truth don't necessarily mix any better outside government circles than inside. Yet this is no counsel for despair about the efficacy of NGOs. The biblical advice about the decent person in an imperfect world best being equipped not only with the heart of a dove but with the wisdom of a serpent seems apt here.

REALISM AND BEING REALISTIC

Striking a pose is a fraught gambit. Once in a while a state actually has to deliver on its commitments, although frequently it may try to sidestep inconvenient ones. So national leaders sometimes are responsive to a mounting pressure for action by domestic interest groups, NGOs, and/or international protest with respect to wars, disasters, and famines abroad. At times, then, states play the "angel's advocate," most particularly when it serves their underlying "realist" thrust for security or gains (whether relative or absolute). Realism, of course, is a multifaceted and sometimes contradictory tradition. This analytic tradition, however, is anchored to an ironclad injunction about the determinants, if not the nature, of all action, which entails an automatic suspicion that any action stems from, or can be readily converted to, the ulterior purposes of advantage-seeking elites. Such is the marked tendency, if not always the reality, among predatory states maneuvering in an anarchic environment, or so say the realists.

Deploying military forces under humanitarian auspices is discouraged under standard realist dogma.[20] Realist doyen Hans Morgenthau always warned that foreign policy ought to be tempered not only by resources available but to a prudent view of the national interest.[21] (Prudent is not the first word that leaps to mind when scanning the ambitious Project for a New American Century.)[22] In the turbulent Vietnam era Morgenthau's caustic antiwar stance startled some LBJ administration members who sincerely believed that they were in utter accord with his dicta.[23] Should realist states gallop off setting wrongs right like a comic book superhero? Is the venerable Hippocratic stricture "First, do no harm" the best advance that progressives can attain for the foreseeable future? Gullibility creates numerous pitfalls. There is nothing—no value and no cause—that is not potentially grist for modern-day Machiavellians operating within and around the state. The urge to induce better state behavior through blends of external and internal pressure, unfortunately, can blind some ardent activists as to the real forces at work in policy decisions, especially those that seem to go their way.

The Vietnam War was conducted, so it was asserted, to rescue a democracy that never existed in a South Vietnam that hadn't existed until the United States interfered in Southeast Asia. Why get upset about Vietnamese boat people but stigmatize their Haitian counterparts? Why ignore the slaughter of half a million in Indonesia in 1965—and, in fact, abet and approve it—while deploring smaller crimes by unfriendly regimes?[24] Why decry torture in Saddam Hussein's Iraq but ignore it in Turkey or Uzbekistan, or engage zestfully in it oneself in post-Saddam Iraq?[25] Foreign policy, to run smoothly, depends on its seamy details being hidden from the bulk of the busy public.

When a Tony Blair or a George W. Bush claims that perilous situations in Iraq or Haiti demand that states with good consciences intervene to restore order so as to bring about social justice, we need to sift out the real motivations and weigh how much human rights matter in the actual political equation.[26] Interventionist enterprises often confer a pleasing impression of blamelessness on the intervener. Witness the British record in Northern Ireland, where the British still represent themselves merely as a mediator between primitive warring communities. No one who knows that case well would ever have believed British claims that they were running a perfectly gentle civil operation in their occupation of the region of Basra in Iraq today.

INTERVENTION AND INTERPRETATION

So how many killings does it take to make a bona fide massacre? How many corpses must pile up to count as mass murder? Does a pit need more than two cadavers to qualify as a mass grave? How many expulsions prove that ethnic cleansing is under way? Is genocide the same thing as extermination? What is the numerical difference between mass murder and genocide anyway? You need not sport a swastika armband to quibble about these macabre measures: they are calculations arising from earthly hell. The point here is not to quibble over macabre measures of earthly hell but to stress that political leaders usually have room to maneuver when seeking to mobilize public support.

According to 2003 Pulitzer Prize–winning author Samantha Power, whose work is a useful proxy of conventional wisdom, the only remotely effective way to stop crazed states on internal killing sprees is to cry genocide and let slip the accountants of war.[27] Genocide is not only the most emotive word in our vocabulary of modern ghastliness but the only one that legally requires action. States come running for nothing less, and hardly ever even then. So if the Nazi Holocaust is the standard, and an advocacy group believes a great crime is transpiring somewhere, the temptation to play fast and loose with an extra zero or two tagged onto numbers is almost irresistible. With memories still fresh of the Nazis' wartime dismissal of Holocaust rumors as "horror propaganda," the contemporary inclination for citizens is to accept such stories, until proven otherwise. It is a different matter for states.

The United States arduously avoided approving a UN antigenocide resolution and, when it finally did, signed a totally ineffectual document.[28] Mass murder must intersect with vital material interests in order for national leaders to grab their white hats and gallop to the rescue. As Henry Kissinger avowed, foreign policy is not "social work." In Armenia, the Nazi Holocaust, Cambodia, Iraq (versus the Kurds), the recent Balkan wars, and Rwanda, the most tragic aspect of some, if not all, of these slaughters is that a minor intrusion at the right stage might have averted them. Realists counsel that virtuous acts depend on political advantages reaped thereby.

We ourselves read 1939 cables by a U.S. diplomat in France arguing that anticipated swarms of European Jewish emigrants only will stir up latent anti-Semitism in America.[29] Hence, bar the gates. Virtue can be exquisitely circumstantial and partial. Former Republican presidential candidate Bob Dole is praised by Power for championing Bosnia (because of an idiosyncratic personal interest and a chance to score points against Clinton), but he staunchly opposed intervening in Rwanda. It is clear now that the Clinton administration knew early on that mass murderous mayhem was going on in Rwanda, but it did not "want to repeat the fiasco of US intervention in Somalia, where US troops became sucked into fighting. It also felt the US had no interests in Rwanda, a small central African country with no minerals or strategic value."[30]

Unscrupulous elites, as analysts observe, often exploit economic troubles by boosting or blaming ethnic groups, and gaining power on that basis. In former Yugoslavia every group played that cynical card—and foremost the Slovenes, Croats, and then the Bosnian Muslims in successive secession movements that the United States and NATO allies never would tolerate inside their own borders.[31] Germany's role in encouraging secession by what one might call "preemptive recognition" of Slovenia is especially troubling.[32] The key question, mostly sidestepped in the 1990s press, was whether wider geopolitical purposes were being served by the breakup of Yugoslavia and, if so, who abetted it?

Power and other pro-NATO intervention advocates consistently omit mentioning the role of Western banking institutions, which in the 1980s heedlessly imposed austerity measures that sent unemployment skyrocketing and rendered hard-pressed people into easy prey for nationalist demagogues.[33] Those

behaviors, as recent testimony of outcast Joseph Stiglitz shows, were not necessarily conspiratorial but par for the course of investor-protecting International Monetary Fund and World Bank policies.[34] Stiglitz notes that human
rights do not concern these institutions, institutions that originally were supposed to ease international adjustment, not just recoup rash lenders' funds.

The good works of fervent human rights advocates become marred by
skewed portrayals. Power depicts Kurds in Iraq as pure noncombatants at a
time when she also admits that armed Kurdish groups were allied with Iran,
and when U.S. ally Turkey was killing and maiming and displacing Kurds in
its territory just as prolifically as Saddam Hussein was in Iraq. She says nothing about post-Armenian Turkish atrocities but does plaintively note that
President Bush Senior, eager to contain Iran, doubled Iraqi trade credits even
after the notorious Halabja poison gas attack on the Kurds. That's realpolitik.

In the Yugoslav wars only the Serbs were portrayed as expansionist insofar
as they tried to hang on to disintegrating pieces of former Yugoslavia that
large Serb "minorities" also happened to inhabit, especially the Krajina. Croatia's secession under the extremely unsavory Tudjman was sure to stir up deep
fears and strife. One must assume from press reports that in the early fighting
the majority of refugees would be non-Serbs, yet Red Cross figures in October 1993 (a year after the Yugoslav Army withdrew) show that four of every
five refugees were Serbs.[35] The first massacres, not widely reported, in the
widening war were of Serbs.[36]

"Almost from the beginning of the Yugoslav crisis, NATO sought to involve
itself," Gervasi points out. "In 1993 NATO began to support UNPROFOR operations in Yugoslavia, especially in the matter of the blockade against the Federal Republic of Yugoslavia and the enforcement of a no-fly zone in Bosnian
airspace."[37] NATO began involvement in Bosnia-Herzegovina a year earlier
when it dispatched about one hundred personnel there to establish a military
headquarters "to help United Nations forces in Bosnia." Severe UN sanctions
against Serbia, as in Iraq, hurt ordinary citizens foremost and only cemented
them to a wayward ruler who conveniently blamed all troubles on unjust
sanctions. The Serbs, especially the Bosnian Serbs, were no angels but neither
were the Croats and Bosnian Muslims, who reaped vastly more military aid
from the United States, Germany, and the Middle East (including imported
mujahideen Afghan veterans) than is usually acknowledged, and who have
their own unpublicized atrocities to answer for. Richard P. Clarke writes in his
recent memoir that the Clinton administration had to badger Bosnian leader

Izetbegovic after the Dayton accords to eject a large contingent of "muj" fighters, renowned for their ferocity and brutality—and links to al Qaeda.[38]

The Kosovo Liberation Army, labeled "terrorists" by the U.S. State Department in 1998, suddenly morphed into bold freedom fighters the following year, in perfect accordance with shifting interests of the United States and NATO.[39] The KLA's ethnic cleansing of Kosovar Serbs after NATO's air war was generously overlooked just as was the Croats' expulsion of hundreds of thousands of long-time Serb residents from Krajina in 1995. Even to human rights advocates one must address the question, does the suffering of atrocities award victims a "free kick," so to speak, to take revenge—even assuming the grounds for revenge are real? Even if every accusation against the Bosnian Serbs and the Serbs were proved, genocide, or an attempt at genocide, was hardly in view. One U.S. Information Agency fact sheet stated that the number of Albanians massacred might be as high as 400,000 at the time. Yet a year after NATO troops entered Kosovo "examination of the 345 most promising sites [for mass graves] had yielded a total of 2,788 bodies of people of diverse origin who had died of various causes."[40] The figure has risen somewhat since but is nowhere near the vicinity of the accusations flung around during the conflict. For that matter, even if the anti-Serb case proved entirely true, the assumption that NATO intervened principally for the sake of terminating an internal European state slaughter is extremely questionable.

Atrocity tales certainly help a cause. Forget Kuwaiti oil for a moment; were ordinary Americans otherwise so keen to sacrifice blood and taxes to restore medieval Middle East potentates to their pleasure domes in 1991? The people you are "saving" may be playing you for fools. Was rape not only the specialty of Serbs but done so on an industrial scale?[41] "The UNCHR found no evidence of a rape camp at Djakovica," and even Human Rights Watch was "concerned that NATO's use of rape camps to bolster support for the war relied on unconfirmed accounts."[42] Yet, as even pro-NATO champion Power acknowledges, Izetbegovic's far-from-multiculturalist Bosnian Muslim government was notorious for "crying wolf" and provoking retaliatory attacks so as to attract Western aid and thereby improve its bargaining position. There remain well-warranted question marks about the identity of the culprits in the very conveniently timed May 1992 market bombing in Sarajevo, and the February 1994 attack as well.[43] Franjo Tudjman's Croatia, steeped in scarcely concealed Ustashe attitudes and symbols, was no liberal or pacifist paradise either.

Power is on the mark when she finds that none of the leaders—Serb, Croat, or Bosnian—"were particularly concerned about the fate of their people." Yet in a civil war with plenty of blame to go around among nationalists, it is only the Serbs who suffered sanctions and who were blasted with twenty thousand missiles and bombs of varying degrees of smartness in 1999.[44] Whether the bombing spurred the Serbs to expel the Kosovar Albanian population, which was never so "autonomous" that it wasn't part of Serbia, is a question always skirted by pro-interventionist analysts. Cluster bombs, depleted uranium weaponry, and civilian-target attacks by NATO are deemed supremely irrelevant. Slobodan Milosevic today is charged with killing several hundreds—not thousands or tens of thousands—of victims. Whatever Milosevic's crimes, the prosecutor has admitted that we are not dealing with an Adolf Eichmann here and that genocide is unprovable.[45] Did the demonization of Serbia serve its geopolitical purpose? Indeed, if Racak or Srebrenica were genocidal events, or part of a chain of genocidal events, what should the "international community" make of its own far larger-scale "silent" killing of hundreds of thousands of Iraqis through employment of sanctions over 1991–2003?

"The state's right to be left alone automatically outweighed the individual's right to justice," is Power's plaintive indictment of realist states. The U.S. interest, as determined by policy elites, foremost is one of securing resources, trade, and bases. So are realists always right? One certainly would be foolish to ignore the concerns they cite when charting very slow progress in civilizing nation-states. Power, like many of us, pillories the duplicitous tactics that politicians commonly use to avoid purely humanitarian intervention. Yet one wonders if human rights advocates are too scornful of the Powell-Weinberger doctrine endorsing intervention only where there is an unambiguous national interest, clear objectives, an exit strategy, and public support. The intention, after all, was to avoid another foreign policy tragedy on the scale of Vietnam, a valid concern that the Bush Junior administration cavalierly disregarded in its implacable rush into Iraq.

CONCLUSION

In the post–Cold War, and especially post-9/11, world a debate has revived regarding the desirability and feasibility of humanitarian military intervention. Activists, and some international relations analysts, are eager for national governments to incorporate a human rights agenda into their foreign policies. At least since the Universal Declaration of Human Rights in 1948, humanitarian intervention has been advocated (if by no means compelled) as a major element in any worthy nation-state's obligations in foreign affairs.

Yet "first do no harm" may not be a bad principle, particularly since partisanship and deception are so hard to detect. Power, for example, acknowledged that massive U.S. bombing of Cambodia contributed directly to the Khmer Rouge reign of butchery. She mentions the United States "looking away" from the bloody Indonesian invasion of East Timor, but does not mention the profitable flow of U.S. and UK arms over there. If one can't stop the killers, can't one stop reloading their weapons? The Vietnamese for their own reasons ousted Pol Pot from Cambodia's killing grounds but the United States saw fit to punish them for the intervention and, for geopolitical reasons, recognized Pol Pot. Who isn't a villain here? Advocates need villains to drive their narratives, and too many villains ruin the uplifting Hegelian human rights story line. Ultimately, there is no principle so pure that it cannot be made to serve unnervingly cynical purposes. This conclusion is not remotely meant to scoff at principles, but one had better know what one is doing before entering the treacherous political game.

Academics might prefer the language of "two logics"—a logic of cold-blooded maneuvers by elites, and a logic of a public-spirited kind that is more ethically motivated, if not exclusively so. The realpolitikers, whenever unable to ignore public groups, invoke ethical backing for their own essentially unchanged goals. One logic often absorbs the other. So long as the public is unable to grasp the leaders' utilitarian logic there is no chance of civilizing those leaders.

No one ought to dabble in politics who ignores realist explanation, inasmuch as the ease with which realists detect self-aggrandizing intentions is hard to surpass (although that is usually all they see). Cynicism is cheap wisdom, but it is still a wisdom to reckon with. Elites want to ground their beliefs in pure material motives, in a bloodstained blueprint where conscience plays no part. No less dubious are people who imply or argue that moral motives, in disregard of secondary or underlying motives, are sufficient and credible forces. Major states concede only to the degree that they are forced to do so or to the degree that they espy a conciliatory way of gaining what they wanted anyway.

Indeed, the fabled "boomerang effect" might be applied in an exquisitely ironic manner to the ways in which a morality-based public clamor enables government to implement plans that it otherwise had simmering on the back burner, such as pipelines across the Balkans or Afghanistan, or the construction of major military bases, such as Camp Bondsteel in Bosnia. Only in this sense is it possible to understand the dramatic eastward expansion and reinvigoration of NATO as a result of the Kosovo intervention as purely "accidental." One's first duty as a citizen, analyst, or activist is not to be gulled.

NOTES

1. This vagueness is more a matter of design than of ill-thought schemes. Major powers, public or private, always strive to write rules in such a way as to allow themselves to escape their strictures, or interpret them, Humpty Dumpty–like, just as they please.

2. See Linda Polman, *We Did Nothing: Why the Truth Doesn't Always Go Out When the UN Goes In* (London: Viking, 2003).

3. Plato, *The Republic* (London: Penguin, 1995), pp. 65, 87–88, 93.

4. Jean Jacques Rousseau, *The Social Contract* (Hertfordshire: Wordsworth Classics, 1998), p. 8.

5. Thucydides, *History of the Peloponnesian War* (New York: Penguin, 1972).

6. University of Maryland Program on International Policy Attitudes in 1999, cited in John Gerard Ruggie, "Taking Embedded Liberalism Global: The Corporate Connection" in *Taming Globalization: Frontiers of Governance*, ed. David Held and Mathias Koenig-Archibugi (Oxford: Polity Press, 2003), pp. 101–2.

7. Chalmers Johnson, *The Sorrows of Empire* (London: Verso, 2004), pp. 74–75.

8. Article 22 of the declaration reads: "Everyone, as a member of society, has the right to social security and is entitled, through national effort and international cooperation and in accordance with the organization and resources of each state, of the economic, social and cultural rights indispensable for his dignity and the free development of his personality." Cited in Youcef Bouandel, *Human Rights and Comparative Politics* (Aldershot: Dartmouth Press, 1997), p. 23.

9. See Franz Schurmann, *The Logic of World Power* (New York: Pantheon, 1974).

10. Ruggie in Held and Koenig-Archibugi, *Taming Globalization*, p. 13.

11. See David Cay Johnston, *Perfectly Legal* (New York: Portfolio, 2003).

12. David Rose and Gaby Hinsliff, "US Guards 'Filmed Beatings' at Terror Camp," *Observer*, May 16, 2004.

13. A point Thrasymachus understood. See Plato, *Republic*, p. 63. Also see J. K. Jacobsen and C. Hofhansel, "Safeguards and Profits," in *Dead Reckonings: Ideas, Interests and Politics in the "Information Age,"* by J. K. Jacobsen (Atlantic Highlands, NJ: Humanities Press, 1997).

14. Thomas Risse-Kappen, "Let's Argue: Communicative Action in World Politics," *International Organization* 54, no. 1 (Winter 2000).

15. See Margaret Keck and Kathryn Sikkink, *Activists beyond Borders* (Ithaca: Cornell University Press, 2002).

16. Keck and Sikkink, *Activists beyond Borders*, p. 19.

17. INGOs currently disburse more money than the United Nations (excluding the World Bank and International Monetary Fund); more than two-thirds of the European Union's relief aid is channeled through them: and in many parts of the world there is a strong trend towards the disbursement of government funds—currently totaling $US 7 billion per annum—more or less exclusively through NGOs. John Keane, *Global Civil Society?* (Cambridge: Cambridge University Press, 2003), p. 5.

18. Florence Levinsohn, *Belgrade: Among the Serbs* (Chicago: Ivan Dee, 1994), p. 33.

19. Keane, *Global Civil Society?* p. 84.

20. "Everything that the new realist find intriguing about the interaction of international economics and politics can be found in the Peloponnesian war": Robert Gilpin, "The Richness of the Tradition of Realism," in *Neo-Realism and Its Critics*, ed. Robert Keohane (New York: Columbia, 1986), p. 308. For a contemporary restatement of realist views see John Mearsheimer, *The Tragedy of Great Power Politics* (New York: Norton, 2001).

21. See Hans Morgenthau, *In Defense of the National Interest* (New York: Knopf, 1951).

22. See the Project for a New American Century website: http://www.newamericancentury.org/.

23. A friend witnessed a debate between Morgenthau and McGeorge Bundy in Berkeley in the mid-1960s where the former chastised the latter for his anti-Communist ideology, which blinded him as to the real stakes, or lack of them, in Southeast Asia. Thanks to Robin Melville.

24. See John Pilger, *Distant Voices* (New York: Random House, 1992).

25. Nick Paton Walsh, "US Looks Away as New Ally Tortures Islamists," *Guardian*, May 26, 2003. Human Rights Watch documented eight torture deaths in Uzbek custody in a briefing paper published in March 2003 at http://hrw.org/backgrounder/eca/uzbek040403-bck.htm.

26. *Observer*, March 7, 2004, p. 1.

27. Samantha Power, *A Problem from Hell: America and the Age of Genocide* (London: Flamingo, 2003).

28. Power, *Problem from Hell*.

29. Archives at the Rockefeller estate, Tarrytown, NY.

30. Rory Carroll, "US Chose to Ignore Rwandan Genocide," *Guardian*, March 31, 2004.

31. Power, *Problem from Hell*. Also see Lloyd and Susanne Rudolph, "Modern Hate: How Ancient Animosities Get Invented," *New Republic*, March 22, 1993.

32. Diane Johnstone, *Fool's Crusade* (New York: Monthly Review Press, 2002), pp. 188–93.

33. See Michael Chossudovsky, "Dismantling Yugoslavia, Colonizing Bosnia," *Covert Action Quarterly* 56 (1996).

34. Joseph Stiglitz, *Globalization and Its Discontents* (New York: Norton, 2003).

35. Levinsohn, *Belgrade*, p. 166.

36. Johnstone, *Fool's Crusade*, p. 29.

37. Sean Gervasi, "Why Is NATO in Yugoslavia?" in *NATO in the Balkans* (New York: International Action Center, 1998), pp. 20–46.

38. Richard Clarke, *Against All Enemies: Inside America's War on Terror* (New York: Free Press, 2004), p. 137.

39. See Noam Chomsky, *The New Military Humanism* (Monroe, ME: Common Courage Press, 1999).

40. Johnstone, *Fool's Crusade*, p. 253.

41. "The 'Serbianizing' of the Bosnian Muslims followed reports by the Muslims of massive rape by the Serbs, an alleged 50,000 by late 1992. As of July 1994 the UN reported that it had 800 documented rapes committed by Serbs, Croatians and Muslims—800 in all." Levinsohn, *Belgrade*, p. 314.

42. See Neil Clark, "There Was No Genocide in Kosovo but Tony Blair Never Allowed Facts to Get in the Way of a Good War," http://www.antiwar.com/spectator/spec15_files/article_line1.gif.

43. Levinsohn, *Belgrade*, pp. 314–15; Johnstone, *Fool's Crusade*, pp. 65–123; Peter Brook, "The Partisan Press," *Foreign Policy*, Winter 1993–1994; and Philip Knightley, "Propaganda Wars," *Independent*, June 27, 1999.

44. In the UK case see Richard Norton Taylor, "MoD Reveal Kosovo Failure," *Guardian*, August 5, 2000. "Fewer than half the bombs dropped by the RAF and just 2% of unguided 'dumb' bombs are known to have hit their targets," according to "an internal report leaked by the Ministry of Defence despite efforts by the Ministry to suppress it."

45. Ian Traynor, "Balkan Butcher Left No Smoking Gun," *Guardian*, February 28, 2004.

15

Human Rights in the Age of Empire

MICHELINE ISHAY

Despite significant human rights progress in the twentieth century, the global epidemic of human-caused misery has yet to be contained. Wherever it strikes, one can record disconnected voices of suffering, voices that demark the spotted landscape of human rights violations. A vast Chinese populace faces growing health problems, from the global spread of AIDS to the stifling air pollution of its industrial centers. Amazonians wander in deforested terrains, searching for ways to remain alive; Guatemalan women are earning their depressed wages in the boiling heat of Central American sweatshops; Thai girls are coerced to sell their bodies as tourist trophies; and impoverished Indians feel compelled to barter their own kidneys for a bite of bread and some rupees. When escape and immigration for the refugee of this or that Golgotha might seem to offer deliverance, deportation becomes her haunting daily fear.

Though globalization has important benefits, its manifold costs have affected people in different ways, creating a plethora of ever more specific and ever more conflicting human rights demands. If the fight for labor rights has been reenergized in recent years, organized labor continues to be divided internationally between workers from rich and poor countries, and domestically between the interests of those who are unionized and those who are not. Similarly, while the unprecedented ravaging of the global environment has prompted the emergence of an active international ecology movement, that movement is animated by different social and economic priorities in the developed and developing world. The abuses of a growing illegal immigrant labor force and the hardships suffered by refugees fleeing from poverty, repression, or war have led to calls for fairer immigration and refugee laws. Yet low-skilled immigration to richer countries conflicts with the interests of unemployed and low-wage workers in the developed world, pitting two needy communities against each other.

There may well be evidence of a growing body of international human rights law. There may well have been signs in the streets of Seattle, Washington, Genoa, and elsewhere that human rights activism may yet overcome its cultural and economic divisions, while broadening and internationalizing its agenda. Despite the revitalization of militant protest, however, cultural and socioeconomic differences heighten tensions within the global human rights community. It is precisely these tensions and the parceling of these human rights demands that can be easily manipulated by ruling elites and tycoons. To conquer, one needs to know how to foment division, co-opt challengers, or hold out false hope. Further, even while the question of which universal principles should be adopted has not yet been fully settled in the streets or in international legal institutions, progressive forces face yet another challenge as they confront a formidable army of illusionists who, since the end of the Cold War, have sought to hijack the human rights discourse in the name of unfettered economic globalization.

With the attacks against America on September 11, that challenge has been further complicated by the United States' growing reliance on human rights discourse to justify its national security policy. Joined by corporate elites, the Pentagon, segments of the popular media, and various private organizations, Washington's propaganda effort has nevertheless proved to be more difficult than anticipated. Gaps between U.S. human rights rhetoric and its actual foreign policy—as it becomes commonplace to describe U.S. preponderance in terms of empire—have created greater discontent in the Middle East and elsewhere, prompting growing opposition to perceived U.S. imperial ambitions. Originating from sources as varied as al Qaeda and left-leaning pacifist groups in the West, this disparate opposition has confused the human rights message of our time.

How can we maintain a cohesive universal human rights agenda beyond the marketing of human rights by political, military, and economic elites? Which is the most strategic level at which to resist this trend: the individual, civil society, international, or state institutions? When U.S. actions are so crucial for either advancing or undermining human rights, how can human rights activists advance their agenda amidst imperial temptations? Considering these three questions will be the subject of this chapter, with a view to demystifying the rhetoric of rights in an effort to recapture the universal foundation of human rights principles, navigating human rights struggle toward the most promising space of resistance, and seizing opportunities whenever they present themselves, even within the context of empire building.

THE MARKETING OF HUMAN RIGHTS

That there is always available work under the new flexible conditions of the modern global market, so that anyone can join the global consumer society, has become a prevalent myth of our times. Another related creed is that economic opportunity under free trade agreements would ineluctably modernize impoverished countries and build the foundation of institutions based on human rights. The United Nations Development Program report, showing that the poorest countries are getting poorer, not just in relative terms but also in absolute terms, gives little pause to neoliberal human rights spin masters, who forecast, for example, that "the economic output of the developing world will soon outstrip that of developed countries and by the turn of the century will account for over 60 per cent of everything the world produces."[1] The new adage in our virtual epoch becomes: what's good business is good for everyone.

This is also what the George W. Bush administration would like us to believe when it rejected the Kyoto agreement and other environment accords. The idea that ozone depletion, marine pollution, deforestation, desertification, soil exhaustion, acid rain, carbon dioxide emissions, and hazardous wastes affect each of us is, according to the Bush dream team, a gross exaggeration, a position widely contested by scientists, or the propaganda slander of lying liberals. When the facts seem incontrovertible, the polluters and their servants do not relent; they instead co-opt and market with superb inventiveness the message of their critics. Witness the incorporation of "green rhetoric" in WTO debates, antismoking commercials by tobacco companies, and corporate advertising exhorting us to protect the environment.[2] Businesses from the cosmetic industry, to paper companies, and even to petroleum companies like Shell seek to persuade their ecologically conscious consumers of their commitment to the environment. These same companies, of course, routinely oppose any environmental regulations that interfere with their pursuit of

profits. Some free market enthusiasts, like Alan Binder, believe it will be sufficient to develop a system in which permits to pollute consistent with Environmental Protection Agency emission regulations are auctioned to the
highest bidders.[3] After all, why shouldn't the wealthiest, who are already increasing their market share of most human rights (e.g., property, freedom of
speech, security, self-government, etc.) also monopolize the "right to pollute"!

Just as environmental concerns can be easily marketed as consumer goods,
so can one capitalize on the fear of losing one's cultural identity—a fear hastened by the ever more extensive movement of people and immigration. Wars,
scarcity, or the lure of greater opportunity have remained throughout the centuries the main factors driving migration. What has changed is the visibility of
refugees, as the global reach of modern mass media has combined with growing recognition that migrants have rights, rights that call into question established conceptions of citizenship and national and cultural identity. As
globalization erodes national distinctions, demagogues peddling cultural
rights revive them, intensifying efforts to protect national patrimonies against
waves of immigrants, foreign imports, or the overall homogenization of the
world into universal consumerism. Over the last third of the twentieth century, the notion of group, or cultural, rights has gained recognition as an important category of human rights, aimed at protecting diverse conceptions of
human needs and values against globalization under Western influence.

Globalization, its cultural rights critics notwithstanding, is not adverse to
cultural diversity, however, so long as globalization offers exotic products of
consumption for a gentrified world athirst for novelties, and insofar as it produces cultural spaces in which one can escape the vicissitudes imposed by
modernity. Let us not forget that despite competing cultural values within and
between the South and the North, cultural assaults against globalization have
often been co-opted by the very forces they challenge. The music of social
protest, like reggae and African-American rap, has lost its political significance
by the time it reaches mainstream audience on MTV, just as sixties counterculture artists found their message radically transformed in the consumer-
oriented hands of 1994 Woodstock promoters, or in the ads of Coca-Cola and
Nike.

After all, "MTV and McDonald's and Disneyland are American cultural
icons," combining in the form of a seemingly innocent Trojan-American horse
that stealthily penetrates other nations' cultures.[4] While some cannot help but
admire the shining steed, and wind up reinterpreting their lives in relation to

soap operas like *Dynasty* and *Dallas* (or more recent shows like *Seinfeld* and *Friends*), a growing number root for heroic resistance figures, like Jean Bové, who defied the great beast by trashing a McDonald's restaurant in the South of France. A far more ominous reaction, however, comes from regions where large segments of society—those most excluded from the benefits of globalization—seek refuge under the veil of religious fundamentalism, where despair is exchanged for rage and hopes of a better afterlife.

The attacks against the Pentagon and the World Trade Center on September 11 epitomized that violent reaction, prompting a broad coalition of influential economic, political, and military actors to unite in action against the new challenge. History teaches us that the effective use of force tends to strengthen the internal cohesion of society, its political resolve against outside aggressors, and to consolidate, in the case of a great power, its economic and geopolitical interests. In this sense, globalization, in the hands of the greatest military power in the world, appears "in the form of a very high tech machine: it is virtual, built to control the marginal event, and organized to dominate and when necessary intervene in the event of the breakdown of the system."[5]

At the same time, imperial hegemony, as Antonio Gramsci understood nearly a century ago, also requires a moral justification of power, and in a world where telecommunication travels at the speed of light, human rights takes on the role of subduing current and future challengers. Improving human rights to win the minds and soul of a defiant Muslim world has becomes the "White Man's Burden" of the new American empire. "Go bind your sons to exile to serve your captives' need," went Rudyard Kipling's account of the British empire, and perhaps the inevitable role of all long-lasting empires. An empire would, according to the nineteenth-century British novelist, patiently endure "through thankless years . . . the blame of those ye better, the hate of those ye guard."[6] One may concede that the American empire has no colonies, in contrast to its British predecessor, yet what is more noteworthy is that America enforces its economic and geopolitical interests with the greatest military machine ever created, and can seek to legitimize its actions, in human rights terms, by mobilizing the greatest network of global telecommunications and advertising power ever put together.

Today, the viziers of the emperor wear different clothes than yesterday. The new allies of the military are Hollywood directors, advertising agents, and cyber-techno magicians, working together to reshape America's image to better sell the idea of America as the lighthouse of human rights. If nineteenth-century British anthropologists were often consulted to inform the imperial masters on the habits and customs of the colonies' indigenous peoples, today public relations specialists such as the Rendon Group, and for a while the advertising doyenne of Madison Avenue, Charlotte Beer, are among those Washington has recruited to "manage perception and truth projection." In a description of himself, John W. Rendon said, "I am not a national security strategist, . . . [but] an information warrior," hired to influence the "emotions, motives, and objective reasoning of foreign audiences."[7]

In a related effort, the Pentagon has also drafted some of Hollywood's best simulators to create an Institute for Creative Technologies. Its mission, as defined by executive director Richard Lindheim, is "to mix showbiz with science . . . to combine Hollywood magic with the real world."[8] Yet this collaboration is not merely technical, aimed to train troops in a simulated war environment. In exchange for providing Hollywood with military advice, personnel, and state-of-the-art equipment for movies and TV shows, the Pentagon will get an advance look at scripts and is provided an opportunity to negotiate changes.[9] After September 11, Washington charged Hollywood with a major wartime role: to help combat terrorism at home by producing movies extolling national pride, and to appease anti-American sentiments abroad by projecting images of America's love for freedom and human rights.

One can document a few cases in which Kipling's "White Man's Burden" has actually been borne in recent years by the developed world. The British intervention in Sierra Leone in 1999 put a halt to massive bloodshed, just as an Australian-led force halted the slaughter in East Timor that same year. The NATO role in Bosnia and Kosovo could arguably also be praised in this context. Yet no one, despite faint gestures of interest, had intervened to interrupt the 1994 genocide in Rwanda, in which hundreds of thousands of women, children, and men met terrible death.[10] And Rwanda was only the most glaring of many cases of inaction. For too many years, the United States had remained motionless in the face of monstrous oppression, particularly against women, under the Taliban regime, until the appalling wakeup call of September 11, 2001. If some response toward a regime as repressive as the Taliban was long overdue, it surely would not have occurred had not the security of the world's most powerful state (not to mention that of the global economy) been put directly in jeopardy.

Cynically enough, morality and interest may well need recurrently to be wed in order to ensure the perpetuation of imperial dominance. Despite a lifetime of apathy toward the subject, Bush enthusiastically declared December 10, 2002, as "Human Rights Day" and the beginning of "Human Rights Week," and December 15–22 as the "Bill of Rights" week. With Jacobin skill, Deputy Secretary of Defense Paul Wolfowitz and friends have repeatedly linked the liberating roles of American troops in Afghanistan and Iraq to human rights themes. As it became clear that weapons of mass destruction in Iraq were nowhere to be found, unearthing mass graves and ending mass torture were retroactively elevated as the principal reasons for committing American troops. Kipling observed more than a century ago that occupying or colonizing forces, no matter how virtuous their endeavor, would soon become objects of scorn. His insight has stood the test of time, as calls across the Middle East to resist the "evil" American empire and its allegedly empty human rights promises spread far faster than in the days of British empire, this time via satellite television and the Internet.

The tension between avowed American human rights principles and post–September 11 practice is noticeable. How can the United States exalt its own values as superior while not portraying an image of openness and tolerance toward other cultures? How can the United States take pride as a country of immigrants, while its surveillance policies violate fundamental rights of both illegal and legal immigrants? How can the United States proclaim a commitment to sound environmental policies, while withdrawing from international "human security" agreements such as Kyoto? How can it support the prosecution of Slobodan Milosevic for his crimes against humanity, while rejecting the authority of the International Court Tribunal? How can it call for the protection of its POWs under the Geneva Convention, while defying the rights of Guantánamo prisoners? How can it pay its overdue debt to the United Nations, and then deride the authority of the UN Security Council as an irrelevant "debating society"? Predictably, many of the United States' European allies have become steadily angrier in the face of U.S. unilateralism, even as pro-U.S. sentiment has plummeted in public opinion polls around the world.

IS RESISTANCE FUTILE? STRUGGLING AT DIFFERENT LEVELS
Confronting the contradictions and hypocrisy of U.S. foreign policy becomes more difficult when the economic and geopolitical interests of an empire are hidden behind human rights rhetoric and when the human rights community remains divided. Is there any hope of resistance within a developed world where each human rights challenge reflects a need that can be promptly com-

modified, and where the outraged mind can be (repeatedly if only ephemerally) appeased by relentless inventions of new placebos? Herbert Marcuse had already prodded the Western public in the 1960s to remain critical thinkers, unveiling the contradictions between the discourse of rights and reality. Those who heeded his call to refuse to conform, nurturing a passionate impulse to protest against the moral pretenses of power, formed the ranks of the counterculture movement of the postwar baby boom generation.

Yet that which brought the student movement together also contributed to its breakup. Negating the system for the sake of negation, or focusing on the particular grievances of blacks, Hispanics, workers, women, gays, and other diverse groups, led not to a strengthened human rights movement but to its fragmentation. The atomizing of the universal discourse of human rights ultimately engendered the postmodern enterprise, as many Westerners became disillusioned with the Cold War hegemonic moral claims of the contending superpowers, the nationalist worldviews of anticolonial fighters, and the cultural rights posturing of Third World elites starving for recognition. Failing to propose universalist and concrete alternatives to a myriad of human rights violations gradually bankrupted the social capital of ever more fragmented progressive movements around the world.

Indeed, embattled efforts to develop peasant solidarity in divided societies like India, Bangladesh, and Sri Lanka were coupled to a failure to broaden what remain disconnected local struggles, from Beijing to Chiapas, and countless other arenas of human rights aspiration. "The paradox is that in our age of communicability," observe Michael Hardt and Antonio Negri, "these struggles have become all but incommunicable," and the very notion of international struggle "based on the communication of common desires seem to have vanished."[11] In the cracks of this fractured social terrain, the irascible seeds of nationalism have sprouted and sunk new roots in Africa, the Middle East, and elsewhere.

The picture is not all grim. There have been some positive trends for human rights institutional and technological opportunities in our globalized age. In 1956, for instance, there were 973 transnational nongovernmental organizations (NGOs), whereas forty years later, there were more than 5,000.[12] Of these 5,000, one may now count more than 200 U.S. NGOs associated with human rights issues in the United States, a comparable number in the United Kingdom, and the spread of similar organizations in the developing world.[13] Human rights websites have also become a major tool for the dissemination of information about human rights violations, for rallying popular outrage, and for pressuring governments to redress human rights transgressions. Repressive states can no longer easily insulate their populations from the diffusion of information, as radio broadcasts of unauthorized views (such as by the Voice of America and BBC World Service) have been supplemented by the interactive capabilities represented by websites and e-mail.

How should we then integrate scattered local struggles for human rights within the broader institutionalization of human rights? If the increase of human rights activism and the subsequent adoption of hundreds of United Nations treaties offer new hope, enduring change will require the coordination of human rights campaigns with democratic agencies at the level of international and local governance. The struggle for human rights needs to continue both within and beyond the legal debates and the corridors of international organizations. It needs to counter the bureaucratization of the institutionalized human rights regime with mobilization efforts in the streets of locales from Gaza to Guatemala, from Genoa to Kabul. Developing solidarity between different social agencies of change in the local and global aspects of civil society in turn requires greater efforts to develop a clear agenda that unites different human rights efforts.

A key part of that agenda must be to strengthen the capacity of the state to resist corporate demands for deregulatory policies. Whether human rights efforts are invested locally or transnationally, they are often conducted outside and against the state: a forum that remains, despite many skeptics of the legitimacy of the Westphalian system, a critical vehicle for the promotion of human rights. The fact that the United States is porous to global market pressures should not imply that human rights activists should abandon in toto its legislative and enforcement capacity to promote democracy and human rights. To do so would be to accept as inevitable the reshaping of state power, in which the strengthening of the coercive machinery to crush domestic or foreign opponents proceeds in tandem with a weakening of welfare, workers' rights, and democratic governance—a world designed to offer carte blanche to corporate and geopolitical interests.

Yet how can one resist that tendency when real security concerns after the September 11 tragedy have provided new rationales for imperial interventions around the world? Resistance for the sake of resistance may prove futile, especially when the new emperor has applied the time-honored model first established by Napoleon of justifying wars of imperial expansion in the name of universal human rights. As the new empire continues to shape, mediate, and resolve conflicts consistent with its interests, the second challenge for human rights activists lies in their ability to confront an imperial security agenda.

SEIZING HUMAN RIGHTS OPPORTUNITIES
IN THE CONTEXT OF EMPIRE BUILDING

While imperial greed should always be denounced, the moral evaluations of empires get complicated when the policies of empire might benefit the Kosovars, Afghans, Iraqis, and others. Hence, human rights strategies need to address differing circumstances and contexts, adopting a critical stand at times, while seizing opportunities to harness imperial power at others. In brief, it is important to follow a skeptical impulse and to hold the emperor and his entourage accountable for actions undertaken in the name of human rights, or to couple denunciations of imperial policies with concrete policy alternatives to counter human rights violations. The following provides some guidelines for advancing human rights in an age of empire.[14]

Considering Human Rights Opportunities amidst Imperial Politics

When security concerns bring an imperial power into conflict with brutal regimes, human rights activists should work to ensure that intervention serves to advance human rights. In this respect, the war against the Taliban, if not undertaken to liberate women from feudal slavery, had considerable beneficial consequences for women's rights, just as NATO's intervention in Kosovo might well have averted a repetition of Serbia's genocidal war, dramatized by Srebrenica, against Muslims in Bosnia. While human rights rhetoric often masks other motives and while the United States routinely maintains a double standard, favoring regimes committing gross human rights violations wherever its serves its own interests, a new human rights realism should nevertheless seize opportunities to advance its cause whenever the empire or Western hegemonic powers confront repressive governments.

Certainly, human rights activists should condemn repressive regimes with equal fervor regardless of whether they are seen as friends or foe by the United States or the EU. While it remains critically important to draw attention to grave human rights abuses that are ignored by the media and on no one's political agenda, human rights advocates should not shrink from actively opposing oppressive regimes, such as that of Saddam Hussein, simply because he became the bête noire of the United States or other major powers. One can support the institutions of the UN, deplore the long record of human rights abuses in the foreign or domestic policies of the five permanent members of the Security Council, and still support those instances when military action advances the cause of human rights.

Considering the Appropriate Means toward Human Rights Ends

Human rights activists have traditionally condemned shortsighted great-power foreign policies that ultimately breed human rights abuses. For instance, many rightly criticized U.S. support of the mujahideen during the Afghan war against the Soviet Union, and the subsequent U.S. indifference to the Afghans' plight after Soviet withdrawal. Yet such critical stands are hardly sufficient. The human rights community should feel obligated to offer viable policies, whether for liberating women from the Taliban regime or for freeing the populations of current repressive and authoritarian regimes. When power politics or the "CNN effect" draws the world's attention toward the brutality of particular regimes, a realistic human rights approach will assess in critical instances whether war is a legitimate last resort, and whether the cost in likely casualties outweighs the prospective ends.

Just as the question of means and ends divided early-twentieth-century Socialists, pitting Karl Kautsky and Rosa Luxemburg against Trotsky and Lenin, over what means were justified for achieving a socialist vision of rights, the question of the appropriate means to forward human rights principles is today equally divisive.[15] For instance, while there might be broad agreement that toppling Saddam Hussein's dictatorial regime and restoring democracy and human rights for Iraqis was an honorable goal, the difficult question remained whether a U.S. military intervention in Iraq would override the envisioned ends and lead only to widening violence in the Arab world. Obviously, there would be fewer critics of military intervention if one could foresee that resistance would be short-lived and the cost in human lives low. While no one knows with certainty the outcome of any impending war, reflexive judgments are no substitute for sober assessments of whether ongoing political and military operations are consistent with human rights objectives, and whether the considered means justify the envisioned ends.

Considering the Limit of Imposing Human Rights from Outside

Even if one could predict with certainty that human rights abuses could be greatly reduced at the cost of very low casualties, the question remains whether external forces can be sufficient for implementing sustained improvements in human rights. If, for instance, one can applaud U.S. policies in Afghanistan that quickly freed women from their burkas, the intervention against the Taliban regime would not have been possible without U.S. cooperation with the Northern Alliance. While one can rightly claim that the groups composing the Alliance were hardly democratic, they nevertheless represented a vital initial source of support for a new post-Taliban government. Generally, finding viable local or exiled sources of resistance remains imperative whenever outside military intervention to redress human rights is under consideration. Not only is domestic support for intervention important in the short term, but in its absence the long-term task of creating the infrastructure to maintain democracy in societies devastated by civil war is prone to being seen as another form of imperialism, resulting in growing resistance.

Thus, one should acknowledge the reasonableness and foresight of Michael Walzer's warning that outsiders' attempts to improve from outside are unlikely to take hold absent strong local support.[16] Taken to its extreme conclusion, however, this position may imply that short of an unfolding genocide, the world should refrain from interfering in cases of severe human rights violations. This line of thinking can inadvertently provide an unacceptable reward for effective totalitarianism—ensuring that once the iron fist of tyranny has silenced all internal resistance, all hopes for outside help disappear as well. In practice, this view marks an unacceptable retreat from the conviction that human rights, including their political, social, and economic dimensions as endorsed by the Universal Declaration of Human Rights, are not a Western privilege, but should be enjoyed by everyone everywhere. Hence, the task confronting a human rights realist is to carve a space between the charge of indifference linked to a noninterventionist position and the possible accusation of imperialism associated with humanitarian intervention.

Considering a New Human Rights Realism in Our Globalized Economy

If security strategies need always to be understood in the framework of our globalizing economy, a new human rights realism should go beyond the critique of globalization to support initiatives, wherever voiced, that integrate security, economic development, and human rights. In July 2000 in Okinawa, Japan, under the Miyazaki Initiatives, the G8 foreign ministers called for "a culture of prevention" in addressing security threats. That culture would be based on "the U.N. charter, democracy, respect for human rights, the rule of law, good governance, sustainable development and other fundamental values, which constitute the foundation of international peace and security."[17] While one may characterize these statements as purely cosmetic rhetoric, a new human rights realism would hold accountable the merchants of human rights ideals and press for the implementation of their decisions.

A campaign to apply that public pressure implies a clear rejection of the conviction shared by many human rights scholars and activists that globalization, with the United States in the driver's seat, is simply antithetical to the advancement of human rights. One should recognize that there are aspects of capitalism that represent dramatic improvement when compared to the feudal arrangements that prevail in much of the global South: its progressive capacity, its formidable power to develop the forces of production, to regenerate new needs, and to kindle humans' unlimited possibilities.[18] That hardly entails an endorsement of neoliberal ideology, which is accountable for rules imposed on developing countries by the institutions controlling globalization (e.g., the IMF) that have perpetuated—or even worsened—poverty.

How, then, could a new human rights realism free globalization from its destructive trends? While a new human rights realism should always condemn the harsh conditions of workers in sweatshops, it should also acknowledge that the often-romanticized alternative of self-sufficient feudalism may be even worse. In reality, millions of young women beyond the reach of globalization are left with no choice but to be subjugated under patriarchal domination, or under the arbitrary tyranny of local mullahs in one or another remote corner of countries like Pakistan or Nigeria. For women and other destitute people within the most impoverished regions of the world, opportunities for change offered by market-driven economic growth should be welcomed when synchronized with redistributive policies that ensure real opportunities to escape poverty as well as with democratic aspirations.

While economic growth is vital to rescuing the poor, so are the institutions of the state, which, kept in check with a vibrant and well-integrated local and international civil society, could thwart undemocratic policies associated with the unfettered march of neoliberal globalization. In other words, realizing some of the advantage of a market economy, a human rights realist perspective would call for more state intervention not less—to develop economic infrastructure, public health and education, and civil institutions.[19] In the same vein, it should call for the implementation of supportive regulatory mechanisms within international financial institutions. Extending the campaign to forgive the debts of

Third World countries, for instance, could help enable many developing countries to combine economic development with a measure of social justice. Needless to say, keeping people alive, controlling the spread of epidemics, and providing clean water cannot be left solely to the work of the "invisible hand." In this respect, from the perspective of human rights, globalization under its imperial guise is not an end, as its proselytes would like to have it, but should be seen as a means to advance political, civil, social, and economic rights not just merely for the privileged but also for the wretched of the earth.

One cannot relegate the task of building such a global welfare mechanism, bridging security, economic development, and human rights concerns, to policy makers or the providential caprices of history. That task belongs to the active intervention of the human rights community, which in the current climate of fear must vigilantly resist narrow and shortsighted security, cultural, and economic pressures. These forces always result in the fragmentation of what should remain the inalienable and indivisible mission of the human rights community, namely, its relentless fight for civil, political, social, and economic rights for the visible, less visible, and conveniently unnoticeable among us, within and beyond every national border.

NOTES

I would like to thank David Goldfischer for his insightful suggestions, and Eric Fattor for his help with my research.

1. Ted Fisherman, "The Joys of Global Investment," *Harper's*, February 1997, pp. 35–42.

2. Michael M. Weinstein and Steve Charnovitz, "The Greening of the WTO," *Foreign Affairs* (November–December 2001): pp. 147–157.

3. Alan Binder, "Cleaning Up the Environment: Sometimes Cheaper Is Better," *Hard Heads and Soft Hearts: Tough Minded Economics for a Just Society* (Reading, MA: Addison-Wesley, 1987), pp. 138–59.

4. Benjamin Barber, "Democracy at Risk: American Culture in a Global Culture," *World Policy Journal* (Summer 1998): 30.

5. Michael Hardt and Antonio Negri, *Empire* (Cambridge, MA: Harvard University Press, 2000), p. 39.

6. Rudyard Kipling, "The White Man's Burden," in *An Anthology of British Poetry of the Empire*, ed. Chris Brooks and Peter Faulkner (Exeter: University of Exeter Press, 1996), pp. 307–8.

7. Sheldon Rampton and John Stauber, "How to Sell a War: The Rendon Group Deploys 'Perception Management' in the War on Iraq," *In These Times*, September 1, 2003.

8. Marc Cooper, "The Army Dream Lab," *Nation*, December 10, 2001.

9. "Pentagon Provides for Hollywood," *USA Today*, May 29, 2001.

10. On the issue of indifference, see Samantha Power, *A Problem from Hell: America and the Age of Genocide* (NY: Basic Books, 2002); Richard Falk, *Human Rights Horizons: The Pursuit of Justice in a Globalizing World* (London: Routledge, 2000), chap. 9.

11. Hardt and Negri, *Empire*, p. 54.

12. Thomas Friedman, *The Lexus and the Olive Tree* (New York: Farrar, Straus and Giroux, 1999).

13. David Held and Anthony McGrew, David Goldblatt, and Jonathan Perraton, *Global Transformations* (Stanford, CA: Stanford University Press, 1999), p. 67.

14. An earlier version of these guidelines was published elsewhere.

15. See Rosa Luxemburg, "The Russian Revolution," in *Rosa Luxemburg Speaks*, ed. Mary-Alice Waters (London: Pathfinder Press, 1970), p. 387; Karl Kautsky, *Selected Political Writings*, ed. and trans. Patrick Goode (New York: St. Martin's Press, 1983), p. 147; Leo Trotsky, "Their Morals and Ours," in *The History of Human Rights Reader*, ed. Micheline Ishay (New York: Routledge, 1997), p. 338; see also Micheline Ishay, *The History of Human Rights* (Berkeley: University of California Press, 2004), chap. 4.

16. Michael Walzer, *Just and Unjust War* (New York: Basic Books, 1977).

17. G8 Miyazaki Initiatives for Conflict Prevention, http://www.mofa.go.jp/policy/economy/summit/2000/documents/initiative.html (accessed December 2001).

18. Karl Marx, *Capital*, vol. 1 (London: Penguin Classics, 1976), pts. I and VIII.

19. See, on this subject, Leo Panitch, "Globalization and the State," in *Socialist Register 1994: Between Globalism and Nationalism*, ed. Ralph Miliband and Leo Panitch (London: Merlin, 1994).

Index

About the Contributors

Alba Alexander is research assistant professor in the College of Urban Planning at the University of Illinois in Chicago. Alexander's articles have appeared in many journals and edited volumes, including the *Harvard International Review, International Journal of Urban and Regional Research, Congress and the Presidency,* and *Critical Sociology.*

Ulrich Beck is professor of sociology at University of Munich. He is the author of *Counterpoison, Ecological Enlightenment,* and *Ecological Politics in an Age of Risk.* He is also a regular contributor to the *Frankfurter Allgemeine Zeitung.*

Carl Boggs is professor of social sciences at National University in Los Angeles. He is the author of a number of books including the forthcoming *Imperial Delusions: American Militarism and Endless War.* He is the editor of *Masters of War: Militarism and Blowback in an Era of American Empire* and coauthor of *A World in Chaos: Social Crisis and the Rise of Postmodern Cinema.*

Stephen Eric Bronner is currently professor (II) of political science and a member of the graduate faculties of comparative literature and German studies at Rutgers University. He is senior editor of *Logos,* an interdisciplinary Internet journal. His works include: *A Rumor about the Jews: Anti-Semitism, Conspiracy, and the 'Protocols of Zion,'" Imagining the Possible: Radical Politics for Conservative Times,* and *Reclaiming Enlightenment: Toward a Politics of Radical Engagement.*

Drucilla Cornell is professor of law, women's studies, and political science at Rutgers University. She is author of *At the Heart of Freedom: Feminism, Sex, and Equality, Declaring Our Freedom: A Feminist Re-Thinking Sex and Equality*, and *The Imaginary Domain: Abortion, Pornography and Sexual Harassment.*

Irene Gendzier is professor of political science at Boston University. She is the author of numerous works on U.S. foreign policy in the Middle East, including *Notes from the Minefield: United States Intervention in Lebanon and the Middle East, 1945–1958*, and the forthcoming study on U.S. policy in the Middle East, *Dying to Forget*. She is also author of works dealing with interpretations of modernization and development and earlier writings on North Africa.

Sam Gindin is Packer Chair in Social Justice in the Department of Political Science at York University. Recent publications include "Global Finance and American Empire" and "Global Capitalism and American Empire," both with Leo Panitch, and "Prospects for Anti-Imperialism: Coming to Terms with Our Own Bourgeoise."

Philip Green is visiting professor of political science at the New School University and a member of the editorial board of *The Nation*. He is the author of *Deadly Logic: The Theory of Nuclear Deterrence, Retrieving Democracy: In Search of Civic Equality*, and *Equality and Democracy.*

David Held is Graham Wallas Professor of Political Science at the London School of Economics. He is the author of *Globalization/Anti-Globalization* and *Global Covenant.*

Dick Howard is distinguished professor of political philosophy at the State University of New York at Stony Brook. His works include *Political Judgments, The Specter of Democracy*, and the forthcoming *Aux origines de la pensée américaine.*

Micheline Ishay is professor and director of the International Human Rights Program at the Graduate School of International Studies at the University of Denver. She has written numerous articles and book chapters and authored and edited several books including: *Internationalism and Its Betrayal, The Nationalism Reader*, and *The Human Rights Reader: Major Political Essays, Speeches, and Documents from the Bible to the Present.*

Kurt Jacobsen is research associate in the Department of Political Science at the University of Chicago. His books include *Chasing Progress in the Irish Republic, Dead Reckonings: Ideas, Interests, and Politics in the 'Information Age,' Technical Fouls: Democratic Dilemmas and Technological Change,* and *Experiencing the State* (coedited with Lloyd Rudolph).

Douglas Kellner is George Kneller Chair in Philosophy of Education at UCLA. He has written a number of books on social theory, politics, history, and culture, including *Media Spectacle, September 11, Terror War, and the Dangers of the Bush Legacy,* and *Grand Theft 2000: Media Spectacle and the Theft of an Election.*

Leo Panitch is Canada Research Chair in comparative political economy and distinguished research professor of political science at York University, Toronto. His books include *From Consent to Coercion: The Assault on Trade Union Freedoms* and *Renewing Socialism: Democracy, Strategy, and Imagination.* For the past two decades, he has been the coeditor of *The Socialist Register.*

Manfred B. Steger is professor of politics and government at Illinois State University and research fellow at the Globalization Research Center of the University of Hawai'i-Manoa. His most recent publications include *Gandhi's Dilemma: Nonviolent Principles and Nationalist Power, Violence and Its Alternatives: An Interdisciplinary Reader,* and *Engels after Marx.*

Karsten J. Struhl teaches political and cross-cultural philosophy at John Jay College of Criminal Justice (CUNY) and New School University. He has coedited *Philosophy Now, Ethics in Perspective,* and, most recently, *The Philosophical Quest: A Cross-Cultural Reader.* He is currently working on the problems of democracy as a universal value and just war theory.

Michael J. Thompson is founder and editor of *Logos: A Journal of Modern Society & Culture* and assistant professor of political science at William Paterson University in New Jersey. His most recent book is *Islam and the West: Critical Perspectives on Modernity.*

Nadia Urbinati is associate professor of political science at Columbia University. She is the author of *Mill on Democracy: From the Athenian Polis to Representative Government* and several books in Italian. She also edited the first English edition of Carlo Rosselli's *Liberal Socialism.*